The Lorette Wilmot Library
Nazareth College of Rochester

Erotic Dawn-Songs
of the
Middle Ages

Erotic Dawn-Songs of the Middle Ages

Voicing the Lyric Lady

Gale Sigal

University Press of Florida
Gainesville Tallahassee Tampa Boca Raton Pensacola Orlando Miami Jacksonville

Copyright 1996 by the Board of Regents of the State of Florida
Printed in the United States of America on acid-free paper ∞
All rights reserved

01 00 99 98 97 96 6 5 4 3 2 1

Library of Congress Cataloging-in-Publication Data
Sigal, Gale.
   Erotic dawn-songs of the Middle Ages: voicing the lyric lady /
Gale Sigal.
     p. cm.
Includes bibliographical references and index.
ISBN 0-8130-1381-X
1. Poetry, Medieval—History and criticism. 2. Erotic
poetry—History and criticism. 3. Albas—History and criticism.
  I. title.
PN691.S54   1996   95–42861
809.1'93538—dc20   CIP

The University Press of Florida is the scholarly publishing agency for the State University System of Florida, comprised of Florida A & M University, Florida Atlantic University, Florida International University, Florida State University, University of Central Florida, University of Florida, University of North Florida, University of South Florida, and University of West Florida.

University Press of Florida
15 Northwest 15th Street
Gainesville, FL 32611

To my loving parents, Max and Frieda

*To David and the Sierra night sky:
the love we share will never see the dawn*

Contents

Preface	ix
Introduction	1
Theoretical and Generic Parameters	3
The Lyric Lady and the Alba	12

Part I: The Alba Lady: Literary and Social Perspectives

1. The Alba Lady: Literary Perspectives	23
The Humanized Ideal	29
2. The Alba Lady: Sex Roles and Social Roles	51
Adulterous Love and the Alba	76
3. Eros in the Socius	94
Power, Gender, and Class: The Love Triangle	94
Fin'amors: Conflicting Loyalties; Divided Selves	110

Part II: Eros and Identity

4. Eros and Dawning Identity	133
Nocturnal Wonders: (K)Night Calls	133
Love's Timeless Utopia: Regressive Fantasies	155
Fusion, Androgyny, Inseparability	160
5. First Light: Mask and Masquerade	169
Janus-Faced Dawn and the Dualisms of Love:	
Pivot and Potentiality	179
Cruel Dawn	186
The Dawn Descends: The Refrain	192
Conclusion: The Fractured Self: Songs of Mo(u)rning	195
Notes	205
Bibliography	215
Index	231

Preface

Erotic Dawn-Songs of the Middle Ages: Voicing the Lyric Lady reassesses female voice and experience in medieval verse from the viewpoint of an overlooked but essential genre, the dawn-song or alba. Whereas most interrogations of medieval attitudes toward women take the canso, the canonical lyric genre, as a model, this study recognizes that in the alba, the lady plays a more active and intriguing role and therefore sheds a unique and colorful light on her poet's and society's view of women. *Erotic Dawn-Songs* launches forth the alba, heretofore viewed as a grace note to the larger troubadour genres, as a powerful lyric instrument in its own right.

Investigating the founding moments of Western conceptions of romantic love, desire, and identity, *Erotic Dawn-Songs* joins an ongoing colloquy among contemporary cultural theorists, feminists, and medievalists. It also reaches out to a general audience of students of literature and lovers of poetry who find the dynamics of romantic love and the creation of the idealized female love object germane, problematic, and provocative subjects. The alba's narrative scenario—the disruption by dawn's light of a passionate love tryst—offers a singular and subtle psychological portrait of the unconscious self arising by way of rebellious, illicit love. Providing a comprehensive overview of the alba's place in the lyric corpus, this work shows how the troubadours' soundings of sexual relations reverberate down the centuries to our own time. Complementing the interpretive endeavor is a series of close readings and detailed commentary on individual lyrics intended to expose the reader to the genre's breadth and poetic virtuosity.

The emerging vernacular lyric of twelfth-century France provided a pioneering impetus for exploring human emotions and also for inventing fresh forms of female speech. The troubadours created their female characters ex nihilo—out of their own vivid imaginations. These indelible feminine figures have not only spawned literary offspring but have also served as models for real women to emulate: if, as many critics believe, the canso lady brought the "lady on the pedestal" into being, the alba lady's progeny are the more lively, clever, and resourceful heroines of medieval romance. Her dramatic intensity and soulful eloquence merit special distinction among the female characters of any time period.

Drawing upon recent feminist approaches, *Erotic Dawn-Songs* offers a new interpretation of the alba by examining its bold female voice. The alba lady assumes her rightful place at the critical center of a lyric continuum in which an array of women are presented from varying points of view. As a marginal figure in the courtly realm, she provides a missing link that unifies diverse attitudes and values. The alba lady voices what the courted canso lady withholds; her expressiveness ties her to the other speaking lyric female, the pastourelle shepherdess, her dignity revealing unappreciated aspects of this hunted peasant woman. A figure who often represents the pastoral and rebellious side of courtly life, she bridges the territorial distance that divides courtly canso lady from pastourelle country girl.

I had the good fortune to attend the City University of New York's graduate school at a time when it boasted an extraordinary grouping of medievalists. Not only did I benefit from taking courses with such accomplished scholars, but I was able to participate in the activities of the New York Medieval Club and other area medieval events. Thanks to the late Helaine Newstead, who established an ongoing medieval seminar for her Ph.D. students, I took my place among a group of student medievalists who discussed our work together as we completed our dissertations. My former classmates are now professors across the country, but we still share our work and collaborate on projects as easily as we did when we were students living in the same city. Among those former classmates, Deborah Sinnreich-Levi has been an indefatigable friend, an empathic and discerning sounding board. Sybbe Tomasch continues to lend a supportive, practical, and wise ear; Diane Marks, Anneke Prinz, Sealy Gilles, Bill McClelland, Lynda Zweborn-Holland, and Sheila Rabin have been solid, reliable, and encouraging compatriots since the Newstead Seminar days. Henry Weinfield offered sharp, helpful feedback as well as astute lyrical insight at an earlier stage of this work. Walter Stiller's endless curiosity and intellectual rigor stimulated my thinking and enriched this work. He encouraged me to enlarge my vision and to trust my creativity; and he taught me, by his example, how poets speak to each other across the centuries.

The primary critical influence on this study has been Frederick Goldin's work and teaching. His tutorial gentleness, vast knowledge, understated brilliance, utter good nature, and respect for his students gave me confidence and knowledge, both much needed and in huge doses. His understanding of lyric laid the foundation for mine, initially inspiring me to take up the subject of this book. Fred's meticulous and perceptive responses to ideas I set out in earlier versions of this manuscript served as a guide of careful and thoughtful scholarship. He is a model of intellect tempered by humanity. Martin Stevens, who also served as a mentor, read an early version of this work, generously sharing his expertise, insights, and wisdom. Robert O. Payne, recently deceased, intuitively grasped the strengths and weaknesses of this study before it took final shape. He advised me with clarity, logic, and precision. At the same time that he taught me to feel for the poet behind the poem, Bob also taught me not to seek real people *in* the poem—that is, not to mistake lyric voices for real people, a lesson that will stay with me throughout my professional life.

More recently, Wake Forest University has provided generous funding for research and a much needed research leave. Dean Thomas Mullen supported the founding of our medieval studies group and helped it sustain a long and rich life. The university has also given me dozens of irreplaceable colleagues. First among them is Gillian Overing, the staunchest of medievalist allies and a model of professional comportment, wit, strength, ingenuity, and compassion; Nancy Cotton, Robert Shorter, Andrew Ettin, Claudia Thomas, Anne Boyle, and Dee Perry have all been vital nurture to my life in the English department; and the warm encouragement and efficient responsiveness of my chairman, Barry Maine, have been crucial. William Meyers, Sarah Watts, Win-chiat Lee, Bob Evans, and Judy Kem have also been essential and beloved mainstays; Nell Gifford-Martin provided intellectual sparks, solace, and flora in abundance. I am indebted to Margaret Supplee Smith for recalling my attention to Joan Kelly-Gadol's work at a crucial juncture. Three graduate student assistants, Elizabeth Ann Jensen, Stephanie Hawkins, and Victoria Schooler, provided indispensable research skills complemented by great patience and good humor.

Margaret Switten, director of the 1987 NEH Institute titled "The Medieval Lyric: Words and Music" at Mount Holyoke College, was a model of humane expertise, wisdom, and organization. Stephen Nichols's energy, creativity, and brilliance made him an inspiring seminar director, lecturer, and listener. Participants in that institute, especially Meredith Jones, Charlotte Gross, and Matthew Steele, generously shared ideas. Brigitte Cazelles and Kevin Brownlee, organizers of "The Quest and the Rose," an NEH Summer Institute (1990) at Stanford University, presented fascinating and exciting material during six weeks of intense and thorough intellectual stimulation. And Bill Burgwinkle's workshops on literary theory at that institute made the crooked straight.

Julie Edelson reviewed this manuscript with clear-sighted objectivity, substantially improving it. Wake Forest photographer Lee Runion gave me professional help on short notice. The University Press of Florida has handled every step of this project with efficiency, patience, and ease. Walda Metcalf, associate director and editor-in-chief, offered expert advice and good humor. I am indebted to Judy Goffman of the press and Dawn Potter for their skillful and smooth editing. The Delaware Art Museum has generously granted me permission to use a reproduction of the Ford Madox Brown painting "Romeo and Juliet" for the cover of this book.

An earlier and different version of part of chapter 1 appeared as "The Pit or the Pedestal?: The Dichotomization of the Lady in Troubadour Lyric," *The Romanic Review* 84 (March 1993):109–42; an earlier version of another part of chapter 1 ("The Humanized Ideal") appeared as "Dignity and Desire: The *Alba* Poet's Liberation of the Courtly Lady," *Papers on Romance Literary Relations: The Creation of Female Voices by Male Writers in Romance Literatures* (Brockport: SUNY, 1987), 9–22. A portion of my analysis of "Reis glorios" in chapter 5 appeared as "'Reis glorios': An Inverted *Alba*?" *Medieval Perspectives* 4–5 (1989–90):185–95; an extended commentary on the psycho-dynamics of parting that my conclusion draws on appeared as "The Poetics of Dismemberment: *Eros* and Identity in the Medieval Dawn-Song," *Tenso* 5 (1990):133–52.

The debt I owe to Matonah Rubin, whose friendship, affection, and integrity have become paradigms for me, is beyond measure. My parents' unconditional love and support have been indispensable; my sister Barbara and her family gave laughter and joy; and the Glass family gave intellectual and emotional encouragement.

Allen Mandelbaum has been a guardian angel whose own work sheds a radiant light for me over the path that does not stray. Through his example, I have come to appreciate the exhilarating potential of dynamic mind wedded to ardent spirit. My husband, David, helped me work through the various pains that coincide with completing a book. He advised, read, and edited—over and over again—all the time with steady and loving encouragement.

Introduction

> An alba is so called because the song takes its name from the hour at which it is sung and because it is better sung at dawn than during the day.
> Jofre de Foixà (?), Doctrina de compondre dictats,
> in J. H. Marshall, The Razos de Trobar of Raimon Vidal, 96

The medieval erotic dawn-song is a lament for the brevity of human love and a celebration of its irrepressibility. The alba, like dawn itself, is Janus-faced: it commemorates and prolongs a love affair while its subject is the love's dissolution. Because the love affair is adulterous, the lovers must confine their meetings in time and place; they need the shield and shelter of darkness, of secrecy. Discovery can bring a violent denouement; and the lady's husband, his spies, or other enemies may perilously circumscribe the tryst. Dawn's ascent disrupts the secret love meeting, providing the impetus for eloquent outpourings of song. Dawn signals parting, its revelatory light invading the shrouded sanctum. The lovers, reluctant but prudent, utter their expressive plaint, their alba. Although outlawed and foredoomed, love contrives to vanquish its opponents and vindicate its value. The dawn-song is the union's final issue; through it echoes resoundingly the intense and fulfilled passion of which it is the abiding monument.

The Old Provençal word *alba* (white) evokes the white brightness of dawn and stands, synecdochically, for dawn itself. The word is frequently used as the generic designation for all medieval dawn-songs, although each language has adopted its own linguistic form for the term. As it descends to us in Old Provençal, Old French (*aube*), and Middle High German (*tageliet,* day strophe), the alba is one of the vernacular verse forms that appeared in southern France around the middle of the twelfth century.

The albas studied here are erotic dawn-songs in Old Provençal, Old French, Middle High German, and Middle English. These songs have enough in common in voice, structure, plot, theme, and characters to be discussed as a group despite the distinctions that make individual members unique. Although far fewer albas than cansos are extant, among the alba corpus many masterpieces can be counted. No poetic forerunners surpass the blend of lyricism, dramatic power, and poignancy of the most accomplished albas, which are to be counted among the great love poems of all time. The alba's elegance, musicality, and expressiveness have made it an enduring form. Once the three greatest twelfth-century German poets—Heinrich von Morungen, Walther von der Vogelweide, and Wolfram von Eschenbach—wrote their tagelieder, the form became a cornerstone of German literature.

The alba introduced into the Western poetic tradition so vibrant and eloquent a female voice and so fresh and fertile a direction that the form was adopted by popular and poetic media. Unlike other genres of troubadour love lyric, it did not play itself out (Goldin, *Troubadours* 124). The genre's flexibility allowed it to find its way into narratives both serious (Boccaccio's *Il Filostrato*, Chaucer's *Troilus*, and Shakespeare's *Romeo and Juliet*, to name the best known) and parodic (*Aucassin et Nicolette*, "The Reeve's Tale," and "The Merchant's Tale"). The genre also had an enduring life in verse subsequent to its medieval flowering, especially in Germany and France, where albas were a favored genre in popular poetry. In England, John Donne picked up the motif to brilliant and original effect in "The Good-Morrow," "Break of Day," and "The Sunne Rising" (see chapter 5).

Although serious treatment of the dawn-parting theme is absent from English poetry after the middle of the seventeenth century, it resurfaces abundantly in the nineteenth and twentieth centuries in the poetry of Tennyson, Browning, and Swinburne as well as in Housman, Yeats, Sitwell, Auden, Ransom, Williams, Shapiro, and Wilbur.[1]

The musical complement to the alba's words, although absent from postmedieval poetry, left its mark on a number of composers. Act 2 of Wagner's *Tristan* has been called an expanded alba. Even modern popular music is not without its examples. The Everly Brothers' "Wake Up, Little Susie" is a poignantly innocent 1960s variation on the alba theme. The later pop song "Angel of the Morning," with its female narrator and melancholy tone, works together an eerie blend of medieval dawn-song and contemporary love lament in which female self-sacrifice is offered in the name of free love.

George Moore, Swinburne ("In the Orchard"), and Pound ("Alba Innominata") each tried his hand at translating the anonymous "En un vergier sotz fuella d'albespi." Pound also translated two others, "Langue D'Oc" and "Alba." The latter is a haunting rendition of the lyrical one-strophe anonymous alba "Quan lo rossinhols escria." Pound's work captures the musicality, energy, and melancholy of the Old Provençal song (1928, 142):

> When the nightingale to his mate
> Sings day-long and night late
> My love and I keep state
>   In bower
>   In flower
>   Till the watchman on the tower
> Cries:
>   "Up! Thou rascal, Rise,
>   and see the white
>   Light
>   And the night
>   Flies."

> Quan lo rossinhols escria
> Ab sa par la nueg e·l dia,
> Yeu suy ab ma bell'amia
>   Jos la flor,
> Tro la gaita de la tor
> Escria: "drutz, al levar!
> Qu'ieu vey l'alba e·l jorn clar."

I hope to leave the reader with an affection for these splendid fresh lyric voices that gathered themselves into a verse corpus powerful enough to spark a literary revolution.

Theoretical and Generic Parameters

Although vernacular poetry of twelfth-century France has been credited with pioneering an exploration of human emotion, the alba plot offers a particular perspective from which to investigate the psychodynamics and emotional consequences of sexual love. The alba paints a complex and subtle portrait of self-consciousness emerging via love in which conceptions of individual identity and self-definition are interrogated. Further, the portrayal of eros modulated within the courtly context throws a distinctive light on the emotional and sociopolitical world of alba poets.

Of all its contributions, the alba's most momentous and original gift to Western culture is its unprecedented array of female voices. It marks a watershed in the history of the poetic idealization of the female in literature. From the alba lady's eloquent voice emerges a strong, courageous, and dynamic heroine. Through her, male poets experimented brilliantly and audaciously with nuances of female characterization. The clear, defiant voice of the alba lady cries out against the confining, stereotypical roles that her gender seems otherwise fated to play.

For the late nineteenth- and early twentieth-century critics who rediscovered medieval vernacular poetry, the alba was especially enchanting. For Saintsbury, the alba, along with the sirventes, was "the most famous, peculiar and representative of Provençal forms" (1897, 366). The Middle High German tageliet was celebrated along with the alba in the late nineteenth century by musicologists and historians as well as literary scholars. Friedrich Engels, although no literary critic in the modern sense, possessed a keen appreciation for the genre in terms of both its social implications and poetic genius. Engels admired the "glowing colors" of the alba, the genre that, for him, was the "flower of Provençal love poetry" (1902, 70). He characterizes albas as lyrics that portray "how the knight lies in bed beside his love—the wife of another man—while outside stands the watchman who calls to him as soon as the first gray of dawn (*alba*) appears, so that he can get away unobserved; the parting scene then forms the climax of the poem. The northern French and also the worthy Germans adopted this kind of poetry together with the corresponding fashion of chivalrous love; old Wolfram of Eschenbach has left us three wonderfully beautiful songs of dawn on this same improper subject, which I like better than his three long heroic poems" (70). For nineteenth-century musicologist and critic Francis Hueffer, alba poets "frequently display an intensity of language, and originality and picturesqueness of description, which we look for in vain in [the troubadours'] more elaborate poems" (1878, 89).

The insights of these early modern critics are more engaging, perceptive, and meaningful than much of the technical criticism that followed in its wake: once nineteenth-century critics established medieval vernacular poetry as a subject worthy of academic inquiry, scholars undertook to survey and classify it. Devoting their attention to tasks such as tracking down the prototype of the alba, they failed to sound nuances of characterization or underlying thematic, social, or political implications. The search for the origins of the vernacular lyric genres was the obsession of several generations of literary medievalists. This preoccupation impeded the study of the poetry because, as Jackson explains, it "set up problems which were incapable of solution and which, even if solved, would add little to our understanding of the works themselves" (1980, 3).

Nevertheless, most of what was written about the alba, like that of medieval verse in general, focused on defining the genre, numbering its members, searching for its origins, and tracing the evolution of its component elements and dramatis personae. The corpus of albas has been variously revised, depending on the criteria used to establish the parameters of the genre. Benedetto Croce's observation that "every true work of art has violated an established genre, and in this way confounded the ideas of critics who thus found themselves compelled to broaden the genre" is, of course, the dictum of a thinker for whom the historic humus of poetic text was, to say the least, somewhat irrelevant (1902, 40). Nevertheless, he does caution us that semiotic codes, structures that frame and inform texts for readers, must always yield, bend, modulate themselves under the pressure of the individual maker.

But a code *is* a code, both prescriptive and helpful. And we can indeed enumerate poems that exemplify the alba code or genre. In his encyclopedic compendium of dawn-songs, *Eos: An Inquiry into the Theme of Lovers' Meetings and Partings at Dawn in Poetry,* Hatto notes: "The formation of a genre of dawn poetry in mediaeval Provençal was so marked that its name of alba has become a type name that can be used in discussions of poems from other parts of the world" (1965, 31). The alba's theme of separation, its preference for dialogue, its "almost obligatory refrain containing the word *alba*," and its inclusion of the watchman figure are the definitive features (31). These elements also differentiate the alba from the aubade, a distinction lost to all but the most specialized literary critics. The word aubade does not appear before the fifteenth century (Saville 1972, 269n.1) and technically designates a waking song addressed to the sleeping beloved from a window or door (Hatto 1965, 22). Many English-speaking literary critics use the term more generally to refer to dawn-songs written in English, of which the first is Chaucer's. But actually Chaucer's dawn-song in *Troilus and Criseyde* is an alba rather than an aubade because it is sung by the wakened lovers to each other. Hatto does not include the aubade or mattinata in his collection of dawn-parting poems. Although Jeanroy felt sure that the aube as a generic designation must have existed in the Middle Ages, no such use of the word has been discovered (1925, 61n).

Whereas Jeanroy counts only eight albas, omitting all didactic or parodic versions, Woledge classifies nine Old Provençal and four Old French lyrics as albas (Hatto 1965, 344–89). I have relied on his scholarship for establishing the corpus, although I have taken the texts of individual lyrics from standard editions where they exist rather than from his chapter in *Eos*. Four other lyrics are related to the genre "but [are] not dawn-songs in the narrow sense" (375). Saville counts nineteen Old Provençal and five Old French albas, including variants or subclasses of the genre (1972, 2). More than one hundred Middle High German dawn-songs exist.

There are a few indications that Provençal albas were sung on the Spanish Peninsula during the thirteenth and fourteenth centuries, but there are no Galician lyrics that can be called albas without qualification. In Portuguese and Spanish poems, dawn signifies the time not when lovers separate but when they meet. Conventional poetry about lovers parting at dawn is absent from Spanish and Portuguese literature until the end of the fifteenth century. The gayta, a form defined in the Catalan treatise *De doctrina de compondre dictats* as a lyric sung by night in which the speaker feigns that the watchman can harm or help him toward his lady when daylight comes, may have been a Catalan subspecies of alba (see Marshall 1972, 139, and Hatto 1965, 379). Several kharjas (Romance verses that appear as tailpieces in Hispano-Arabic and Hispano-Hebraic strophic poems in which female-voiced erotic utterances have been preserved) have some relevance to dawn poetry but lack the idea of a night spent together or of separation brought about by dawn. Medieval Arabic poetry has no independent poems of a fixed structure whose sole theme is the separation of lovers at dawn. Although Italian literature took its inspiration as well as many verse forms from Old Provençal lyrics, there are no albas in the whole of the poetry of the Sicilian school nor in the corpus of poems written in the *dolce stil nuovo*. The first comparable material appears not in lyric but in Boccaccio's *Il Filostrato* (Hatto 1965, 215, 299–391).

Mindful of Croce's general caveat, we can note that Poe, with reference to the members of the alba family, observes that each scholar puts forth his or her own idea about which poems are true members of the genre and which can be eliminated: "It is unlikely that any of these disagreements will ever be settled, since practically all of the arguments advanced in favor of one position or another depend either on missing evidence or on an arbitrary and highly disputable chronology of texts. . . . The *alba* underwent a number of changes, as evidenced by the striking contrasts among the members of the corpus. Without presuming to arrange the various stages in order, we posit that the *alba* was a dynamic concept moving across erotic, didactic, burlesque, and pious registers" (1984, 140, 148). Poe's view of the alba as a "dynamic concept" moving across numerous registers is supported by genre theorists such as Jauss (1982, 88). Although modern readers prize originality, the most innovative artistic works often fit least easily into existing categories. For Jauss, a masterwork never stays wholly within the rigidly definable boundaries of a genre (94). The more a text merely reproduces generic components, the easier it is to classify but the more inferior it will be. When Hatto prints only eighteen of the more than one hundred Middle High German tagelieder, he explains that despite their numbers, the later tagelieder lack the charm and originality of the earlier ones (1965, 441). The historical end of the genre is often manifest in a lack of originality (Jauss 1982, 94).

Poe's broader and more orderly redefinition of the genre, in many ways a vast improvement over earlier efforts, yields eighteen Old Provençal texts subdivided into "three modalities": profane alba, counter-alba, and religious alba (1983, 260):

> An *alba* is a courtly (i.e., opposed to popular) lyric piece whose distinctive formal trait is its use of the word "alba" in the final verse of each stanza. The constant theme, love, articulates itself in terms of contrasting motifs: night/day, sleep/wakefulness, union/separation, joy/sorrow, all of which find poetic resolution in the image of the dawn, which connotes awakening, leavetaking, and a mixture of conflicting emotions. The three roles basic to the representation of the *alba* theme are: the sleeper, the object of desire, and the vigilant figure. The corpus of known texts, composed in Old Provençal and dating from the late twelfth through mid-thirteenth centuries, embraces a broad range of registers: erotic, didactic, burlesque, religious. (1984, 148)

Like Bec, Poe believes that the Old Provençal alba and Old French aube developed independently of each other and that the aube, adhering more closely to popular sources, was less rigorous, formal, and elaborate than the alba (Bec 1977–78, 91, 95). She excludes the aube with the explanation that Old French dawn-songs remained a separate genre (1984, 147). Our lack of information, the possibility of missing texts, and the small number of Old French lyrics (which seem to replicate alba conventions) make the case for distinguishing between Old Provençal and Old French dawn-songs less than persuasive. I see no need to separate them into two distinct genres.[2]

The distinction between alba and aube has been at issue, in part, because our knowledge of the evolutionary process of the genre is imperfect. According to experts, troubadour verse forms evolved from primitive song, most likely originating from folklore. This core developed via the gradual accretion of characters and poetic devices into a genre. For the alba, the primitive core is, according to some critics, the lady's lament, developing into a dialogue between two lovers to which a third figure— the *gaita*, or watchman—was later added. According to others, however, the alba grew out of the watchman's cry, announcing the night hours and the return of day. Because there is no external evidence that permits us to place the poems in chronological order, no evolutionary theory is tenable (Woledge in Hatto 1965, 348–49; Poe 1984, 140). The editors of the *Princeton Encyclopedia of Poetry and Poetics* favor the view that the watchman is the originating character, but there is no chronological evidence to support this theory over any other (1974, 8).

Because it features a female narrator, the alba was classified as "Woman's Song" by the early critics despite its courtly elements and authors. Scholars such as Theodor Frings, "a founding father of modern study of woman's song" (Jackson 1981, 53), examined them for proof of the popular origins of the courtly love lyric, believing that vernacular female-voiced lyrics of the Middle Ages derived from an unrecorded tradition of women's oral folk poetry, *Frauenlieder*. A number of articles and book chapters in the 1960s and 1970s manifest more recent critical interest.[3] But reading the alba in light of folk-song theory distracts us from the more fruitful path of considering its lady as a literary construct rather than a real woman and viewing her song as purposeful fiction presented in the guise of autobiography rather than a directly autobiographical account.

Baskerville, in his pioneering study "English Songs on the Night Visit" (1921), attempts a realistic or socioanthropological approach to alba origins based on studies in ancient folk culture. He proposes that the genre developed around the actual night visits paid by unmarried men to women. Particular phases of the night visit, according to his theory, were commemorated in song: "It is to be expected, I think, that the . . . aube should have developed first and been the most widespread since the parting offered the dramatic moment for the expression of lyric passion"

(570). Baskerville's study was ground breaking in its time because of its extensive range, suggestiveness, attempt to synthesize courtly and popular poetry, and use of recently collected ballad and folk materials. But he was unable to provide substantial proof of the European pagan practice he describes; his only evidence is the songs that he believes reflect them. If he feels that parting would have "offered the dramatic moment for the expression of lyric passion," that is because we have tangible proof of the expression (but not of the event it ostensibly reports). Although interesting in itself, Baskerville's work does not explain why a genre of intricately wrought poetry on this subject suddenly appears in medieval France nor why England lagged so far behind. (He notes that the English material is "very fragmentary.")

Dronke also sees the alba as developing out of oral Romance folk culture: "It is possible that a popular tradition of erotic albas went back to the very beginnings of Romance patois, and that the dawn-songs of Ambrose and Prudentius were themselves a learned and sacred rejoinder to a vogue of profane albas that have not survived in writing" (1977, 172). And Rieger considers the alba a blending of the folk and the courtly—a folk poetry clothed in courtly raiment (1976, 8–13).

Classifications of the alba have rested on the presence of either a structural or linguistic device (such as the word alba or the refrain) or a particular character (such as the watchman). Saville's definition, on the other hand, focuses on the alba plot. Although faulted for favoring the genre's plot over its "essential lyrism" (Poe 1972, 141), Saville's definition does draw the outlines of the narrative scenario accurately (1972, 1). Poe's view that the alba is best defined in the broadest possible way so as to incorporate as many variations as possible seems the most reasonable approach.

Definitions of the alba typically exclude the religious dawn-song from the genre even though scholars have long speculated on the kinship between secular albas and their sacred counterparts. Medieval dawn-hymns are linked to secular albas primarily by the repetition in the refrains of the word "alba" or "tac" (dawn, day). Sacred dawn-hymns recall people from their life, or night, of sin; sung in an omniscient voice never signaling a specific gender, these songs depict no lovers or dawn partings. If night is a time of bliss for alba lovers, it is the domain of danger, inhabited by demons, in Christian dawn-hymns. Night is equated with sleep and sleep with symbolic death. Dawn's burst of light is a welcome revelation, forcing into flight the evil ministers of night.

The erotic alba, despite its contrast with the sacred dawn-hymn, is nonetheless charged with the sacred. The line between sacred and profane in medieval poetry cannot be firmly drawn; to enrich their songs, medieval poets expertly and consciously manipulated erotic, secular, and sacred motifs, conventions, and registers. In the language of *fin'amors*, physical relationships are spiritualized, just as spiritual relationships are sensualized in sacred works. For the medieval artist, the boundary between sacred and secular is fluid, especially with regard to the theme of love, which can be either. Giraut de Bornelh's alba "Reis glorios, verais lums e clardatz" and Folquet de Marseilles's sacred poem "Vers Dieus, el vostre nom et de sancta Maria" begin with similar addresses to God and are set to the same melody. The piety that pervades "Reis glorios, verais lums e clardatz" heightens its apocalyptic overtone and appears more emphatic when set against Folquet's song. The intermingling of sacred and secular that reaches its full culmination in Dante's *Divine Comedy* makes futile the effort of determining to which of these traditions Dante is more indebted. My study excludes the religious alba not because it is of lesser value but because the themes under discussion here—the female voice, the psychological and metaphorical dynamics set in operation during the dawn parting of alba lovers—are present solely in the erotic alba.

After all the evolutionary and generic theories are assessed, if the most significant conclusion we can draw is that classification alone sheds little light on the meaning of the poems, the need to establish the originating elements of the genre or its definitive boundaries becomes less imperative. No matter how many poems end up in the count or in what way it is classified, the alba remains a subsidiary genre. The canso (Old French *chanson*, Dante's *canzone*) is considered the major genre not only because its poems far outnumber those in other lyric genres (forming 40 percent of the extant troubadour corpus, which includes fourteen or fifteen genres) but also because it has, almost since its inception, been viewed as the most aristocratic and highly wrought of all the genres. Dante, in *De vulgari eloquentia*, pronounced the canso to be the most exalted genre of lyric: "Of [the metrical molds], we consider the form of the canzone the most excellent; and so if the most excellent things are worthy of the most excellent, as we have proved above, then those which are worthy of the most excellent vernacular are worthy of the most excellent form, and consequently should be treated in canzoni" (Purcell 1981, 41).[4] Nor did the medieval author(s) of *Las leys d'amors* think otherwise when they defined the canso as a poem of five to seven *coblas* (strophes, stanzas) treating of love or praise "with beautiful, pleasing words and with gracious subject matter, for in the canso one should not set any ugly words nor any vulgar or badly placed words" ["am bels motz plazens et am graciozas razos. quar en chanso no deu hom pauzar deguna laia paraula. ni degu vilanal mot. ni mal pauzat"] (Gatien-Arnoult 1841, 1:340).

Jeanroy, following these early definitions, classifies the canso as the preeminent genre, the one most deserving of an exalted place within the corpus of troubadour poetry. Subsequent scholars have agreed that the canso is the genre "most in tune with the ideals of medieval vernacular in general, and most representative of its poetic techniques" (Saville 1972, 3). For Zumthor, the canso is the prototypical medieval love song (1972, 144); for Topsfield, who combines Dante's criteria with that of *Las leys d'amors*, it is the supreme genre because it "treated of the highest subject, love, in the highest style, which was free from base words and thoughts, and demanded a fresh scheme of versification for each new composition" (1975, 4). Nichols's view of the canso as "that most canonic of all poetic forms of twelfth-century aristocratic culture" is the most useful and accurate (1988, 88). The wide dissemination of the canso evinces what great popularity it attained.

Among scholars who pioneered interpretive approaches to the troubadour corpus, Frederick Goldin's now-classic 1967 study, *The Mirror of Narcissus in the Courtly Love Lyric*, heralded a major scholarly breakthrough with its perceptive exploration of unrequited love and the underlying dynamics of the singer's obsessive pursuit of his elusive female love object. For the alba specifically, the first full-length study of the genre in English was Jonathan Saville's *The Medieval Erotic Alba* (1972). Saville poses penetrating and useful questions about the genre, demonstrating how it elucidates specific aspects of medieval culture. He presents the larger literary context into which the alba fits but fails to appreciate the genre's significance within its more immediate lyric and romance contexts. And while he provides insightful general commentary from a number of perspectives, his study falls short, especially in its superficial analysis of the alba lady. For all the merits of Saville's study of the alba, the genre's elasticity, originality, and range are not given their due.

Hatto's *Eos* (1965) documents the motif of dawn-parting lovers in poetry of diverse cultures from ancient to recent times. A study of encyclopedic scope, this indispensable work makes a huge quantity of material easily accessible. But the work does not aim to examine in depth individual periods, languages, or songs. The chapters, arranged according to language and prepared by distinguished scholars in each linguistic field, provide brief surveys and interesting commentaries, original texts, translations, and manuscript data. Hatto's chapter on Middle High German tagelieder, although too brief, is expert and enlightening. Woledge's chapter on Old Provençal and Old French dawn-songs offers an excellent introduction, reliable English prose translations, and useful technical information about each lyric. But in so voluminous a work, neither scholar has much space to enlarge.

Dronke's comparative approach to the alba in *The Medieval Lyric* (1977) places a welcome emphasis on the lyrics' varied poetic qualities. While appreciative, engaging, perceptive, and learned, his chapter on the alba is again too brief. Of these works only Saville's provides in-depth analysis.

My study intends to fill this critical gap. The female presence in the alba is closely examined along with the more general problems posed by the male troubadours' creation of this new feminine voice. The changing conceptions of eros that unfold along with evolving vernacular verse forms, especially as they reveal themselves in the alba, are likewise studied in depth. *Erotic Dawn-Songs* strives to fathom the alba's depths, to comb the modulations of tone, theme, mode of presentation, character, and point of view. I aim to highlight the poetic virtuosity of these masterpieces and facilitate the reader's appreciation of their particular beauties and innovations. With that goal in mind, I have retained my own translations of the albas in order to furnish the most literal meanings. I hope that the rich lyricism of the genre will nonetheless be conveyed. All the albas under discussion have been translated, often brilliantly, by others; occasional borrowings from those translations are noted.

I trust that this book, like those works of scholarship that have inspired it, will provoke further debate and study.

The Lyric Lady and the Alba

> Know truly by my faith
> That he does us wrong—may God give him worse—
> Whoever parts me from you, sweet love!
> Anon., *"L'abe c'apiert au jor"*

The alba lady transgresses the boundaries erected to safeguard the courtly lady. She resides within the court but pursues an illicit romance that violates its mores. Her outlaw behavior and her outspokenness about it declare her an outsider inside the court. The elements that make her marginal—her voice and her illicit behavior—also make her pivotal. The alba lady's eloquent voice fills a void in the court as well as in the troubadour corpus. When we gather the entire array of lyric ladies into our line of vision, a considerably expanded spectrum of female figures becomes visible; the silent, iconic, courtly *domna* of the canso whom we customarily call *the* courtly lady is fleshed out by the alba lady. The alba lady is the link between the mute but exalted canso domna and the loud but lowly pastourelle shepherdess.[5] What purpose should such variety serve if all these women are to be seen as the same woman? The Middle Ages no more created a monolithic view of woman than it did of man. As Bynum notes in another context, "there is no such thing as . . . *the* medieval attitude toward women" (1991, 40). With its many poets, rich variety of genres, and array of registers, medieval literary art (despite the conventionality that appears on the surface to constrict originality) offers a number of avenues for differences to be expressed.

Yet when critics turn to medieval poetry to investigate the development of the idea of romantic love in the Middle Ages, they see only one woman: the silent, worshipped lady created in the canso. They discount or ignore other female presences even though such figures play more active and intriguing roles than the canso domna. The alba lady often sets the parameters for the illicit rendezvous and takes the discursive initiative. Embedded in her defiant song is a fictionalized confession that explores the boundaries of feminine desire and identity. Among lyric females, she plays a vital central role; her plaintive voice cries out for a hearing.

Because critics have failed to hear her, the alba's inventiveness and brilliance have not been fully appreciated. Even those who have written on the alba have neglected to explore its lady's uniqueness; instead, they view her as a recapitulation of classical and medieval female stereotypes or as an exemplary folktale figure. Maureen Fries, one of the few scholars to include the alba in her discussion of the female voice, sees the alba lady as a victim, representative of the otherness of woman in medieval lyric. Doris Earnshaw's *The Female Voice in Medieval Romance Lyric* (1988) makes four short references to the alba; but in both her remarks and Fries's, Saville's stereotyped view of the lady is accepted as a given rather than interrogated for its accuracy or logic. My study will correct these misreadings of the alba lady, revealing her distinctiveness when contrasted with literary precursors as well as contemporary models.

Furthermore, the alba sheds a different light on fin'amors. Its sympathetic stance toward adulterous love does not participate in the virulent misogyny of the antimatrimonial tradition: while the alba is clearly antimatrimonial, it targets the husband, sometimes referred to as the *gilos* (the jealous one), who is vilified and mocked throughout.[6] No critic has explored the alba's ridicule of the husband; nevertheless, Gaston Paris long ago (1883) expressed dismay over the fact that the *chanson de mal mariée* presents marriage "as a servitude from which the wife had the right to escape, and the jealous husband as the enemy against whom everything may be permitted, even though the only charge against him was precisely that of being the husband" (quoted by Nichols, "Medieval Women," 81n.12). Although significant exceptions exist (for example, in the poetry of Marcabru), scorn of the husband is a general convention of the troubadour corpus. But the alba poet, who gives vent to the lady's rage against her spouse and sides with her against her more powerful husband, must be making some kind of social commentary. Although the alba vilifies the husband and sometimes marriage, the lyric does not disparage women; to the contrary, it exalts both the lady and her lover. Her antimatrimonial protest is taken seriously enough to be answered in the form of a lover. The lover's presence and his words (when he sings) frame the audience's compassionate reception of her plight. The alba encircles a private space in the lyric landscape in which female experience, both joyful and sad, is treated with respect and sympathy. The alba is one poetic form in which the ambivalence toward and mistreatment of women that appears so blatant in other lyric genres vanishes.

The alba never enters the misogynistic discourse that, in R. H. Bloch's view, underlies the idealization of the lady generally present in the courtly lyric.[7] The eloquent and impassioned alba lady cannot be reduced to the silent, immobile canso domna. Because the canso lover envisions his lady as the best part of himself, the danger of rejection or disappointment if she should speak or otherwise assume a life of her own is too threatening. The perfect canso lady remains enshrined in perfect silence. Enthroned in a p(a)lace where ladies don't talk back, she reflects her suitor's glorified self-image at twice its size. Perhaps not surprisingly, the expressive alba and pastourelle women, who serve functions other than ennobling or aggrandizing the male wooer, are marginalized by poet and critic alike. But while the pastourelle shepherdess is all too often mocked or sullied, the alba lady is consistently presented as dignified and self-assured.

The symbiotic relationship between alba lovers who feel so intimately bound that separation is physically painful greatly differs from the scenario of the canso or pastourelle in which the lover's pursuit of his love object involves an implicit power struggle between the sexes. Furthermore, the alba lady is portrayed as having a life of her own: she speaks, acts, moves, and is moved; at the same time, she remains dignified. She is not diminished or rejected when she responds. In fact, the very act of speaking out—and its converse, remaining silent—emblematizes the dichotomization of the female image in courtly lyric. If the silence of the canso domna has come to signify a suppressed female other, the alba lady's *prise de parole* represents an entry into the public sphere of social interaction (Bruckner 1992, 865). The marginal speaking woman becomes much more central from this angle. Although predominantly crafted by male poets, the lyric female voice reveals itself to be a potent vehicle. It may not be a great wonder that the silenced canso lady is given center stage by poet and critic when speech is so empowering a force. But it is a wonder, then, that speaking females, however disenfranchised (and ignored by critics), are allotted any place at all in the troubadours' lyric landscape. If we persist in remaining deaf to the voices of alba ladies, we are as guilty of silencing an aspect of female experience as those who promoted the idealization of the mute canso lady.

The courtly lyric has been described as the juncture where "romantic love, virginity and the ascetic impulse" meet (Bloch 1991, 143; see also 147, 151). A number of critics argue, as does Bloch, that the unrequited nature of love in the canso is definitive for fin'amors. But this lack of reciprocation should not be broadly accepted as the defining act of courtly lyric. Mutuality is a vital aspect of the alba, as it is of numerous medieval love stories. This mutuality is so common a theme in early courtly love literature that we must seriously question the view of fin'amors as a form in which a distanced and virginal lady spurns intimacy. The renunciatory aspect was but one facet of the literary invention of courtly love; as courtly love evolved in the later Middle Ages and early Renaissance, especially in the hands of the *dolce stil novo* poets, it was increasingly transformed into a kind of Madonna worship. Before that transformation, mutuality rather than renunciation, both within and outside of marriage, was presented as the ultimate ideal in courtly lyrics and romance. The sexual aspect of courtly love, the voluntary character of romantic reciprocation, and the nonpatriarchal structure of its relationships in numerous works of literature should not be overlooked (McCash 1990, 430).

Although Bloch's characterization may be accurate for the canso, it contradicts the very nature of the alba: how can courtly lyric be the nexus for "romantic love, virginity and the ascetic impulse" if, from the alba's perspective, fin'amors is mutual and the lady courtly but not virginal because she is typically already married to someone else? Despite the fact that the canso is only one genre among many that present an array of stances toward women, love, sexuality, and sociopolitical concerns, many critics take the canso as representative of the entire lyric corpus and erroneously apply its conventions to the other genres. In the past, when these conventions failed to fit other genres, the critics marginalized those genres, categorizing them as derived from folk song or based on real-life experience. For earlier critics, this kind of categorization, which made such lyrics noncourtly, also made them, by extension, unimportant. The critics dichotomized the corpus into courtly and noncourtly and thereby dismissed those they classified as natural and realistic rather than courtly. Because reciprocation and sexual activity occur with a vengeance in the alba and the female voice dominates the genre, early critics excluded it from the courtly category. Thus, of the genres that include women, only the canso (in which the lady appears but is mute) was deemed worthy of study.

In setting up a definition of courtly love that ignores the reciprocated love of the alba (as well as the mutual love relationships that appear in many romances), Bloch reenacts the early critics' dismissal of the alba. But there is no longer any doubt that the alba is a courtly genre. Hence, even if the "deprecation of the feminine" that for Bloch "lurks just below the surface of the courtly idealization of woman" (1991, 148) can be found everywhere in the canso, it is evident nowhere in the alba.

The kind of generalities set forth in recent wide-ranging studies ignore differences among genres and between individual lyrics. These differences are crucial not only because such distinctions reveal individual poetic genius and artistic innovation, but also because the colloquy among courtly poets shaped the corpus. To overlook these differences is to misread and distort a poetry that thrives on them. We must recognize the "complex dialectic of opposite tendencies and seek the individual place of each poet in this dialectic" rather than devise a sweeping theory of courtly love that does not accommodate all its modulations and variations (Roncaglia 1964, 7). The troubadours and the poets who followed them mocked, parodied, mimicked, and vied with one another, variously affirming, negating, and attempting to surpass one another's songs. While the troubadours adapted other poets' patterns—rhyme schemes, sounds, key words—each poet stamped his or her song with a recognizable hallmark or idiosyncracy (Gaunt 1989, 71). The strong sense of self that emerges from many troubadour lyrics comes across through the interplay between the troubadour's ability to allude to the work of rival poets and his or her originality in performance and style (Kay 1990, 1–16; Nichols 1968, 374). Awareness of the intertextual dynamic of the corpus is vital to our ability to interpret its words: these poets valued, commented upon, and rivaled one another's ideas and skills; and their responses to one another were a more vital catalyst for their art (and should be for our understanding of it) than their attempt to perpetuate the misogyny that may be found embedded in it.

Although the alba may be a reaction to the objectification of women, this does not preclude the fact that canso and alba poets can be the same. An attempt at deprecation in one genre could well be undermined in another. The values dramatized in an individual lyric no more represent the poet's entire world view than an individual song by a performer today represents his or hers. The troubadours consciously invented stage personalities (Sutherland 1962–63, 96). In a lyric tradition that flourished on performance, experimented with varying self-images and diverse voices (sometimes even within a single song) and thrived on repetitions and variations of what others had to say, direct, spontaneous feeling on the part of the authorial "I" becomes elusive.[8] The song's aim is to present a fiction so persuasively that the audience believes it comes from the heart: "The poem will fail if the poet cannot make us believe the emotional experience is the shaping principle of the speaker's existence" (Nichols 1968, 355). Medieval poets created a repertory that established their range and virtuosity. Their combination of rhetorical skill and performance magic makes their art seem real.

In sum, any analysis of gender issues in medieval literature must grapple with the alba precisely because of its marked distinctiveness from all other models. Whether or not Bloch's interpretation, which is a summing up of many recent theories, accurately reflects the canso, the canso itself should not be taken as the sole or even most representative expression of love in the lyric, no matter how numerous its exemplars. The alba views fin'amors from an equally important but widely differing perspective, one that has left a lasting legacy of its own.

The alba presents a new feminine paradigm: she is reducible neither to Ovidian infiltration (derived from his sympathetic female-voiced *Heroides* heroines) nor to allegorical representations (akin to Dante's Beatrice). The voices that emerge in the letters of Ovid's heroines, noble and full of pathos as they are, are also formal, stilted, and rhetorically flamboyant. They possess none of the spontaneity and directness of the alba lady. And unlike her contemporaries—the ladies created in other medieval vernacular lyric genres—the alba lady is not mediated through the eyes of a male narrator or lover (as is the pastourelle shepherdess or canso lady). She speaks to us directly and dramatically, taking on the role of spokeswoman in vernacular courtly lyric. In that capacity, she sparks an original, nonconjugal discourse (one destined for critiquing by Dante in his creation of Francesca da Rimini in *Inferno* V). Her song, defiant yet dignified, celebrates consummated, reciprocal love even as it laments the aftereffects.

The alba lady's voice is, presumably, *man*-made: all the albas for which authorship is known are by men. Although we cannot rule out the possibility that, in the case of the ten anonymous albas, anonymous was a woman, scholars have found no evidence to suggest that a significant number of anonymous vernacular lyrics were composed by women. But this ventriloquism rather than a misogynistic usurpation of the female voice (as it is in medieval Latin verse) is empathic. It identifies with female passion, unites male and female experience; and poet, characters, and audience are swept up in the intensity of the moment and the emotions.

In response to the charges of misogyny leveled at medieval lyric poets, I would argue that the vision of love that emerges in the alba transcends the antifeminism so often expressed in medieval writing and offers instead a universalizing empathy.[9] The alba implicitly critiques the frustrated posturings of the canso lover as well as the silence of its iconic lady; the genre becomes a dialogue with or reaction to other courtly representations of love and ladies. And it makes explicit a sympathy for women that, more masked, may even lurk beneath the surface of the other genres.

In its opposition to the communal values of feudal society, the alba favors an antimatrimonial, individualizing, rebellious, and, by extension, ennobling love. If Bloch contends that the "invention of Western romantic love" is a manifestation of the antifeminism so pervasive in the Middle Ages that the term "medieval misogyny . . . seems redundant" (1991, 7), I counter that the idea of romantic love passed down to us by our medieval forebears embraces the dignity, mutuality, and passion that emerge exclusively and for the first time in Western literature in the alba, not in the canso, where "renunciation of the flesh" becomes "the great equalizer" (Bloch 1991, 81). The alba presents fin'amors from an angle not visible in other genres. But in the lyric corpus, love is a many-splendored thing.

In the alba poet's shaping hands, the stylized courtly lady springs to life. She is humanized into a lively, forthright, and spontaneous character. She is as dignified as the canso domna, but as emotive as the pastourelle peasant girl. The poet-lover's need for the real (pastourelle) woman that conflicts with his aspiration toward the ideal (canso) lady is beautifully resolved in the alba drama. For the first time in Western literature, an essential and unmistakable female link is forged between idealized/silent lady and lowly/loquacious woman. As a warm, sympathetic, and eloquent noblewoman, the alba lady reconciles the opposed aspects of an otherwise dichotomized female.

Alba poets, rather than being mired in conventional, oppressive conceptions of women or promoting female subordination, were obsessed with depicting, investigating, and anatomizing the anarchic emotions of sexual love. They tacitly criticize the stultifying societal gender roles and expectations that the love they create/portray seeks to transcend and that the characters in the alba heroically decry. Within the courtly corpus, the outlet for subversion is the alba.

This is not to claim that alba poets were social reformers nor to propose that their poetic achievements effected social change. Nor do I mean to deny that women were disenfranchised in the Middle Ages or to claim that the troubadours necessarily intended to liberate real women in the real world. It is time, however, to acknowledge the alba poets' utopian reenvisioning of the relations between the sexes within a larger society that is strongly misogynistic. The alban vision of love is a new, vital, and liberating contrast to the subjection and mocking of women in real life as well as in other literary forms: consider, on the one hand, the fabliau (where women are often mocked) or the pastourelle (where, as Gravdal has proven, the threat of rape is usually lurking); or, on the other hand, the canso (where the idealization of the courtly lady as a form of objectification leaves her no voice and no choice).

The alban vision of love is completely new. Despite its fictionality, the alba expresses feelings so poignant, sincere, and profound that its influence can still be felt, however unconsciously, in our own, ostensibly modern conception of romantic love. After all, our fictions are constructed from and ultimately may become part of our reality. The alba charts the changes of the heart and launches forth brave new ways of configuring eros. Alba poets convey their lovers' voices so sympathetically, richly, and authentically that they demonstrate for the first time in Western literature the equalizing alchemy of romantic love as well as the evolution—through the processes of fusion and separation—of the emerging self. What a marvel it is that in so misogynistic an age, the newly emergent self, as depicted in the medieval erotic alba, is female.

I
The Alba Lady

Literary and Social Perspectives

1

The Alba Lady
Literary Perspectives

Because the alba centers on female experience and is often sung by a female voice, contemporary critics have taken a special interest in the alba lady's character and voice.[1] However sympathetic to the female viewpoint they are, these scholars have unwittingly violated the spirit of the lyrics and produced a reductive and distorted view of the alba. Although most listeners lend compassionate ears to the alba lady's lament, we are apparently hearing very different songs.

For Saville and Fries, the lady of the alba shares the qualities attributed to women by almost all of the literary traditions known to the Middle Ages; there is nothing new in "her passion, her exclusive concern with love, her upholding of erotic values above all others, and her violent opposition to reality" (Saville 1972, 155). Characterized as an abandoned, wailing woman, the alba lady, like Dido, is degraded by her lover and deserted by Love. Seen from this perspective, she becomes merely another link in the long chain of powerless and passive females; and her genre becomes notorious for illustrating the "otherness of woman in medieval lyric by positing her ultimate desertion by her lover as well as her exclusion from the male community of action" (Fries 1981, 158).

By fitting the alba lady so neatly into existing categories, these critics cannot see her singularity. Far from reiterating the role of the passive, victimized female, the alba lady is neither ignored nor rejected by her lover. Rather than being destroyed by love, she gains strength. She sings to an audience of presumed sympathizers; and even though her activities are ostensibly secret, she serenades us so ardently about them that we become willing accessories to her "crime." Her active control over her romantic life, her rebellion against her expected subordinate role, and her articulation of her experience to the listening audience are as unprecedented as they are distinctive.

In ancient and medieval Western literature, women are presented from an abridged and constricted vantage point. The limited range of female models available to medieval authors has been cause for much commentary, especially among feminist scholars. But the scholars' much-needed correctives have not altered the fact that the portrayal of women in this literature is predominantly negative. Whether women are depicted as weak, wicked, abandoned, pitied, degraded, or mocked, they are not to be emulated. In the rarer instances when female figures are praiseworthy, as in the sublime perfection of the Virgin Mary or the idealized lady of courtly lyric, they are so transcendent that they cannot be emulated.

Female figures may appear with increasing frequency in larger or more central roles as literature approaches the modern period, but they are still presented primarily from unsympathetic viewpoints. Artists and thinkers of either sex who sought to challenge the prevailing derogatory attitude lacked the power to influence mainstream views. Female authorship was so isolated and rare a phenomenon that its influence was likewise negligible. Medieval literature, like other aspects of its culture, was dominated by the aristocratic and clerical classes and their elitist, masculine perspectives that by definition excluded women as well as the illiterate lower classes.

Yet the troubadours who began to sing praises of women in eleventh- and twelfth-century Europe infused fresh air into age-old literary gender conventions. The courtly lady, given a founding role in the building of a new cultural image, represents an entire class and aesthetic evoked in the word *cortoisie*. The majestic lyric lady of the troubadour canso, the canonical love-song, reflects her poet's vision of a mode of life that is peaceful, refined, and cultured. This courtly *domna* is an idealized blend of femininity and power, a regal emblem of virtue, strength, autonomy, and beauty. Courting her requires deference, verbal dexterity, tact, and personal worth; it becomes a major preoccupation of the lyric singer. But when the beloved canso lady is exalted, she is raised to such heights that only her reflection is discernible; she says and does nothing.[2]

The alba lady takes a detour from the narrow path down which her literary foremothers and sisters were led. She does not resemble the wife, betrothed, or helpmate of the epic hero—a provident, prudent, faithful, and supportive minor figure—although women of the epic may lament their men's departure as sorrowfully as does the alba lady. In epic, "women are fixed objects in the landscape through which men travel. They are often almost metonymical extensions of the home castle or town" (Bossy

1986/1990, 24). Odysseus moves across the epic landscape, encountering stationary female creatures and moving beyond them, passing from one woman to another. In classical epic, women are possessions traded among men. They are "exchanged, as gifts, as valuable prizes of war. The Trojan War is caused by a violation of proper exchanges, since Menelaos, the recipient of Helen, loses possession of her"; and Achilles' wrath at Agamemnon's taking away from him the captive Briseis opens the *Iliad;* (DuBois 1984, 99, 100). Aeneas likewise passes a succession of fixed female landmarks that include Creusa, Dido, the Sibyl, Camilla, and finally Lavinia (Bossy 1986/1990, 25). Women are used and then discarded when they no longer serve a purpose. Heilbrun's characterization of women's place in classical literature summarizes recent views about their representation: "The traditional place for women in literature may be seen clearly, if distantly, in the *Aeneid.* Which of us can forget the picture of Aeneas as he leaves the burning city of Troy? On his shoulders he carries his aging father, Anchises; by the hand he leads his son, Ascanius. Of his wife, Creusa, we seem to have lost account; so has Aeneas, so almost has Virgil. She has produced Aeneas's son, and can now only be an encumbrance to everyone. Aeneas's other hand is not offered to her; she is left to follow, and is lost in the shadows" (1973, 51). The famous manly trio "symbolizes the salvation from Troy of the masculine element, the family and future conceived in exclusively patrilineal terms" (Arthur 1984, 101). Aeneas does return to Troy in search of Creusa, risking life and mission in the process, only to discover that she has (conveniently) perished.

Women in feudal literature before the twelfth century function as sex objects, noble and virtuous wives and mothers, or deranged and monstrous creatures. Raising their children, facilitating their menfolk's success, nurturing their sons' martial instincts, or mourning or avenging their murdered kin, epic females exist to support the work of men. In Old English poems such as *Beowulf* or *Widsith*, they function as peace weavers or symbols of power or of monstrosity. Romantic passion between the sexes is absent from the Old English corpus (Robinson 1984, 118–19). In *Beowulf,* women are marginal figures, having "no space to occupy, to claim, to speak from"; love is "a means of developing solidarity" among men, and marriage, too, "is essentially an alliance of men" (Overing 1990, 72, 74). In Norse literary sagas, the female figure functions primarily as the *Hertzerin,* the instigator whose only power is to incite men to war or revenge (Jochens 1986, 40).

Ladies who appear in the *chanson de geste* are "stock characters who symbolically complete the hero's experience; their marriage to the hero provides a resolution of the action" (Feinstein 1986, 253). Female characters in these works often assure, counsel, and encourage men in their activities. Should a woman have a personal agenda unconnected to the success of a man, she becomes a destructive force, a mad or evil woman who must be subdued.[3] The woman allowed to speak at will in a chanson de geste speaks for men. Women's views, when voiced, "tend to be those of a chorus close to the wings which upholds the values of the masculine heroes performing on center stage. They witness rather than question. They do not seek to convey an illusion of personal introspection" (Bossy 1986/1990, 29, 34).

The fair Aude, Roland's fiancée, receives great honors at her burial, her heroic (and only) action being to fall dead at Charlemagne's feet upon learning of her valiant betrothed's death (Goldin, 1978, 155, 3708–22). Ferrante describes such epic ladies as "passive victims of power struggles and war, ignored when they attempt to participate openly, forced to maneuver behind the scenes, which they often do quite successfully" (1988, 216).

The alba lady does not resemble the lewd, obsessed, sometimes evil creature in medieval narratives who often threatens the hero or his marriage—a figure used primarily to test him, such as Arthur's treacherous queen in Marie de France's "Lanval," Kilydd's second wife in the Welsh "How Culhwch Won Olwen," or the ravishing maiden who tries in vain to seduce the loyal hero of Chrétien's *Lancelot*.[4] The alba lady is as different from the crude and comic pleasure-seeking fabliau women as from their more elevated sisters. The women of the vernacular fabliau scheme either to seduce or prevent seduction.[5] While the fabliau woman's perpetually deceived husband is often the object of derision, in numerous examples she, too, is duped: "Male domination and aggression take an expected place . . . [and] male sexuality is given somewhat more prominence than female." Nevertheless, the emphasis on female appetite is one of the form's persistent topics (Muscatine 1957, 110–12, 121). Fabliau women are presented as naive, illiterate, unrefined, or coarse. Their speech often reflects their lack of elegance—their noncourtliness. The consequences of their sexual activity (seduction, rape, pregnancy, abandonment by the lover, or discovery by the lady's husband) are often the impetus of the tale, subjects absent from courtly verse.

Medieval Latin lyrics, written by and for clerics, mock and degrade women. Even those narrated by a female voice portray women primarily as victims of male predation and present their love experience as ultimately thwarted or unhappy. Schotter's study of female-voiced medieval Latin poetry reveals how these lyrics not only "constitute a [male] projection of woman's erotic experience," but also scorn or mock women's vulnerabilities (1981, 19, 21). In contrast to vernacular verse, the medieval Latin love lyric "was written not only by men but for men, to be performed before a male clerical audience" (19). There are, indeed, Ovidian infiltrations in these lyrics—from those antifeminist works of Ovid (unlike his *Heroides*) that celebrate deception and seduction of women. These works present love for women as an experience whose invariable unhappiness met with the audience's approval: "The genre as a whole is, in a sense, an extended use of prosopopoeia, in that it is an attribution of thought and feeling to a group which was historically mute. . . . The majority of woman's songs, however, are cynical, showing approval of the woman's abandonment" (30). The use of Latin simultaneously served the misogynistic aim of excluding women while expressing contempt for them.

Medieval Latin poetry does have a strain that invites sympathy and pity for the abandoned lady, echoing works such as Ovid's *Heroides* that present dignified female figures. The *Heroides* explores tragic love through the unique device of female-authored letters. Because he gives voices to women formerly silenced in their own stories, Ovid has been designated "the father of the female voice" (Calabrese 1993, 1). As such, the *Heroides* provides something of a prototype for the alba, regardless of whether the later poets demonstrate familiarity with this particular work.[6] Ovid's ventriloquism ranges over an array of abandoned but faithful female lovers, victims of their overwhelming passions. In writing their autobiographical accounts, his heroines tell a personal love story in which their point of view comes across richly, sympathetically, and intelligently. But for all the dignity of Ovid's ladies, there is no sense that love itself is dignified. Ovid marshals great sympathy for his heroines, but love has not been a good in itself; rather, it has been destructive. The medieval Latin songs written in a similar sympathetic vein depict the female narrator's grief and often her regret over an unhappy love affair and focus on the solitude and desolation that now await her—her punishment for having loved so rashly. None of the positive or ennobling effects of love that the troubadours cultivate are apparent.

Nor does the alba lady resemble female figures inscribed in other genres of courtly lyric contemporary with her own: the canso and pastourelle. She is as different from the outspoken, defensive (but often defenseless) pastourelle shepherdess as she is from the isolated and mute canso lady. The canso lady's perfection depends on her silence, whereas the pastourelle shepherdess, a peasant, has no sublimity to lose. Like the alba lady, the pastourelle shepherdess, or *pastora,* is vivacious and approachable. But in the duet between knight and shepherdess that is the body of the song, the shepherdess's words are conveyed indirectly through the narrator-knight's recounting of their meeting; it is his story he is telling. Her voice seems to come across loud and clear but is actually mediated through her boastful narrator's. The alba lady's voice, on the other hand, is unmediated by a male narrator (even though her words, like the pastourelle shepherdess's, are fashioned by a male poet). So clear and authentic is the alba lady's voice that past scholars saw in her an actual woman singing about a real love affair (a subject that did not compel their attention).

The revered and distant domna is already perfect; speech would only jeopardize the illusion. Worshipped but unresponsive, elevated but immobile, she is a virtual prisoner of the pedestal. Like Tennyson's "Lady of Shalott," the canso lady must remain within the static confines of the ideal. Were she to venture beyond these boundaries, she would automatically lose her sublimity: she would crack the image that mirrors, and freezes, her perfection. Response on her part would make her human rather than perfect, mortal instead of transcendent, simultaneously "killing" her sublimity and dispelling her lover's fantasy.

The definitive difference between the alba lady and her female lyric counterparts is that she reciprocates rather than disdains or ignores her wooer's affections. Unlike the canso and pastourelle, the alba is not a song of seduction. Rather, the alba bemoans the imminent separation of lovers who have spent the night together. The canso, on the other hand, laments the present distance between the lover and his lady; and the song is an attempt to bridge that distance. When Saville comments that "the mutual love relationship we see in the *alba* is scarcely unique in Medieval Literature. It is found with great frequency in the romance (e.g. Chrétien de Troyes, Gottfried's *Tristan*)," he fails to appreciate the uniqueness of this mutuality in the context of the lyric corpus (1972, 218). What occurs in medieval romance is often a working out of lyric emotions and scenarios, particularly in reference to the dynamics of falling in love (Ferrante 1975; Goldin, 1967, 107–8). Medieval poets, intrigued by the literary possibilities and psychological dimensions of the mutual, secret love introduced in the alba, perhaps began to explore its ramifications in romances as well. The happy union between hero and heroine that occurs in courtly romance cannot be a working out of the canso scenario because the canso is predicated upon nonreciprocal love. It is, rather, an elaboration of the genre that celebrates mutual love—the alba. Further, when the romance heroine is smitten, when she ruminates about love, when she suffers over her confusion and pain, when she responds, and, finally, when she parts from her beloved, her dignified reactions and heartfelt sorrow are modeled on the alba lady's.[7] How could it be otherwise? The canso domna, the only other aristocratic female model, never speaks. The female paradigm for the noble, loving, clever romance heroine is the alba lady. In other words, the germ of the kind of love presented "with great frequency" in the romances that Saville refers to (218) may well be found in the very albas he claims are unoriginal.

In sum, when courtly literature of the twelfth century provides an unprecedented role for women, the alba gives her the richest part (Ferrante 1984, 67). Although three characters typically take part—the lady, her lover, and the watchman—the female voice dominates. And that voice is dramatic, energized, vibrant. The alba lady possesses the beauty, dignity, and refinement that are hallmarks of the stately domna; but she is also given something the mute domna lacks—personality. That is, she is dramatized as expressing thoughts and emotions. Consequently, the alba lady offers a sharp contrast to the "motionless and emotionless" canso lady, whose lofty position on the pedestal makes her responses to experience, including those to her lover's suit, indecipherable (Goldin, 1967, 76).

Less idealized than the canso domna, the alba lady loses neither her desirability nor her respectability by reciprocating love or singing out. Even though she often lashes out against her enemies—her jealous husband, his spies, and local gossip-mongers—she does not lose courtly stature in the eyes of her lover or audience. The words and images used to describe the alba lady paint her as elevated and dignified, a domna.

Because the canso lady is perfect and the pastourelle peasant girl all too human, the alba lady reconciles these two opposing aspects of the female; she combines elements of each. Although she is less than perfect—possessing idiosyncratic tastes, personal opinions, intense emotions, defiant and loving actions, and forceful speech—the alba lady is completely courtly. That the troubadour gives her a voice is all the more remarkable considering that the courtly domna is otherwise silenced.

The Humanized Ideal

In the alba, the poet humanizes the perfect canso lady; he allows her to speak for herself, confront danger stoically, participate fully and joyfully in sexual activity, and bemoan and suffer the departure of her lover. In the face of imminent dawns, jealous husbands, envious spies, and wicked slanderers, the lady risks her reputation and possibly her life to pursue love. Although she is far less realistic than a three-dimensional character in later literary forms such as the novel, the alba lady is multidimensional. She is full of feeling and possesses true dignity. The alba poet adheres to the conventional stylization of courtly verse, but his attempt to portray a more rounded feminine figure and an aspect of female experience is as conspicuous as it is remarkable.

The lady's responsiveness liberates and energizes the alba. It humanizes and levels the rigid, hierarchical, and ineradicable conditions established in the canso. Through her voice, the poet calls rare attention to the feminine aspect of the love experience, capturing its vitality and power. Even if his portrayal is an inherently masculine idealization or projection (that is, a distortion) of the feminine experience, he centers on an aspect of love that up to this point had been sorely neglected in literature.

Unique, for example, is the realistic self-portrait of Cadenet's alba lady as she depicts her plight. In this lyric, which speaks most explicitly about the unsatisfactory marital situation that we should take as the generic given, the lady vividly presents her rationale for engaging in the adulterous liaison. She explains her situation directly, making no attempt to conceal her responsibility for the love affair; on the contrary, she boasts in her final strophe of her eager participation. The purely mercenary marriage arrangement may have been typical for its time, but her depiction of it is a rare moment in the alba. This is the only poem in the genre that portrays the *mariage de convenance,* and her opening strophe reveals what is even more rare and essential—a wife's reaction to it.[8] However frequent and acceptable this arrangement may have been, Cadenet's female creation deplores it:

> If ever I was fair or prized,
> I am turned from high to low,
> for to a boor I am bestowed
> all for the sake of his great wealth;
>   and I would die
> had I not my true love by
> to whom to tell my sorrows
>   and a pleasing watchman
>   who warns me of the morrow.

> S'anc fui belha ni prezada,
> ar sui d'aut en bas tornada,
> qu'a un vilan sui donada
> tot per sa gran manentia;
> > e murria
> s'ieu fin amic non avia
> cuy disses mo marrimen
> > e guaita plazen
> > que mi fes son d'alba. (ll. 1–9)

Given the opportunity to tell her side of the story, the lady describes her elevated premarital status. The opening conditional—"if ever" ("s'anc")—emphasizes her feeling that her former worth and beauty, for which she was much admired, seem part of a past existence so remote from her present circumstances that she has begun to doubt its reality.

Shifting to the present tense in the second line, she relates in quick succession what has followed since marriage: she has literally "been turned" ("sui tornada") from prized to despised. Although she herself has not changed, her worth has dissipated. She has taken the typically unpropitious ride on Fortune's wheel—once she was up; now she is down. This descent has occurred by the mere turn of events in her life, not by any real action she has taken. Given her use of the directional words "aut" and "bas," we should also interpret her turn as vertical rather than horizontal—that is, as a fall. Her fall has occurred because of a single event: marriage. She has been "given away" (and when she says "sui tornada," she speaks in the passive voice), sold into union with "un vilan" whom she later identifies as her spouse (l. 38). Although she was married off to a man of considerable means ("tot per sa gran manentia"), he has no worth in her eyes. As a vilan, her husband cannot know how to esteem her; consequently, she is removed from the sphere in which she was properly valued. Her beauty and refinement, like her husband's wealth, were assets, bargaining chips, that made the couple a desirable match (but that also dooms them, or at least her, to unhappiness).

In the lady's presentation of her marital plight, she is the victim. All the verbs in the first half of her strophe are in the passive voice, implying her lack of choice about the mercenary marital arrangement: events happened to her. The lady's agony is curtly expressed in the brief central line that connects the two halves of the strophe: "e murria" ("and I would die").

Her shift from passive to active voice in the second half of the strophe is telling; she reveals now how she rescued herself by taking a lover. She justifies her adultery by presenting it as a desperate reaction to her victimization. Under such circumstances, the audience may pity her; yet it cannot help but admire her self-assertion and courage.

The lady's determination to pursue her romantic attachment despite the dangers it entails takes on heroic overtones. She boasts in her final strophe:

> Never through threat or bluster
> that my wicked spouse might muster
> shall I fail to stay
> with my love until day
> for it would be
> ignorant vulgarity
> to part ignobly
> one's worthy lover
> from herself, before dawn.
>
> Ja per guap ni per menassa
> que mos mals maritz me fassa,
> no mudarai qu'ieu non jassa
> ab mon amic tro al dia,
> quar seria
> desconoissens vilania
> qui partia malamen
> son amic valen
> de si, tro en l'alba. (ll. 37–45)

Opening the strophe with the stark, startling "ja" ("never") and scorning her husband as "wicked" ("mals maritz"), she lauds her steadfast clinging to her lover until the last possible moment. She proudly defies all obstacles.

The lady's voice comes across not only in her words, but in the tight rhythms created by the demanding *coblas unisonans* versification. The strophes all begin with three isometric lines rhyming together followed by three *b* rhymes, two *c* rhymes, and a *d*. The lady not only relates her story and expresses a range of emotions, but Cadenet compacts it into this narrow and difficult form. We are meant to admire the artistry involved in such a presentation.[9]

Although her remedy for her marital ills breaks the law, she follows a law of another kind; for she invokes certain principles, employs key terms, and sings according to a fashion that frames her love within a courtly context. She disdains ignorance of a code of manners ("desconoissensa") that leads to discourteous ("malamen") behavior; her churlish husband is "un vilan" in contrast to her lover, who is noble and worthy ("fin'amic," "valen"). Indeed, her self-portrait is designed to forestall any hint of ignoble behavior, of "vilania," on her part. She may break her marital vow and vehemently denounce her despised spouse; but this, in the fin'amors ethic, never constitutes boorishness ("vilania"), the ultimate disgrace. Only her comportment toward her fin'amic concerns her. She so prizes refinement that, even in the anguish of being forced apart from her lover, she refuses to part "ignobly" ("malamen"), implying that to banish one's love before the moment of utmost necessity would be poor form. Her fin'amic valen, unlike her wicked spouse, must be treated with perfect courtesy; for he values it as much and is as deserving of it as she. She would be unworthy of the designation of fin'amics if she behaved otherwise.

The lady of "S'anc fui belha ni prezada" not only risks danger but defies it; and with the backing of the code of love to which she alludes, she does so in style. She adheres to a code that dictates a careful and calculated refinement, courtesy, and grace, the type of behavior that distinguishes her from her vilan spouse and any others—the uninitiated—who might dispute her point of view.

Although her tone is explanatory rather than self-pitying, forthright rather than manipulative, one of the lady's aims must be to inspire compassion in those who hear her song. She explains her actions according to a set of behaviors that she defines as courteous. Her success in winning our sympathy is testament to the efficacy and power—the eloquence—of her voice. Further, by presenting herself as an adherent to a preestablished code, she builds a case for her behavior as ethical. If she persuades us that her behavior is justified, she becomes a social critic, a spokeswoman for other unhappily wedded wives.

In addition to letting the lady proclaim her courtliness and in order that we do not have to accept only her word for it, Cadenet intersperses her monologue with a three-strophe soliloquy by the watchman, whose primary function is to corroborate the love's worthiness:

> "I am a courteous watchman who
> would never wish to be untrue

          to loyal love rightly made
       wherefore I watch for night to fade
             and at day-rise,
          he who with his lady lies
       may take his leave more boldly,
             kissing and holding,
             for I cry out, when I see dawn."

       "Were I watching in a castle where
       false love lodged its lair
       false I'd be, not to hide
       the day as long as I could abide;
             for I would never fear
       to part lovers insincere,
       but to aid the loyal pair
             loyally I watch with care
             for I cry out, when I see dawn."

       "Well pleased am I by long night's dark
       in wintertime, when it's most stark,
       and never shall I fail, for the cold,
       to be a loyal watchman bold
             always,
       so that the lover rests secure
       when he takes his pleasure pure
             from his worthy paramour
             for I cry out, when I see dawn."

       "Eu sui tan corteza guaita
       que no vuelh sia desfaita
       leials amors a dreit faita,
       per que·m don guarda del dia,
             si venria,
       e drutz que jai ab s'amia
       prenda comjat francamen,
             biazan e tenen,
             qu'ieu crit, quan vei l'alba.

       "S'ieu e nulh castelh guaitava
       ni fals'amors y renhava,

> fals si'ieu, si no celava
> lo jorn aitan quan poiria;
>   car volria
> partir falsa drudaria,
> et entre la leial gen
>   guait ieu leialmen
>   e crit, quan vei l'alba.
>
> "Be·m plai longua nueg escura
> el temps d'ivern, on plus dura,
> e no·m lais ges per freidura
> qu'ieu leials guaita no sia
>   tota via,
> per tal que segurs estia
> fins drutz, quan pren jauzimen
>   de domna valen,
>   et crit quan vei l'alba." (ll. 10–36)

The watchman boasts of his ability to distinguish true from false lovers. He claims to conceal day's approach from false lovers who deserve exposure for demeaning the ideals of fin'amors, of "loyal love rightly made" ("leials amors a dreit faita"). His talent for discerning types of lovers makes him the arbiter of love; the subtlety of his judgment exemplifies his own knowledge of love ("conoissensa"). The watchman, like the lady of the lyric, crafts a revealing self-portrait in which his own courtly conduct is manifest. His importance and usefulness reside not in his own skill at love but in his uncanny gift for assessing the loyalty and depth of the others' love; he is a watchman in more senses than one! He actively assumes the burden of defending true love. Perhaps we might consider such an outsider a figure for the poet himself, as Shapiro proposes (1976, 609, 620).

The alba poet dramatizes a woman in love. Like Cadenet's lady, the alba lady often narrates a large part, if not all, of the song. She not only sings, but the variety, intensity, and flexibility of her verbal responses reveal an extraordinary range of emotion. She expresses joy, desire, resentment, anger, sorrow; she praises, pledges loyalty, and wishes; she curses, commands, and threatens. Unlike the canso lady, the alba lady is so vehemently involved that she forswears all signs of distance and passivity; she sings out her joys and cries out her grief.

The alba lady's emotional range is reflected in the first strophe of "Cant voi l'aube dou jor venir," an alba that intermingles love and hate:

"When the dawn of day I spy,
Nothing do I more despise,
For it causes me to part
From my friend who holds my heart.
Now I hate nothing so much as day,
Love, which sends you far away."

"Cant voi l'aube dou jor venir,
Nulle rien ne doi tant haïr,
K'elle fait de moi departir
Mon amin cui j'ain per amors.
Or ne hais riens tant com le jour,
Amins, ke me depairt de vos."

Although expressing hatred, she still addresses her lover endearingly as "amins." The range from love to hate encompassed in the lady's song expresses not only the full spectrum of her emotions but also their fluidity as she swiftly shifts from love to hate and back again. The words "love" and "hate" pervade the strophe, intertwining: the intensity of her love may be said to engender her feelings of hate. Her range is extended by the use of the intensifiers "nulle rien" and "tant" in the strophe and repeated similarly in the refrain—"Or ne hais reins tant com le jor."

The theme of the intermingling of joy and sorrow prevalent in the alba is treated most powerfully in its Middle High German examples, the tageliet. The lady of Walther von der Vogelweide's "Friuntlîchen lac" learns to associate love and pain—"That which they call love, it is nothing except the pain of longing" ("daz si da heizent minne, deis niewan senede leit"). So, too, does the lover of Wolfram von Eschenbach's "Der helden minne ir klage," for whom the aftermath of love is "the bitter after the sweet" ("daz sûre nâch dem suezen"). In Wolfram's tagelieder, joy and sorrow are so intermingled that they physically merge: in "Ez ist nu tac," "enjoyment went along with their lament" ("dâ ergíe ein schimpf bî klage"); in "Den morgenblic," "the love indeed bore many sorrows between them" ("ir beider liebe doch vil sorgen truoc").

The alba lady's virulent anger is directed sometimes at her husband, invariably hovering on the periphery of the scene; sometimes at the watchman, who may be either friend or foe; and sometimes even at dawn itself. This anger clearly distinguishes her voice from all other domnas. Here is a lady capable of feeling intense emotion and expressing it emphatically. Her forceful, defiant language reflects an equally strong will. She chooses when to be refined; at other times, she lashes out in rage, most notably when she defies her husband. At those times, her manner contrasts markedly with the delicacy and refinement she displays toward her lover. We have seen this at work in "S'anc fui belha ni prezada" and "Cant voi l'aube dou jor venir." It is also present in "En un vergier sotz fuella d'albespi," where the lady graciously invites her lover to defy her spouse: "Let's do it all in spite of the gilos" ("Tot o fassam en despieg del gilos"). In Raimon de las Salas's "Dieus, aydatz," the lady is undaunted by the power of not only the gilos but an entire host of armed enemies:

> Never believe
> that for fear of armed men
> I would leave the games
> Of my friend
> Who in my arms
> Rejoicing lies.
>
> Non crezatz
> Per armatz
> Que jogars
> De mon amic lais,
> Qu'e mon bratz
> Jauzen jatz. (ll. 49–54)

The choppy rhythm and sharp sounds augment the sense of defiance expressed in her words.

Although the gilos is the main object of derision and defiance, the watchman, whose clamor ("schalle") distresses the lady in Wolfram von Eschenbach's "Sîne klâwen," also receives his share of abuse:

> "So it please you, watchman,
>   sing and leave him be,
>   who brought love here and love received.
> By your racket
>   he and I are ever startled
>   while the morningstar has nowhere yet arisen
>   over him, who came here seeking love,
>   nor any gleam of day.

> You have often stolen him away
> from my white arms, but never from my heart."

"Swaz dir gevalle,
  wahtaer, sinc und lâ den hie,
    der minne brâhte und minne enpfienc.
von dînem schalle
  ist er und ich erschrocken ie,
    sô nínder der mórgensterne ûf gienc
      ûf in, der her nâch minne ist komen,
        noch ninder lûhte tages lieht.
du hâst in dicke mir benomen
  von blanken armen, und ûz herzen niht."

(ll. 31–40)

The strophe ends with the lady's accusing the watchman of being the agent of separation. In the tageliet especially, he is maligned by the lady for his poor form and lack of consideration. In the Margrave of Hohenburg's tageliet "Ich wache umb eines ritters lîp," the lady damns the watchman and his singing: "Your life be damned,/ Watchman, and all that singing of yours!" ("Dîn lîp der müeze unsælic sîn,/ Wahtære, und al daz singen dîn!" [Hatto 1965, 457–58]). The tageliet lady's great rage toward the watchman is in keeping with the larger role the watchman assumes in Middle High German versions. By attacking the watchman, who functions in the tageliet as the lovers' ally, the lady displaces her attention from the real enemies of love, those powerful social forces that dictate love's secrecy. She also diverts the audience's potential suspicions about her own morality.

In Wolfram's "Ez ist nu tac," the lovers curse the dawn, which is accused of cheating and envying the lovers, rather than the watchman: "gevlouchet wart dem tage." The lady of Walther von der Vogelweide's "Friuntlîchen lac" threatens: "Woe betide you, Dawn,/ since you do not let me lie longer by my love" ("wê geschehe dir, tac,/ daz dû mich lâst bî liebe, langer blîben nieht"). The lady of the Old French "L'abe c'apiert au jor" beseeches God to punish anyone who disrupts the love union: "And know truly in good faith,/ That he does us wrong—God give him recompense—/ Whoever parts me and you, sweet love!" ("Et sachiés en bone foi,/ Ke malz nos fait, Dex li dont prix,/ Ki moi et vous depairt, dous amins!").

Despite her diatribes, however, the alba lady's dignified stature remains constant in the eyes of her lover and her audience. Her anger and scorn testify to the intensity, steadfastness, and depth of her love, the only justification for such behavior. The words and images used to describe her demonstrate her worthiness and respectability. The lady of "En un vergier sotz fuella d'albespi" is the very image of a domna—beautiful and pleasing:

> The lady is gracious and pleasing,
> for her beauty many regard her,
> and she holds her heart loyally on loving.
>
> La dompna es agradans e plazens,
> per sa beutat la gardon mantas gens,
> et a son cor en amar leyalmens. (ll. 21–23)

Her loyalty to love, the final image with which her anonymous poet leaves us, is especially prized. Dronke, correctly observing that "no other *alba* ends this way," believes that the poet concludes like this because the lady, "glowing with life and passionate," is meant to contrast with "the accepted 'portrait of a lady' in his society. That is why he ends by deliberately insisting on her courtly qualities, affirming that she is all that a *domna* should be. He is, one might say, forestalling objections: she is not impious in invoking God, not unrefined in spiting her husband, not unbecomingly lascivious in luring her lover; she is perfect, even by courtly standards" (1977, 175, 176).

Although "En un vergier sotz fuella d'albespi" may be the only alba that ends on such a note, all albas demonstrate this respect toward the lady. She is often spoken of in the superlative: she is "the best and most beautiful" ("plus . . . bon e bel" ["Gaita be"]); "the one of greatest worth" ("e so qu'eu plus voilh ai" ["Gaita be"]), "the being most beloved" ("la re que plus volia" ["Us cavaliers si jazia"]), "the very summit of beauty" ("de biauté le monjoie" ["Gaite de la tor"]), and "the noblest and best of all creatures" ("la gensor . . . la mielhs aibia" ["Ab la gensor que sia"]). Such descriptions tell us that her stature cannot be diminished; she is inherently courtly, and her actions are always appropriate. In fact, she is the measure by which courtliness in others, and in her lover, is assessed. And her loyalty to love is the overarching, definitive characteristic.

Another of the alba lady's humanizing characteristics is her willingness to confront the danger of the love affair, a danger that adds to the intensity of its pleasure. Unlike the passive and isolated canso lady, the alba lady assumes a fulfilled, intense, and active presence. Her courage establishes the strength and depth of her love. Her attachment to her lover is so physical and strong that she clings to him despite all threats. She actively denies the watchman's warnings, suspecting the world, nature, and sometimes even the watchman himself of miscalculating time in order to cheat her. In Wolfram's "Sîne klâwen," the watchman warns the lady to let the lover depart; but she scolds him instead for his interference:

> "By your racket
> > he and I are always startled
> > > while the morningstar has nowhere yet arisen
> > > > over him, who came here seeking love,
> > > > > nor any gleam of day.
> > > > You have often stolen him away
> > > > > from my white arms, but never from my heart."

> "von dînem schalle
> > ist er und ich erschrocken ie,
> > > sô nínder der mórgenstern ûf gienc
> > > > Ûf in, der her nâch minne ist komen,
> > > > > noch ninder lûhte tages lieht.
> > > > du hâst in dicke mir benomen
> > > > > von blanken armen, und ûz herzen niht."
> > > > > > (ll. 34–40)

Other tagelieder also focus on the lady's persistence. In her audacious willingness to risk all for the sake of love, the alba lady, like a valiant knight, is heroic. Her resistance to the watchman's warnings, her anger at his message, and her reluctance to part intensify our sense of the passion and power of her love.

The alba lady's passion contributes to the genre's realization of a more fully fleshed-out woman. In the alba lady, the icy indifference of the canso lady is transformed into flames of love. The depth of the couple's sorrow at the thought of parting touches us more fully because their union has been so intimate; their sacrifice also increases their dignity in our eyes.

Leonard Forster argues that the sexual activity implicit in the alba is undercut by an actual avoidance of explicit attention to it. In the alba, "the only way in which [love's] consummation may be treated is one which concentrates attention, not on the night of love (which in the best examples is barely indicated), but on the lament of the lovers because they have to part. In this way the senses have their due, but there is no coarse dwelling on sensual detail; however passionate the poetry, an atmosphere of discretion and delicacy is preserved. The safety valve for repressed sensual desires has been found and maintained on a courtly level and integrated into the convention" (Forster 1967, 121). It is crucial to note, however, that contrary to Forster's view, the alba really is explicitly sexual and sexually explicit. Most albas clearly place the lovers in compromising positions: the poets, although ignoring all details of conventional setting and description, consistently describe the lovers' physical closeness and bonding and carefully specify their reclining postures.

The lovers' side-by-side positioning demonstrates the mutuality and equality of their love relationship. This reciprocity is a factor of its sensuality, from which there is no reason to shy away. Meeting his paramour, the lover of "Ab la gensor que sia" describes not only his own supine position but also the activities in which he engaged while "asleep":

> By the noblest who could be
> and the fairest
> I lay me down the other day
> > all alone;
> > playing, laughing
> I slept until day.
>
> Ab la gensor que sia
> et ab la mielhs aibia
> mi colgei l'autre dia
> > tan solamen;
> > jogan rizen,
> m'adormi tro al dia. (ll. 1–6)

At the beginning of the second strophe, he again refers to this relaxed position and their activities:

> While I lay
> supine, sleeping,
> a sweet kiss she tendered me
> > so pleasingly

> that I feel it still
> and all my life I will.
>
> Mentre qu'ieu mi jazia
> e·n sobinas dormia
> un dous bais mi tendia
> tan plazenmen,
> qu'enquer lo·m sen
> e farai a ma via. (ll. 7–12)

While mundane details of place are omitted, the poem carefully details the lover's reclining posture. In "Gaite de la tor," the lovers' lying position is twice referred to: first by the watchman: "courtly lovers,/ who are at rest,/ lying in the quiet chamber" ("cortois ameor,/ qui a sejor/ gisez en chambre coie" [ll. 45–47]); and later by the lover himself: "Much I have lain/ In the chamber of joy" ("Pou ai geü/ En la chambre de joie" [ll. 63–64]). The lover recalls both the scene of the tryst and the "chamber of joy" ("chambre de joie")—a pun not only in English. Walther's "Friuntlîchen lac" also opens with a portrait of a reclining knight:

> Companionably lay
> a splendid knight
> in the arms of a lady.
>
> Friuntlîchen lac
> ein rîter vil gemeit
> an einer frowen arme. (ll. 1–3)

Later the lady implores the knight to stay longer: "now just lie awhile: you could never do so well" ("nû lige eht eine wîle: sô getæt dû nie sô wol" [l. 40]). The lover's supine posture is often mentioned at the opening of the poem as though it in itself is a generic marker. In "Dieus, aydatz," however, the lover's position is withheld until the conclusion, when the lady declares her reluctance to relinquish her lover, "who in my arms/ rejoicing lies" ("qu'e mon bratz/ jauzen jatz" [ll. 53–54]).

Simple phrases such as "ab son amic" or "pres de mi" or the tageliet phrase "bi mir" also indicate the lovers' side-by-side intimacy. The motif of attachment introduced in the opening lines of a well-known alba—"En un vergier sotz fuella d'albespi/ tenc la dompna son amic costa si"—is further marked by the juxtaposition of the words "la dompna son amic," which accentuates the lovers' conjoinment (literally, "in a park beneath the hawthorn leaves/ holds the lady her lover at her side"). The lady of "Cant voi l'aube dou jor venir" laments that she misses the presence "at her side" ("encoste mi") of her lover's body. The "breast-to-breast" embrace referred to in the tageliet echoes the Romance poets' use of the word "costa," which etymologically means "rib." These references to specific body parts emphasize the physicality, corporeality, and intimacy of the attachment. No virginal coyness veils these portrayals.

Furthermore, one need only glance at many of the lyrics to see the frank and often detailed manner in which sexuality is portrayed. The lady of "En un vergier sotz fuella d'albespi" actively initiates an escalating physical engagement with her lover: "let's kiss" ("baizem"), "let's play a new game" ("fassam un joc novel"), and "let's do it all" ("tot o fassam"). The lady of the beautiful and simple Old French "Entre moi et mon amin," coyer but no less involved in the erotic dimension of the rendezvous than her Old Provençal counterpart, playfully expresses her attraction to her lover while gracefully and artfully undercutting the blatantly sexual aspect:

> My love and I alone
> In a wood nearby Bethune,
> Played together Tuesday
> All night there by the moon,
>   Until the night turned gray
> And the lark arising, sang,
> As if to say: "Lovers, away";
> And he responded softly:
>   "It isn't nearly day.
>   Sweet noble heart,
>   so help me love,
>   The lark lies to us."
>
> Then he drew himself to me,
> And I did not draw back;
> Three times at least he kissed me,
> And I returned them back;
>   Now that did not tire me.
> Then how glad we should have been
> Had that night lasted one hundred.

> But we would not need to say:
> > "It isn't nearly day.
> > Sweet noble heart,
> > > so help me love,
> > The lark lies to us."

> Entre moi et mon amin,
> En un boix k'est leis Betune,
> Alainmes juwant mairdi
> Toute lai nuit a la lune,
> > Tant k'il ajornait
> E ke l'alowe chantait
> Ke dit: "Amins, alons an";
> Et il respont doucement:
> > "Il n'est mie jours.
> > Saverouze au cors gent,
> > > Si m'äit amors,
> > L'alowette nos mant."

> Adont ce trait pres de mi,
> Et je ne fu pas anfruine;
> Bien trois fois me baixait il.
> Ainsi fix je lui plus d'une
> > K'ainz ne m'anoiait.
> Adonc vocexiens nous lai
> Ke celle nut durest sant.
> Mais ke plus n'alest dixant:
> > "Il n'est mie jours.
> > Saverouze au cors gent,
> > > Si m'äit amors,
> > L'alowette nos mant."

Rather than affirming her eagerness, she understates the intensity of her desire with negative declarations (litotes): "I did not draw back" or "that did not tire me." Her lack of specificity with regard to numbers—"three times at least he kissed me/ And I returned to him more than one"—calls attention to the dizzying effects of the pleasure, a sense augmented by the contrasting evocation of one hundred nights. Moreover, the preponderance of understatements emphasizes the disproportion between the elegance of her description and the intensity of her emotion. The resulting impression suggests the inadequacy of words to convey the intensity of her feelings. Indeed, the Old French poet masterfully centers on the lady's pleasure and the delicacy of her expression of it.

In commenting on the discretion and delicacy of the alba, Forster singles out one of the genre's most extraordinary and appealing aspects. This sensibility is not a result of the poets' intentional veiling of sexuality, as Forster posits, but rather a function of their emphasis on the lovers' inherent refinement—delicacy and discretion shown in their excellent and graceful manners. Such characterization demonstrates that sexuality and passion can be depicted and explored with good humor and decorum. Further, the poet's pleasing and courtly portrayal blazons forth his own refinement and proves his ability to explore love with dignity as well as finesse without renouncing its sexuality. This is significant in a broader way because it contradicts prevalent theories that courtly love in general is chaste.[10]

The alba's sexuality is taken up with particular gusto by Wolfram von Eschenbach, author of four highly regarded tagelieder and one "antitageliet" (in addition to the narrative masterpieces, *Parzival*, *Willehalm*, and *Titurel*). In "Den morgenblic," he sharply focuses on the lovers' intimacy: "the lady pressed her lover fast to herself" ("diu vríundîn den vriunt vast an sich dwanc"). In the concluding stanza, the lovers' embrace is analogized to artistic endeavor:

> The sad man swiftly took his leave like this:
>   their smooth bright skins
>   came nearer, thus the day shone in.
> crying eyes—a sweet woman's kiss!
>   thus they could then intertwine
>   their lips, their breasts, their arms, their white thighs.
> Whichever painter were to portray it
>   companionably as they lay, that would indeed have been enough.
>   Although their love bore them many sorrows,
> They cultivated love without any hate.
>
> Der trûric man nam urloup balde alsus:
>   ir liehten vel, diu slehten,

> kômen nâher, swie der tac erschein.
> weindiu ougen—süezer vrouwen kus!
> sus kunden sî dô vlehten
> ir munde, ir bruste, ir arme, ir blankiu bein.
> Swelch schiltaer entwurfe daz,
> gesellechlîchen als si lâgen, des waere ouch dem genouc.
> ir beider lieber doch vil sorgen trouc,
> si pflâgen minne ân allen haz. (ll. 21–30)

The graphic and lively depiction of physical intimacy demonstrates Wolfram's interest in the specific activities of human love. Although stark and direct, the portrait does not violate the narrator's sense of propriety. The allusion to pictorial beauty in the evocation of the "shield painter" ["schiltaer"] endows the scene with a decorum that justifies Wolfram's wholly unconventional detailing of sexual activity.

In the poem's final stanza, Wolfram shifts from the lovers' direct discourse to omniscient narration, distancing us from the immediacy and closeness that the lovers' voices had given us earlier. We turn to a more objective, aesthetic point of view as Wolfram prepares us for the most graphic scene in the poem. The idea of satisfaction alluded to in the word "enough" ("genuoc") is not conveyed directly by the lovers but by the outsider. The closer the lovers get to each other, the further the narrative point of view recedes from them.

In his reference to the shield painter, the narrator implies that the lovers provide fertile subject matter for art.[11] The lines invoking the painter have been given varying interpretations and translations:

> Whichever painter were to portray it
> companionably as they lay, that would indeed have been enough.
>
> Swelch schiltaer entwurfe daz,
> geselleclîchen als si lâgen, des waere ouch dem genouc. (ll. 8–10)

Hatto, making the passage a comment on the lovers' movements, translates: "If a painter were to sketch it, companionably as they lay, he would have enough to do" (1965, 451). In other words, the complexity and confusion of the scene are a challenge to any artist. To capture such frantic and tumultuous action, the artist would have to freeze motion itself.

Sayce, in her note, centers on the idea of artistry: "Lit. 'that would satisfy even him,' i.e. could he paint them as they really were: 'he would indeed be equal to his task'" (1967, 121n). In other words, no artistic embellishment would be necessary because the scene is already a work of art; a reflection of reality would achieve the greatest artistic success. Richey's verse translation has a slightly different tinge (1969, 99):

> If a shield painter could have limned them there,
> Where they lay clasped, no other picture could have been so fair.

Her reading also stresses the beauty of the scene as it is—not to indicate the difficulty an artist would have in capturing it but to suggest the consummate glory of the scene, the unsurpassable delicacy and refinement of the lovers' actions.

Both Hatto's and Sayce's interpretations, unlike Richey's, focus on the traditional topos that the scene defies representation. How can an artist depict such turbulent and swift motion, such complex intertwinings, such confusions and profusions of parts? Not surprisingly, Wolfram solves the riddle he poses: only an artist of the greatest magnitude could do justice to such a scene—an artist only as supremely gifted as Wolfram himself! In this brilliant rhetorical maneuver, Wolfram becomes the master painter to whom he alludes. He furthermore proclaims the superiority of poetry over any other art, for it is in poetry rather than paint that the representation is achieved.

That such a vivid and detailed private love scene would be appropriate *matière* for a medieval shield painter or a painter in any other medium—or a poet, for that matter—is almost shocking. Yet in creating and animating this scene, Wolfram applies the conventional artist-defying topos to very unconventional subject matter without veiling, understating, or euphemizing it. He has painted the act of human passion in all its splendor and has made his depiction not only acceptable but an artistic triumph.

This depiction of the lovers' embrace, although powerful and explicit, is neither coarse nor animalistic. Sympathy and admiration for the lovers are expressed: their skins are "liehten" ("white," "bright," or "shining"); the lady is "süezer" ("sweet"); their legs are "blankiu" ("white," "shining"; Hatto translates this nicely as "gleaming"). Wolfram's allusion to the artist encourages us to view the lovers as objects of beauty. Despite their sorrow, they are able to "cultivate" their love. The concluding phrase, "without any hate" ("an allen haz"), is the kind of understatement that emphasizes the intensity of the opposite emotion.

Wolfram's use of the motif of artistry in portraying the lovers' embrace is apparent also in "Ez ist nu tac," where he presents his lovers so inextricably entwined that they achieve new heights of intimacy:

So nobly together did these friends fit,
that never had two been so tightly knit;
    wherefore still now Love retains the renown.
        If three suns (instead of one) had been shining
            even their light could never glance through such entwining.

Si hâten beide sich bewegen,
ez enwárt sô nâhen nie gelegen,
    des noch diu minne hât den prîs:
        ob der sunner drî mit blicke waeren,
            sine möhten zwischen sî geliuhten. (ll. 29–33)

That three poetic suns cannot detect any space between the entwined lovers is an ironic allusion to the actual disruptive effect that the one real sun will have, making visible the lovers' disengagement. Wolfram's tagelieder demonstrate that explicit sexuality does not in any way compromise courtly comportment and status. On the contrary, the alba proclaims the idea that the consummation of love can provide as acceptable matière for courtly poetry as unrequited passion can.

If the alba lady experiences love in its fullest, most passionate moments, she must also suffer its saddest, most painful ones. She often dreams up fantastic resolutions to her sorrow, expressed in rhetorical figures known as *adynata* that proclaim simultaneously her desire and desperation. In "En un vergier sotz fuella d'albespi," the lady implores God to perform the miracle of altering reality in accordance with her wishes, requesting His aid in Love's cause. By expressing wishes that contradict reality, the lady implicitly acknowledges reality. In "Entre moi et mon amin," the lady echoes a sentiment from Psalm 84: "For one day in thy courts is better than one thousand." But she has changed the time of the wish to night—a very secular inversion of the sacred meaning: "And so glad we should have been, if that night had lasted one hundred" ("Adonc vocexiens nous lai/ Ke celle nut durest sant"). The desire to extend precious nighttime is echoed throughout the genre. Saïz comments that "since the *alba* is a genre that stresses realism, the lady's wish is never granted" (1976, 33n.25). Because the lovers are pleasure-oriented, their wishes assume great importance. Valuing primacy of feeling, alba lovers attempt to make reality accommodate itself to desire; and they fantasize that God, too, will make circumstances accord with their wishes. But the genre does not stress realism any more than it stresses fantasy: the alba focuses, rather, on the clashing of fantasy and reality that occurs at dawn.

The alba lady also voices her despondency more directly. The lady of Walther's tageliet "Friuntlîchen lac" focuses not on dawn but on her newly discovered definition of love, a definition that pervades the tageliet far more than its Romance counterpart: "that which they call love, it is nothing except the pain of longing" ("daz si dâ heizent minne, deis niewan senede leit"). Her personal experience of love alters her; she arrives at new, sobering knowledge. She anticipates being overwhelmed by sorrow and dreads the length of time that must pass before she will be able to see her lover again. She says such empty time "will seem endless/ . . . Indeed, I do not see an end to how long I must do without you" ("jon weiz ich niht ein ende, wie lange ich dîn enbir"). Her concluding complaint, though rarely articulated by Romance alba ladies, is in tune with the sorrow with which albas in any language leave us: "now I lie without love just like a woman filled with longing" ("nû lige ich liebes âne reht als ein senede wîp"). In the alba couple's suffering, we discover an eternal truth about what it is to be human: it is a condition of change and loss. As loss weighs upon them and despite their grief, alba lovers must reorient themselves to the inevitability of parting, a prefiguring of love's eventual total dissolution. Such comprehension endows their grief with depth and dignity.

The alba lady has become the obverse of the chill and distant canso lady; fired by love and torn by grief, she sings with sincerity and immediacy, fathoming the depths of her complex humanity. The qualities that humanize her—voice, anger, desire, grief—do not undermine her exalted stature or the elevated tone of the alba. Like the lady of "En un vergier sotz fuella d'albespi," all alba ladies are clearly courtly; their behavior is dignified, decorous, and fitting. Unlike the pitied, vulnerable ladies who become victims of their sexuality or love, such as Ovid's *Heroides* narrators or fabliau women, the alba lady is intelligent, shrewd, strong, defiant. She punishes neither herself nor her lover for her sorrow. If she laments parting from her lover, she also claims responsibility for her active choice of the illicit relationship. In albas, it is loveless marriage, not requited passion that victimizes the lady (see chapters 2 and 3).

Despite the authenticity and eloquence of her voice, it is nevertheless a male poet's projection. The poet allows the alba lady a voice of her own—even if it is only a vehicle for his vision. The male lover, although he is no less humanized than his alba lady, is portrayed in a sympathetic way in other genres. His compassion, tenderness, humor, anger, sorrow, and fear are fully apparent in the canso, although from the perspective of the unrequited lover. His personal traits do not emerge as the result of innovative treatment in the alba.

The figure of the alba lady, on the other hand, is utterly new. Her poet may not have succeeded in capturing the essence of womanhood or the totality of the female experience, but what artist, male or female, has? Yet in its sympathetic portrait of a woman who is actively loving as well as dignified, the alba reaches out toward a far more complex and expansive vision of womanhood and, indeed, of love itself.

2

The Alba Lady
Sex Roles and Social Roles

> Who peyntede the leon, tel me who?
> *Geoffrey Chaucer, "Prologue to The Tale of the Wife of Bath"*

Rather than recognizing the fundamentally anticonventional nature of the alba, some critics have sought to show how the genre upholds conventional sex roles. Kaske, Saville, and Fries apply various sex-role theories to it. But most scholars today understand that sex-role theory is a dangerous tool: many of the assumptions that lie behind our perceptions of the differences between male and female roles are so deeply ingrained and automatic that those who are most bound by them are often the least conscious of their presence. Because our most powerful impulses frequently turn out to be those we have most deeply repressed, it is difficult to be fully aware of our own perspective—hence, our own biases. Assessments of male and female roles are particularly vulnerable to such subjective treatment, for gender-based assumptions are intertwined with our fundamental understandings of our culture. Consequently, when we study gender-related subjects, we must be especially careful not to allow our own conceptions of sex roles to cloud our view. Many errors of perception have been made by past—and mostly male—scholars; feminist critics have taken the lead in correcting the record in many disciplines.[1]

In *Female Strategies,* a fascinating exposé of past omissions and errors of biological researchers, biologists Evelyn Shaw and Joan Darling claim that most biological researchers have been so blinded by their own preconceptions about animal sexual behavior that they fail to observe it accurately. One of the authors' most significant conclusions is generally applicable: "The feminine stereotype is so tightly etched in scientific thought that a female [animal] who is brightly colored, promiscuous and a gadabout is described as showing 'sex role reversal'—in other words, taking the expected masculine role. . . . Many scientists are reluctant to relinquish their cherished image of the male's monopoly on courtship behavior and sexual drive" (1985, 11–12). Male animals showing nurturing behavior are seen as acting maternally when, Shaw and Darling contend, they are simply showing a parenting impulse not alien to either sex. But researchers who record data that conflict with their notions of appropriate or expected behavior designate such behavior sex-role reversal. Of course, scientists are not the sole culprits of such flawed perceptions. As scholars, we must be wary of imposing personal views about sex roles onto literary characters or narrative voices; such designations reveal more about our own preconceptions of masculinity and femininity than the poetry our studies are intended to elucidate.

In "The Aube in Chaucer's *Troilus*" (1961), Kaske introduced the idea that alba lovers consistently illustrate specified sex roles. He posits that there are definitive sex roles in albas and that Chaucer intentionally reverses those roles in his alba in Book III: "In particular, Chaucer seems to have bestowed on Troilus several speeches usually assigned to the lady in an aube, and on Criseyde certain speeches usually assigned to the lover, thus enriching a theme sometimes detected in other parts of the poem: the reversal of the roles of man and woman as they are popularly or romantically conceived" (171). Even today assessing how sex roles are "popularly or romantically conceived" is no simple matter; to speculate about how they were conceived in the Middle Ages in general, or in a particular genre of lyric, seems nearly impossible.

Kaske qualifies his interpretation with a proviso that it is inconclusive, noting that the number of his examples are "suspiciously slight" and that exceptions to his patterns are present "in every instance" (176). Nevertheless, his cautions have not been heeded. Because the extant corpus of albas is small (and that corpus is possibly only a fraction of what was composed and popularly known), one should at the very least hesitate to make large generalizations about its male and female roles, especially considering that there are many exceptions to the posited norms, as Kaske carefully acknowledges. Yet Kaske's interpretation has never been challenged; it has instead been accepted and elaborated. Consequently, sex-role analysis and its corollary, the sex-role reversal theory, have engendered a view of the alba that has become not only more entrenched with time, but also increasingly distorted. Rather than examining the albas themselves to corroborate Kaske's initial impressions, subsequent critics have relied upon his hypothesis *as a closed case* (except for Saville, whose full knowledge of the genre does not prevent him from applying sex-role theory).

Kaske's quest for consistency in sex-role presentation reveals his concern with prescribed gender roles far more than it illuminates the medieval genre. And subsequent scholars' continuing preoccupation with this line of inquiry reflects not medieval but modern cultural anxiety about the proper roles of male and female and the catastrophic consequences of not conforming to these roles. Hence, Kaske's hypothesized sex-role reversal between Troilus and Criseyde may conveniently explain the disasters that inevitably follow.

In characterizing the role of alba males and females, Saville likewise invokes the sex-role reversal theory: "While the knight is usually the first to give in and accept reality, the lady usually accepts it only grudgingly, if at all, and only when the man is already taking his leave. In a few albas the lady is much concerned with the knight's safety, and seconds the watchman's urgings that he leave. But this is so unusual a state of affairs that we are probably justified in considering it a conscious reversal (on the part of the poet) of the norm" (1972, 154). Saville further describes the alba lady as "much more passionate than the knight; and much more eloquent in her expression of feeling" (153). Although the genre's artistry often resides in the lady's eloquent lament—the song's raison d'être and centerpiece—and albas are sung more often by the lady than any other character, one finds that whenever alba men (be they watchmen or lovers) address the lady or the audience, their voices are intense and ardent—complementary to rather than competitive with the lady's.

The idea that because the alba lady is passionate and eloquent her lover cannot be so as well may be a modern bias. Theatrically minded or psychologically aware critics bring to their view of lovers in dramatic poetry the idea that they are competing for external recognition (that is, from either the inscribed or extradiagetic audience), a contest more relevant to siblings competing for parental attention or actors vying with one another for the spotlight or the audience's acclaim than to parting lovers. No such rivalry is evident between alba lovers. In other lyric genres, male and female are inherently unequal: in the pastourelle, the peasant girl is accosted by an aristocratic knight, however errant; in the canso, the exalted lady is worshipped by one who feels (and may be) morally and socially inferior. But the alba never postulates one lover's or gender's superiority over the other, an aspect that is one of the most significant and touching innovations of the genre.

Ironically, while Kaske and Saville have sought to distinguish gender-defined behavior as well as significant divergences from a posited set of norms in the alba, they have overlooked the more pervasive and obvious similarities between the sexes. Interpretations based on sex-role stereotypes overlook both the genre's variety and its major concerns. Equality and reciprocity, not difference or indifference, are at the heart of the alba. Kaske twice notes, in an offhanded way, the free assignment of roles in the alba, ignoring the definitive value of such fluid role adoption: "Criseyde's wish for longer night (1427–28) is a commonplace, freely assigned to either of the lovers in an aube.... This commitment of the loved one to God's care is a frequent motif in the aube, where it is freely assigned to either the lover or the lady" (1961, 172, 174).

Disregarding the active and aggressive role the alba lady regularly takes as initiator and celebrant of the love affair, Fries considers the alba lady an exemplification of the philocentric, passive, and impotent female, desperate to retain her lover within her narrow world: "The woman speaker is absorbed in the experience of the beloved's presence in or absence from her arms, a passive experience as opposed to that world of male activity which occupies most of his life.... She may be rhetorically dominant but is actually powerless in her attempts to confine her man within the bounds of her feminine world, as most dramatically illustrated in the *alba*" (1981, 159). She ignores the alba male's equal obsession with his lady; and in contrasting the lady's presumed passivity to an opposing "world of male activity," Fries presumes that the lady's experience is personal and passive ("her feminine world"—that is, domestic and stultifying) as opposed to male experience, which is public, active, and free. These loaded terms illuminate Fries's (and typically modern) biases more than they do the alba.

Before we turn to the lyrics that contradict such sex-role analyses, let us note in passing that the "world of male activity" is so remote from the alba landscape as to render it irrelevant to the lovers' laments. The exclusion of the outside world is an essential generic attribute: alba love strives for a self-enclosed autonomy that shuts out external forces. *Both* lovers long to escape from the "world of male activity," which for them is synonymous with the despised authoritarian obstruction to their love, self-expression, and freedom. That the lovers try so hard to shut out the world is testimony to its pervasive, tyrannical presence in their lives.

Moreover, when one reads through the alba corpus, it becomes quite clear that there is no rigidly defined sex role for lady or lover. On the contrary, one discovers a more expansive and liberating view of traditional gender roles. Alba lovers are, if anything, anticonventional. The lady's role is significantly less confining than that of other lyric ladies: she is forced into neither the icy silence of the canso lady nor the lewdness of the pastourelle peasant girl. In her varied and artful voices, her adoption of diverse roles, and what could be called her exchanges rather than reversals of roles with her lover, she escapes the confinement of traditional female roles both social and literary. She fully indulges in the creative expression inspired by the liberating, though secret, love she pursues. But her freedom and self-indulgence reveal a shedding of conventional roles rather than a substitution of one set of roles for its opposite.

Examination of the corpus reveals that either alba lover can be passive or aggressive, but both are powerless—and equally desperate—to change their situation. Both desire to perpetuate night. And the male lover, like his beloved, is totally absorbed in the love experience rather than any other activity. In the Old Provençal alba "Ab la gensor que sia" the male lover longingly recounts an idyllic tryst with his lady. He recollects how, after their joyful play, he fell asleep beside his beloved until dawn:

> By the noblest who could be
> and the fairest
> I lay me down the other day
> > so alone
> > playing, laughing
> I slept until day.

> Ab la gensor que sia
> et ab la mielhs aibia
> mi colgei l'autre dia
> > tan solamen
> > jogan rizen
> m'adormi tro al dia. (ll. 1–6)

Passively receptive to his lady's actions, the lover reminisces with as much longing as any alba lady:

> While I lay
> supine, sleeping,

> a sweet kiss she tendered me
> > so pleasingly
> > that I feel it still
> and all my life I will.

> Mentre qu'ieu mi jazia
> En sobinas dormia,
> Un dous bais mi tendia
> > Tan plazenmen,
> > Qu'enquer lo·m sen
> E farai a ma via. (ll. 7–12)

The lady in this dreamlike sequence appears as the more active partner, while the lover paints himself as passive, reclining, sleeping, responding—a self-portrait that might tempt some readers to characterize him as "feminine," especially because he presents himself as the object of another's desire. But to so typecast him would be distorting. In the remainder of the lyric, he angrily threatens the watchman and the gilos. His aggressive side is revealed in strophe 3:

> Watchman, if I held you,
> in my hands, I'd kill you;
> Nothing would ever help you one bit
> > neither gold nor silver
> > nor living man,
> nor anything in the world.

> Gaita, s'ieu ti tenia,
> De mas t'auciria,
> Ja res pro no·t tenria,
> > Aur ni argen
> > Ni hom viven
> Ni res que e·l mon sia. (ll. 13–18)

He calls down curses on the watchman: "Gaita, dieus ti maldia" (l. 19).

The contrast between his loving affection for his lady and his verbal (and potentially physical) aggression toward the watchman reveals his complexity and emotional range, his humanity. Ironically, *he* resembles Fries's "rhetorically dominant but . . . actually powerless" lady. At the same time, the reader who, bound by sex-role stereotypes, evaluates the lover's initial self-presentation as "feminine," would now be forced to reappraise him in light of his subsequent "masculine" behavior.

In fact, all alba lovers, male and female, are "rhetorically dominant but ... actually powerless" to do anything about their predicament. Nevertheless, the power of rhetorical dominance, especially on the part of a gifted narrator or poet, should not be underestimated. That the poet gives his lovers license to cry out against their pain is an empowering recognition, even legitimation, of their plight. The powerlessness indicated by vigorous complaint or desperate wish is undercut by the literary or performance context in which it is the rhetorically dominant voice that is heard and endures. The voice of the husband, however authoritative, is excluded from the alba and effectively silenced.

Although the poet of "Ab la gensor que sia" endows the lover with particular behavioral traits, he nowhere suggests that they are gendered. The lover of the poem behaves with discrimination: he is gentle and passionate toward his lady but not toward the gilos or watchman. He adjusts his emotions according to their object, demonstrating an elasticity of response, a capacity for making distinctions within a range of possible responses. But for all his range, he resists reality as much as any alba lady.

If this lover reminisces with longing, so, too, does the lady of the Old French "Entre moi et mon amin." She recalls a tryst in which she and her lover were also "playing" ("juwant") one moonlit night until dawn. Like the male lover of the previously cited lyric, she then relates her lover's actions:

> Then he drew himself to me
> And I did not hold back
> Three times at least he kissed me
> More than once I kissed him back
>   For that did not bore me.
> Then how glad we should have been
> Had that night lasted one hundred.
>
> Adont ce trait pres de mi,
> Et je ne fu pas anfriune;
> Bien trois fois me baixait il,
> Ainsi fix je lui plus d'une,
>   K'ainz ne m'anoiait.
> Adonc vocexiens nus lai
> Ke celle nut durest sant. (ll. 13–19)

The activities in which these two alba couples engage are almost identical: in the first poem, the male recalls his lady's actions; in this one, the lady remembers her lover's. Both narrators recount their reciprocating responses. From these parallel portrayals, we cannot draw the conclusion that one of the two poets is consciously reversing a norm, for we cannot establish a norm in the first place. What we can perceive is that lady and lover can be active or passive—or sometimes *both* active and passive.

The knight of the alba "Us cavaliers si jazia" tells his beloved of his great desire for her—so strong that living without her would kill him: "For without you I have no life" ("Que ses vos vida non ai"). Pledging to return quickly, he bewails the emptiness of life without his beloved, like many an alba lady. These sentiments do not feminize him any more than strong emotions masculinize a lady; rather, we learn that the male alba lover is as obsessed, declares his devotion as forcefully, sorrows as poignantly, and loves as intensely as his lady.

Mutuality is the most essential and distinctive aspect of alba love. Lovers address one another as "friend" or are described as "friend with friend" ("amic d'amia" ["Us cavaliers si jazia"]), friend being a synonym (or euphemism) for lover in many languages, including Old Provençal, Old French, Middle High German, and English. In the tageliet, Wolfram von Eschenbach tells us that the lovers form a "fellowship" ("geselleschaft") or lie together companionably ("geselleclîchen as si lâgen" ["Sîne Klâwen," "Den morgenblic"]), making ironic allusions to the knightly bonding he cherishes elsewhere in his oeuvre. While such companionship is primarily sexual and the words "friend" and "companionship" euphemistic, these terms nonetheless manifest a specific aspect of their intimacy: the lovers provide one another with emotional gratification, reciprocated affection, and the sharing of confidences. Alba love is not sexual gratification alone.

The lover of either sex anticipates a sympathetic hearing from his or her paramour. If the male lover of Walther's "Friuntlîchen lac" asks for his lady's confidences—"Now tell me in our brief moments all that you wish" ("nû rede in kurzen zîten allez daz dû wil" [l. 19])—the lady of Cadenet's "S'anc fui belha ni prezada" declares that her lover is one in whom she freely confides: "And I would die/ Had I not my true love by/ To whom to tell my sorrows" ("E murria/ S'ieu fin amic non avia/ Cuy disses mo marrimen" [ll. 5–7]). Sharing secrets typifies alba lovers, making it a measure of their companionship and closeness.

Despite its idyllic reciprocity, the alba is elegiac, a song of loss and separation. When Fries claims that the alba posits the lady's desertion by her lover as well as her exclusion from the male community (1981, 158), she fails to see that the loss is felt by both lovers, not by the lady alone. To see the alba as centered on the desertion of women by men is reductive, one-sided. Such a view creates a distorted portrait of the alba lady as abandoned and victimized by the one person whom she has freely chosen and with whom she shares her most intimate feelings. The enforced leave taking does not constitute desertion; in fact, the lovers might meet secretly every night and still sing their alba at dawn. The fact that more albas are narrated by the lady than by her lover does not indicate that she is more often deserted or that the man's plight (even when it goes unsung) should be lightly dismissed. Indeed, when the male lover is given a singing role, he expresses sorrows similar to those of his lady.

Fries's observation is representative of a more general critical myopia: even when a man does expose his sorrows or fears to public view, they are overlooked. If noticed, they are considered exceptions, and the sex-role reversal theory is put into operation. In this way, extremities of emotion— the heights of passion and desire; the depths of sorrow, dread, and fear— can be relegated to the female domain. We can persuade ourselves (or be persuaded) that such profound or intense emotions and their eloquent renderings in song are or should be alien to the masculine norm. Alba poets portray suffering and loving men who never indicate that they are violating a masculine code. In writing albas, poets identify with the anguish that love parting entails; and that sorrow is presented similarly whether it is voiced by the male or female lover.

The lover of "Us cavaliers si jazia," after expressing his great desire (cited previously), goes on to relate the unparalleled anguish he feels about parting:

> Gentle one, whatever they say,
> Never believe there could be such grief
> Like that which parts lover from lover,
> For I myself have proved it.
>
> Doussa res, que qu'om vos dia,
> No cre que tals dolors sia
> Cum qui part amic d'amia
> Qu'ieu per me mezeys o sai. (ll. 19–22)

The lover of "Gaita be" suffers as well:

| But grievous to me | is the thought of dawn |
| and the distress | that daytime spawns |

        displeases me
        more than the dawn,
        the dawn, yes the dawn!

| Mays enics | sui de l'alba, |
| e·l destrics | que·l jorn nos fai |

        mi desplai
        plus que l'alba,
        l'alba, oi l'alba! (ll. 10–14)

Tageliet men are no less sorrowful. The narrator of Wolfram's "Von der zinnen" laments: "Sadness never so utterly destroyed the fund of happiness of any man" ("allen mannen/ trûren nie sô gar zerstôrte/ ir vröiden vunt" [ll. 34–36]). Why pass over or turn these expressions into sex-role reversals except to minimize such emotions or their appropriateness for male behavior?

    The lady of Wolfram's "Ez ist nu tac" sings of the sorrow that she and her lover share, never doubting that he feels it as deeply as she: "I know full well that it is the same with him" ("Ich weiz vil wol, daz ist ouch ime" [l. 7]). Her intuition is corroborated when, like his lady, the lover cries out: "I never knew such a sad and sudden parting" ("jôn erkande ich nie/ kein trûric scheiden alsô snel" [ll. 18–19]). The narrator does not neglect to recount the sharing of pleasures as well as sorrows: "that he kissed her enough they both liked it well/ . . . Her wet eyes then grew wetter, sorrow also oppressed him" ("Si beide luste, daz er kuste sî genouc./ . . . Ir ougen naz dô wurden baz. ouch twanc in klage" [ll. 25, 37]). Wolfram binds their joys and sorrows into the same line. For Wolfram, only the loss of the greatest pleasure and fulfillment could warrant such dread-filled agony. In "Den morgenblic," the lady's tears "moistened the cheeks of both" lovers ("diu beguzzen/ir beider wangel" [ll. 15–16]). Although she alone cries, they both concretely share her tears.

    Wolfram surpasses his poetic rivals in showing how fluid the roles can be by portraying the turns his lovers take in embracing each other. He twice depicts the lovers' embrace. First the lady and next the lover initiates it: "the good woman her friend's body fast embraced/ . . . He pressed her to his breast" ("Daz guote wîp ir vriundes lîp vaste umbevie/ ... an sîne bruste dructe er sie" ["Ez ist nu tac" ll. 13, 17]). Wolfram's portrayal of their reciprocity ensures that the audience will understand how mutual and equal alba love is. Under these circumstances, it is disheartening to come across critical appraisals that make gender distinctions where none exist in the poetry. Paden, for example, declares that in the alba "the lover has enjoyed the lady's favors from the start" (1975, 158), assuming a power relationship in which only men enjoy ladies' favors and failing to recognize that both sexes participate, love, and enjoy.

Although Fries claims that the alba is about the desertion of women by men, no consistent pattern can be found in the lyrics. If the lady of the Old French "Cant voi l'aube dou jor venir" asks her lover to remember her, it is the male partner who begs for remembrance in "Us cavaliers si jazia." The lady of "Cant voi l'aube dou jor venir" warns her lover:

> Fair gentle friend, be off,
> To God may your body be commended.
> In God's name, I beg you, do not forget me.
> I do not love anything as much as you.
>
> Biaus dous amis, vos en ireis,
> A Deu soit vos cors comandeis.
> Por Deu vos pri, ne m'oblieis.
> Je n'ain nulle rien tant com vos. (ll. 19–22)

The lover of "Us cavaliers si jazia" begs his lady: "In God's name, don't forget me one bit/ For the heart of my body remains here/ And from you shall I never part" ["Per Dieu, no m'oblidetz mia/ Que·l cor del cors reman sai/ Ni de vos mais no·m partrai"] (ll. 33–35). On either side of the gender fence, lovers invoke God when imploring the beloved's remembrance. The lover of "Us cavaliers si jazia" speaks of his "cors," playing with the same association between heart and body as the lady of "Cant voi l'aube dou jor venir." Whereas the lady of "Cant voi l'aube dou jor venir" commends her lover's body into God's keeping, the lover of "Us cavaliers si jazia" pledges his heart to his mistress, leaving it in his lady's keeping. Even Kaske notes that the commitment of the loved one to God's care is freely assigned to either sex (1961, 174).

Furthermore, despite Fries's assumption, not only the male is capable of abandoning. Indeed, if we consider the most famous of all medieval alba scenarios and the only extant example in which the tumultuous secret love affair is worked out in some detail, we find that the desertion is perpetrated by the lady—Criseyde—not by ever-faithful Troilus. The fact that Criseyde rather than Troilus is unfaithful does not, however, justify Kaske's conclusion that a sex-role reversal, which can be traced through the alba, has taken place. Kaske contrasts Troilus's "hesitant request for assurance (III, 1485–91) and Criseyde's long answering promise of faithfulness (III, 1492–1518)" with the "prevailing pattern" of the medieval alba: "Though there are strong exceptions, its prevailing pattern seems to be that in which the lady introduces the question of faithfulness, and the lover replies with an elaborate pledge in what might be described as the superlative mood" (1961, 173). But we have clearly seen that the interchange between lady and lover takes a variety of forms, that both speak of their faithfulness, and both make pledges. Indeed, the poets may have known each other's lyrics and have been experimenting with role playing and responding to one another's motifs long before Chaucer was able to discern "prevailing patterns."

Kaske further observes of the alba generally that the male is "more nearly resigned to the necessity of parting, while the lady emotionally opposes or laments his departure and begs for his quick return" (173). Although examples of this type certainly exist, there are also albas that contradict these patterns. Such strong exceptions within so small a corpus suggest that the theory does not hold. In fact, the absence of sex roles rather than their establishment and subsequent reversal is at the heart of the alba.

My conclusions suggest that alba poets had a much less rigid conception of sex roles than modern critics do. There is no sex-role reversal from the early alba to Chaucer's in *Troilus and Criseyde* because sex roles are not assigned in the alba in the first place. Indeed, this lack of sex-role differentiation is one of the genre's unique and miraculous aspects; for some alba poets, it may also have been a truth about love itself.[2] Chaucer uses the dawn-song at the center of *Troilus and Criseyde* to highlight very real differences between the lovers; yet crucial as they are for the denouement of his narrative, these character differences are neither based on gender stereotypes nor the product of an intentional sex-role reversal.

Like their alba forerunners, Troilus and Criseyde joyfully transcend their differences along with their bodily boundaries at their first union. Chaucer captures their reciprocal abandon in the image of the twining honeysuckle: "And as aboute a tree with many a twiste/ Bytrent and writhe the swote wodebynde,/ Gan ech of hem in armes other wynde"

(III, 1230–32). Regardless of the behind-the-scene machinations required to bring about their union, once it occurs, their love takes on the symbiotic quality common to all albas.

For a brief time, Troilus and Criseyde relax their personal boundaries as they grow together in love. The romantic situation that Chaucer plays out is embedded in all albas: the idealized and distant lady, warmed to responsiveness, is not diminished by returning her wooer's affections nor is love destroyed when she reciprocates. On the contrary, love deepens and intensifies.

But while his alba predecessors take the similarity, mutuality, and symbiosis of alba lovers as their lyric subject, Chaucer portrays love as having only a temporary power to obliterate personal boundaries and differences. That dawn's light reimposes Troilus's and Criseyde's individual personalities is made clear when each addresses a different aspect of dawn at sunrise. Replacing the image of dawn with night and day in his dawn-song, Chaucer simultaneously discards the symbolic fusion of alba lovers in favor of fragmentation and difference.

Unlike his alba predecessors, Chaucer presents Troilus's and Criseyde's laments not as a concerted outcry uttered in a single song but as two discrete lyrics across a stanzaic divide that portrays Troilus's heartache:

> But whan the cok, comune astrologer,
> Gan on his brest to bete and after crowe,
> And Lucyfer, the dayes messanger,
> Gan for to rise and out hire bemes throwe,
> And estward roos, to hym that koude it knowe,
> *f*ortuna Maior, that anoon Criseyde,
> With herte soor to Troilus thus seyde,

> "Myn hertes lif, my trist and my plesaunce,
> That I was born, allas, what is me wo,
> That day of vs moot make disseuerance;
> *f*or tyme it is to ryse and hennes go,
> Or ellis I am lost for euere mo.
> O nyght, allas, why nyltow ouere vs houe,
> As longe as whan Almena lay by Ioue?

> "O blake nyght, as folk in bokes rede,
> That shapen art by god this world to hide
> At certeyn tymes wyth thi derke wede,

That vnder that men myghte in reste abide,
Wel oughten bestes pleyne and folk the chide,
That there as day wyth labour wolde vs breste,
That thow thus fleest and deynest vs nought reste.

"Thow doost, allas, to shortly thyn office,
Thow rakle nyght, ther god, maker of kynde,
The for thyn haste and thyn vnkynde vice
So faste ay to oure hemysperie bynde,
That neuere more vnder the ground thow wynde:
ƒor now, for thow so hiest out of Troie,
Haue I forgon thus hastili my ioie."

This Troilus, that with tho wordes felte,
As thoughte hym tho, for pietous distresse
The bloody teris from his herte melte,
As he that neuere zet swich heuynesse
Assayed hadde, out of so gret gladnesse,
Gan ther-with-al Criseyde, his lady deere,
In armes streyne and seyde in this manere:

"O cruel day, accusour of the ioie
That nyght and loue han stole and faste i-wryen,
Acorsed be thi comyng in-to Troye,
ƒor euery bore hath oon of thi bryghte yen.
Enuyous day, what list the so to spien?
What hastow lost, why sekestow this place,
Ther god thi light so quenche for his grace?

"Allas, what haue thise loueris the agylte,
Dispitous day? thyn be the peyne of helle!
ƒor many a louere hastow slayn and wilte:
Thy pourynge in wol nowher lat hem dwelle.
What profrestow thi light here forto selle?
Go selle it hem that smale selys graue—
We wol the nought, vs nedeth no day haue."

And ek the sonne, Titan, gan he chide,
And seyde, "O fool, wel may men the dispise,

> That hast the dawyng al nyght by thi syde,
> And suffrest hire so soone vp fro the rise,
> ſorto disesen loueris in this wyse.
> What, holde zoure bed ther, thow, and ek thi Morwe,
> I bid god, so zeue zow both sorwe." (III, 1415–70)

As if to stress the lovers' distance from one another, Chaucer fractures the dawn image as each lover addresses one aspect of it. Rather than huddling together in united opposition to dawn's dissolution of love, they turn away from each other, facing one aspect of dawn's two constitutive elements. Their individual responses prefigure their separate though intertwined fates. The symbolic shattering of their intimacy foreshadows not only the imminent separation that inspires their song but the more permanent parting that ultimately awaits them.

Troilus and Criseyde each abide by a different aspect of the Janus-faced dawn. When she begins her lament, Criseyde implores night—which sanctions and protects love—to delay, not to hasten away. Troilus addresses day, which he views as a merciless invader that offers no harbor to lovers.[3]

Chaucer bestows upon Troilus and Criseyde very different personalities, needs, and motives. This choice does not indicate, however, that he intentionally plants a sex-role reversal that will destroy their potential happiness. Their laments highlight temperamental tendencies that in the course of the poem receive fuller development. The differing response each has to the necessity of parting paints in broad strokes the lovers' contrasting personalities. Criseyde's portion of the alba is elegiac, a song of wish and desire. She laments the coming dawn without formulating any practical solutions for it. Her love pits itself against natural, social, and cosmic law. She advocates, in defiance of all law, perpetual night; she desires to be engulfed by the womblike oblivion of darkness and love; she yearns for integration in Love's night.

Troilus's half is divided from Criseyde's by a stanza of narrative in which his "pietous distresse" and "blody teris" are portrayed in all their melodramatic pathos. The separation of Troilus's address from Criseyde's on the textual level parallels their emotional disengagement from one another. On the narrative level, it serves to occupy enough time for the cosmic movement from night to day to occur.

Troilus centers on day, signifying that the transition from night to day has occurred during the intervening stanza. It has dawned, although the narrator neglects to describe it and Chaucer allows neither lover to cry out specifically against it. Troilus's and Criseyde's individually focused songs reflect in which half of a bisected world they abide. Criseyde, looking back toward a happy past as it flees, attempts to cling to its last seconds of grace. Troilus, however, across dawn's divide, looks ahead toward a dreaded future. The present, as a time of readjustment, is made palpable. And the song carries that present across the centuries, even to our own time. The alba becomes the vehicle through which each lover verbally and emotionally reorients him- or herself to time's tragic alteration of their circumstance.

Troilus personifies day as a violently willful antagonist. Like a vicious rapist, daylight forcibly exposes the shrouded sacraments of love. It penetrates the hearts and souls of its victimized lovers as it invades Troy, which stands, in Troilus's lyric, as a metaphor for the lovers. Day forces the lovers asunder, leaving dissolution, fragmentation, and death in its wake. This conception of day is consistent with the flow of the larger narrative, for day brings back not only the reality of everyday Trojan public life (in which love must be concealed) but also the reality of war with the Greeks. In terms of the poem's resolution, the oncoming day truly may be seen to portend apocalypse, for the imagery of Troilus's lyric blatantly presages the invasion and conquest of Troy by the Greek army.

If Troilus perceives day in militaristic terms, his response to it is also defiant and martial. In keeping with his warrior reflexes, he aggressively retaliates against day's onslaught, barraging it with a series of antagonistic rhetorical questions. Troilus's warrior-like responses do little to support the gender-role reversal theory. But although he is a valiant warrior, Troilus confronts a kind of ferocious adversary he cannot vanquish. He realizes the futility of attempting to shield himself from day's infiltrations, protesting that no lovers are safe from day's incursion: "Thy pourynge in wol nowher lat hem dwelle." Instead, he hurls insults at day, calling it cruel, envious, spiteful. As though facing a triumphant rampaging enemy, Troilus lashes out verbally while frantically seeking respite from its wrath.

Where Criseyde is concerned with the joys of love bestowed by night, Troilus focuses on the pain of separation enforced by light. Whereas Criseyde devotes her song to pleasure and the wish to prolong it at all costs, Troilus struggles with feelings of impotent rage at his inability to defend his love from the incursion of light. Criseyde feels deserted by night, while Troilus feels deluged by day.

Chaucer's bifurcation of dawn into night and day suggests that we view the lovers similarly, as components of a divided whole dramatized in terms of its parts. Regarded as either complements or contrasts to each other, the parts, in the final analysis, can be summed up only in terms of a negative whole. Whether apostrophizing night or day, Troilus and Criseyde's dawn-parting lament addresses the irremediability of their situation. Both stances to the day's advent manifest the catastrophic nature of the love affair; no matter how dawn is perceived by the lovers, the result is dread and sorrow. All that remains of joy is a past that is swiftly receding. The future brings only loneliness and anguish. Although each lover maintains a different point of view, both suffer deeply; despite the fact that Chaucer presents the dawn in terms of polarities, neither pole offers a future of hope. One pole reveals the (passively lamented) loss and retreat of love; the other, the (aggressively confronted) impossibility of averting heartbreak. This duality serves to compound the negativity of love because from both angles the love provides pleasures that are transient but pain that is certain and enduring. In the end, Troilus and Criseyde's love has a dual negativity: it withdraws and abandons; it engenders misery and the desire to avoid reality.

Chaucer's poetic dichotomization of the alban dawn into night and day gives his dawn-song an original turn, but this bifurcation also expresses a pessimistic attitude toward love not shown by his generic predecessors. Whereas the earlier poets explored how love enables an individual to transcend himself or herself, Chaucer's romance ultimately demonstrates that love's reciprocity does not enable lovers to overcome their more enduring individual character differences. Chaucer's greater interest in the idiosyncrasies of personalities within the couple rather than the sharing and attachment between them demonstrates his, and possibly his age's, new way of problematizing individuality as it encounters erotic love. For Chaucer, the differences within the couple are more dominant and enduring than the intimacy the lovers share; and these differences, in combination with potent external forces, direct the downward spiral of the love affair.

Despite its deeply satisfying and intense joys and its ability to endow individuals with resilience, compassion, and fortitude, love in Chaucer's pagan Troy is genuinely benighted: it flourishes in shadow and clandestine concealment; it is unenlightened. Night and day, as viewed by the lovers, are forces of deterministic inevitability. Troilus and Criseyde are continually beset by social and cosmic forces beyond their control. Ruled equally by the overwhelming passions and needs within them and the potent forces outside, the lovers have lost sight of any recourse or escape. Through the dark maze that has become their existence, these pagan lovers can find no lighted, united path.

Although their differences divide and destroy Chaucer's lovers, he nonetheless portrays how their desire for one another—and their love—deepens after their first night together. Their parting sorrow is mutual; and alone after dawn, each meditates upon the other. If sleepless Troilus burns for Criseyde, Criseyde likewise longs for him:

> And in his thought gan vp and down to wynde
> Hire wordes alle, and euery countenaunce,
> And fermely impressen in his mynde
> The leeste point that to him was plesaunce;
> And verraylich of thilke remembraunce
> Desire al newe hym brende, and lust to brede
> Gan more than erst, and зet took he non hede.
>
> Criseyde also, right in the same wyse,
> Of Troilus gan in hire herte shette
> His worthynesse, his lust, hise dedes wise,
> His gentilesse, and how she with hym mette,
> Thonkyng loue he so wel hire bisette,
> Desiryng eft to han hire herte deere
> In swich a plit she dorste make hym cheere.
>
> (III, 1541–54)

In a similar reminiscence about their night together, the lovers of Heinrich von Morungen's beautiful "Owê, sol aber mir iemer mê" display the togetherness that Chaucer's lovers have lost. Heinrich's poem, the tageliet that Dronke calls "the summit of the genre" (1977, 181), is unique because it is also written in the form of a *wechsel*, a form in which characters sing alternating stanzas but do not address one another; their speeches are, instead, interlaced monologues. Independently, each character in the poem reminisces about the shared evening. One might logically assume that the wechsel form would stress the lovers' different responses, but surprisingly, it is the similarity of their responses—their memorialized joys, their desperate sorrow—that is most notable:

> "Alas,—
> shall never again for me
> shine through the night
> whiter even than the snow
> her body so beautiful?

It tricked these eyes of mine:
I thought it must have been
the light of the moon shine.
Then it dawned."

"Alas,—
shall he never again
await the morning here?
May night go in such a way for us
that we never need complain:
'Alas, now it is day.'
As he did complain
when last he by me lay,
Then it dawned."

"Alas,—
wondrous times, she kissed
me in my sleep.
Then there fell down
her tears upon themselves.
Wherefore I comforted her
so that she left her crying
and embraced me all around.
Then it dawned."

"Alas,—
that he so often lost
himself in contemplating me!
When he uncovered me
he wanted so without covering
my arms to see.
It was a wonder great
that it never wearied him.
Then it dawned."

"Owê,—
Sol aber mir iemer mê
geliuhten dur die naht
noch wîzer danne ein snê

>   ir lîp vil wol geslaht?
>   Der trouc diu ougen mîn:
>   ich wânde, ez solde sîn
>   des liehten mânen schîn.
>   Dô tagte ez.
>
>   "Owê,—
>   Sol aber er iemer mê
>   den morgen hie betagen?
>   als uns diu naht engê,
>   daz wir niht durfen klagen:
>   'Owê, nu ist ez tac,'
>   als er mit klage pflac,
>   dô er júngest bî mir lac.
>   Dô tagte ez.
>
>   "Owê,—
>   Si kuste âne zal
>   in dem slâfe mich.
>   dô vielen hin ze tal
>   ir trehene nider sich.
>   Iedoch getrôste ich sie,
>   daz sî ir weinen lie
>   und mich al umbevie.
>   Dô tagte ez.
>
>   "Owê,—
>   Daz er sô dicke sich
>   bî mir ersehen hât!
>   als er endahte mich,
>   sô wolte er sunder wât
>   Mîn arme schouwen blôz.
>   ez was ein wunder grôz
>   daz in des nie verdrôz.
>   Dô tagte ez."

If the lover begins with a question, the lady's first words also frame a question. Her words echo her lover's, even though she hasn't heard them. If the lady's kisses and tears were "without number" ("âne zal"), her lover's gaze and desire were tireless: "it was a great wonder/ that in this he never tired" ("ez was ein wunder grôz /daz in des nie verdrôz"). Describing how his lady's beauty eclipses the brilliance of the snow, the lover instills the scene with a sense of wonder. His wonder is matched by the lady's marveling at her lover's tireless gazing on her. Both lovers' marvels are jarringly shattered by day. The staccato refrain echoings "then it dawned" ("dô tagte ez"), sung by both lovers, tie their individual monologues tightly together and leave us with a haunting sense of the deprivation and desolation dawn brings.

Their similarity unites these lovers once they are apart. Both lament the passing of their bliss, doubt that they will ever again attain such rapture, and treasure the remembered tryst as miraculous and sacred. Although each lover concentrates on his or her own experience, each is brought into union with the other by the mutuality of their respective responses. Ironically, the simultaneity of their responses heightens the audience's sense of the separated lovers' isolation. Such togetherness even when apart bespeaks the symbiotic nature of alba love. The ubiquitous alba watchman, the gaita, is absent from this lyric; his interfering presence does not jar the tranquil splendor of the remembered scene. Perhaps the audience, witness to the lovers' fidelity and sorrow, takes on the watchman's sanctifying role.

Because both sexes in the alba show the same preoccupations with pleasure, love, and loyalty as well as pain, anger, and fear of abandonment, alba love is portrayed as an equalizing and humanizing experience not dichotomized into male-female polarities. Fries, however, sees the alba as a dramatic enactment of the conventionalized, polarized, sex-linked roles of lady and lover: "The necessary absence of the male is epitomized in the alba, in which the watchman and/or the omnipresent dawn of the masculine Day (as opposed to the feminine Night) interrupt the joyous lovemaking of Lady and Knight and cause them to enact dramatically their sex-linked roles: the Knight goes off to his world of male affairs, for him the important one, while the Lady remains behind" (1981, 158). But there is no sense in the alba that the knight considers "the world of male affairs" to be more important than the world of love or even that he values "the world of male affairs" at all. Although conventional, it is nonetheless inaccurate to assume that "the male community of action" mentioned by Fries (but not by alba poets) is central to albas or that alba characters perceive such a community as the more desirable and important sphere of action, as a community into which the lady desires admission, or even as a community at all. On the contrary, the lady's court rather than the knight's wanderings, battles, or jousts provides a sense of community both in twelfth-century secular life and in its (court) poetry. Further, Fries's gender oppositioning of Night/Day, while a traditional classical topos, is utterly alien to the medieval vernacular alba. In classical myth and verse, dawn is represented as the goddess Eos or Aurora; but this reference, while it may have been familiar to alba poets, is absent from the alba.

Saville's view of the alba lady is singularly limited: "She lives only for love. She is the chief upholder of the erotic values of the inner world, having no existence anywhere else. The knight at least has a social function in the outer world although not much is said about it. The knight leaves the love-chamber. The lady does not. She remains in the inner world, her only world, and since that inner world has meaning only when it is the scene of love-making, the lady must go into a kind of inanimate suspension during the daylight, when her lover is away" (1972, 153). If we want to consider aspects of life that extend beyond the purview of the alba, then does not the lady, like the knight, exist in a fictive social realm where she, too, has a function? And isn't it solely because she exists in this context that he must depart at dawn? In fact, her social context is even more vital to the alba than the knight's because it is her realm into which he desires entry and her realm, with its jealous guardians and clever spies, that threatens them.

If we conjure the lovers' social context, the lady, a central member of the castle complex, occupies a secure and significant place within a vibrant social world; her lover, an outsider, roves from place to place, perhaps homeless. Which of these worlds is more public? Were we to speculate about the historical knight upon whom the alba lover could have been modeled, he might well fit into the class of dispossessed bachelors or "youths" ("jovens") described by Duby—young men without fixed or important positions in the world. Like the bachelor that Duby proposes as the prototype for the *compagno* of troubadour poetry, the alba lover was perhaps envisioned as a member of the "relatively new and still fluid class" of knights, "many of whom were landless sons of noble families" (1977, 118). These younger, disinherited sons of the nobility sought to make a place in the world in a relative's (usually maternal uncle's) or a foreign court. According to Duby, such a knight could demonstrate valor "by seducing and abducting the lady of the house." Envy of the lord was sublimated into a desire for his wife, inspiring a "sophisticated form of love" that was used as "a means of disciplining young knights" (1987, 82).

Presumably blinded by modern biases created, in part, by expunging from the historical record the lady's central place in the court (a lacuna only beginning to be filled), Saville and Fries ignore the alba lady's pivotal public role. If we examine her status from recent sociohistorical research, we find that regardless of her premarital status she derived power through her relationship to the man she married. As Duby tells us, "she, too, dominated" even though always from a position subordinate to her husband (1987, 68). According to historians, she was the center of court life, acquiring a special status of great authority particularly during the lord's frequent absences: "As the lord's substitute (*midons* < Lat. *meus dominus*, referring to the lady, meant 'my lord') she became the center of the court and an object of respect, even veneration, on the part of these often unmarried knights" (Bullough et al. 1988, 91). The noble wife functioned as the head of the women in the household, her spouse's first assistant, and his deputy assuming his duties when he was away: "When the nobility of Europe went forth to do battle it was their wives who managed their affairs at home, superintended the farming, interviewed the tenants, and saved up money for their husband's next expedition" (Bullough et al. 1988, 153). Although subject to her husband, the lady was mistress of the household, in charge of all its activities. Some noble wives oversaw substantial financial transactions and record keeping, such as the collection of taxes from peasants. Women remained a separate sphere within the noble family, and the noble wife was responsible for their care; younger children received their training from her (Duby 1987, 70–71, 79).

Although some contemporary critics may consider the lady's wifehood and homebound domesticity confining or insignificant, for the alba's contemporary audience, home was an entire castle community with the lady situated at its heart. Considering that this may have been about as public a place as there was in twelfth-century French society, the alba lady's intense wish for privacy takes on some realistic urgency.

The life of a noblewoman with these kinds of responsibilities does not become any more meaningless than her lover's when he has ridden off. It may be convenient to believe, as Saville does, that the lady "must go into a kind of inanimate suspension during the daylight, when her lover is away." Nevertheless, this is not the contention of alba poets, and not one lyric approaches the subject from this angle. Indeed, the lover-knight's world is more likely to be isolated, lonely, and deprived, however glamorous his roving may seem to modern eyes. If the knight goes off to his "world of male affairs," it is solely because he cannot remain where he would rather be.

Only rarely does the alba depict the knight outside the lady's presence; and although the couple continually refer to the lover's having to leave, the poem concludes before he actually does so. This must be deliberate because elsewhere the same poets (Giraut de Bornelh, Wolfram von Eschenbach, and Walther von der Vogelweide, for example) *do* talk about "the world." Only in the few albas narrated by a third party is a glimpse given of the knight after he has left the lady's chamber. Indeed, nothing is mentioned about the knight's social function in most albas. Although he is sometimes referred to as *cavaliers* or *ritter* (denoting a "horse-mounted man"; Scaglione 1991, 18), he is even more frequently simply called "friend" (amics), a social relationship reciprocated explicitly by the lady in the lyric.

If we do not opt to extrapolate what may happen to these fictional characters beyond the alba's boundaries and consider only the context of the poems, we must admit that both lovers lapse into "inanimate suspension" when they are no longer together. Their being together is the heart and raison d'être of the song, which concentrates almost exclusively on them together, assiduously avoiding the question of what will occur thereafter as it has ignored all prior action. Everything that occurs outside the lady's chamber is anticlimactic, irrelevant, insignificant.

It is the knight who must leave, but his departure is not portrayed as an entry into exciting and eagerly awaited masculine adventure. Rather, it is a withdrawal from his love, an exile. He falls from lover's heaven into time, history, conflict, consequence, and longing. Secret love sets the alba couple apart from the community; it also makes a space for itself free from conventional power and gender relations.

In sum, there is little sex-role differentiation in the alba. One of the most distinctive characteristics of the lady's relationship with the lover as opposed to her relationship with her husband is the lack of sex-role differentiation that exists between them. With her lover, the lady is on equal footing; with her husband, she is a subordinate, undervalued: "in conjugal partnerships . . . the woman must consent to her subjugation" (Duby 1987, 144). There is an implicit struggle for power and dominance reflected in the alba; but it takes place between the lady and the powerful though caricatured and much despised gilos, the jealous spouse who is the greatest obstacle to alba love. (See the next section of this chapter.)

When alba lovers are together, there is no other world. Their sex-linked roles may be enacted once they separate. But this extension into the future—or "reality"—is purposefully evaded in the alba. In fact, this differentiation is enforced by the social codes the lovers desperately seek to escape. The alba depicts lover and lady while they are together, and at that time they are portrayed as equals, as friends. It is their equality and freedom rather than their separate, prescribed roles that the alba strives to portray. And this openness to experience gives the alba its marvelous appeal and makes the genre truly avant-garde.

By creating women who adopt a variety of roles, whose voices are fluent, artful, and independent, alba poets provide metaphors as well as vehicles for their own creativity. They sympathize with lovers who desire to transcend the limitations of confining, conventional roles just as the poets themselves desire to transcend the confinements of established poetic conventions. That alba poets were able to convey the lovers' voices so movingly speaks an eloquent tribute to their own desire to represent some human truths that transcend gender altogether.

Alba poets were launching forth a new vision of love that valued reciprocal passion and equality. And even if, like most other medieval literary female creations, the alba lady is a male-constructed ideal, she reveals something about the poets' aspirations and dreams. She is a more humane and humanized woman than the ladies of antiquity or medieval epic; she is more responsive than the canso domna and more dignified than the pastourelle shepherdess.

Those who view the alba lady as victimized by her lover and the social conventions that (they believe) endow him with superior status to hers inaccurately interpret the genre. In so doing, they falsify the lady's role in the lyrics as well as the man's; but they also miss the poets' most momentous innovations. Far from being a recapitulation of literary and social conventions, the alba puts forth a subtle, understated, but nonetheless revolutionary critique of the social order. In the alba, lady and lover construct a space apart from the sordid conventions that place the sexes in disequilibrium.

Rather than viewing the male alba partner as more powerful or free than the lady, we should acknowledge that the alban love triangle implicitly places the lady's husband at the apex. Lady and lover are equal, but both remain at the triangle's base—that is, unless they can convince us through their eloquent lament that their ennobling love can turn the triangle upside down.

Adulterous Love and the Alba

> Never through threat nor bluster
> that my wicked spouse might muster
> shall I fail to stay
> with my love until day,
> for it would be
> ignorant vulgarity
> to part ignobly
> one's worthy lover
> from herself, before dawn.
> Cadenet, "*S'anc fui belha ni prezada*"

In "The Troubadour's Lady," Paden claims to debunk "two cardinal tenets of received literary history": the first, that "courtly love" (a term he, like a number of other critics, considers suspect) is adulterous; the second, that the courtly lady is the lover's social superior (29). The emergence of romantic love in twelfth-century literature, however, whatever term one applies (courtly love, fin'amors) and whatever one's opinion of the concept, is one of the lasting literary legacies of the Middle Ages. And the adulterous nature of that love is indeed one of the primary tenets of received literary history.

Paden believes that this received view is founded upon the misinterpretation of certain key terms in troubadour verse, among them the word *gilos*, in combination with "a tendency on the part of the critic to express his own perspective, not that of the poet" (29). We have already seen how distorting critical misconceptions can be as well as how they take on a life of their own. But "the critic" to whom Paden refers here necessarily designates the majority of critics if the interpretation is now part of received literary history. Since the late nineteenth and early twentieth centuries, scholars have found the adultery inscribed in early vernacular verse a fundamental underpinning of medieval sexual love. Friedrich Engels, for example, speaks of the "improper subject" of adultery, which, he says, was a vital aspect of the medieval chivalric code. By chivalrous love, he means the "first form of individual sexual love," a love "by no means conjugal. Quite the contrary. In its classic form among the Provençals, it heads straight for adultery, and the poets of love celebrated adultery" (1902, 70).

Paden argues that the figure of the gilos cannot be proven either by etymological or philological analysis to refer invariably to the husband, concluding that the term may sometimes refer to a *lauzengier* (slanderer) or some other figure: "Even when the *gelos* threatens to beat the poet's lady, we cannot be certain he is her husband, for he might also be her lover or a member of her family, such as her brother. Since *gelos* denotes an emotional relationship rather than a legal bond, and since the troubadours were perfectly capable of using *marit* when they chose, we must not gloss *gelos* simply as 'husband.' Doing so distorts the poetry" (1975, 31–32). Although we may wince at the reminder that not only a lady's husband but a host of males can beat the lady, this array of possibilities does not exclude the husband. The alba would seem to be the best test case for Paden's theory: the gilos is frequently referred to in albas, and a lady's husband might be among those enemies of love who spy on alba love (and therefore be designated as gilos). Nevertheless, Paden makes only a passing reference to the genre. Of the 503 troubadour lyrics he surveys from the philological angle, Paden finds 47 percent of the poems to center on the narrator's love, "but there is no evidence that his lady was married or that she was superior to him" (36). That a lyric does not explicitly use the word "husband," "adultery," or "marriage" (the required evidence) does not prove that the lady is unmarried, especially if a convention of adultery, of which poets are aware, is already in force. Lancelot and Guenevere join together in Chrétien de Troyes's *Le chevalier de la charrete* (or *Lancelot*), sparking an entire romance convention of adulterous love without the author's explicit use of the word adultery. And the exploration of love in Chrétien's romances works hand-in-hand with the Old Provençal lyric tradition despite Paden's unsubstantiated claim that "Provençal lyric does not provide a background for Chrétien's *Lancelot* in which adultery formed a common theme" (49).

Troubadour ideas on love and courtliness were absorbed into Chrétien's romances as well as those of other authors (see Topsfield 1975, 5; Ferrante 1975). Dante, a keen observer deeply steeped in lyric conventions, roots the tragedy of Paolo and Francesca in the Lancelot and Guenevere story without using the word adultery. Yet Dante's disapproval of adulterous love manifests itself in his depiction of his lovers' suffering and punishment. The couple, irresistibly drawn together by a reading of the Lancelot and Guenevere story, is led astray by their love, fused into the "one death" they suffer at Francesca's husband's hand that set them in Hell. Why would a poet as immersed in the Old Provençal lyric tradition as Dante punish the adultery of courtly lovers if courtly love were not adulterous in the first place?

Further, Paden notes: "A few troubadours make clear that the ladies they love are maidens. The trouvères, too, reveal here and there that courtly love could concern unmarried women" (1975, 42). That revelation leads one to believe that love with a single girl was the exception rather than the rule. The troubadours present romantic love as adulterous without denying that alternative forms of romantic passion exist. Many medieval couples may have enjoyed fulfilling, passionate marriages. Romances such as Chrétien's *Erec et Enide* or Wolfram's *Parzival* portray couples who fall in love and marry, and, in reality, adultery may not have run riot in medieval courts. But in the numerous stories of marital strife that pervade medieval literature, both courtly and popular, the jealous husband is as ubiquitous as the unhappily married wife. Marie de France "makes the lament of the unhappily married wife central to the narrative motivation of her lay, reworked into a kind of biography, contextualized and extended, of the *mal mariée*" (Nichols 1988, 15). Marie's *Lais* provide a fund of such figures: the husbands in "Guigemar," "Yonec," "Milun," and "Laüstic" guard their wives zealously, virtually imprisoning them. The wives in "Guigemar" and "Yonec" are, like Cadenet's alba lady, married against their wills to begin with; and the wives in "Equitan," "Chevrefoil," and "Milun" are also unhappily married.

Lyric poets react in various ways to the idea that husband and wife are not necessarily monogamous. Cercamon and Marcabru sing out the wrongs of the adultery that rival poets (at the least) were promoting. In "Ab lo pascor m'es bel q'eu chant," Cercamon scorns husbands who become lovers and wooers, indicating that the practice is familiar, at least in poetry:

> I know well that it is unseemly
> That husbands become wild
> Lovers and wooers;
> And the guerdon they get for it
> The peasant recounts in his proverb:
> Whoever takes the sword, with the sword
> Is struck by his own mortal blow.
> . . . .
> Since you have asked for it
> Lover, wife, and husband—all three—
> May you be joined together by your shared sin.
>
> Ben sai qe lor   es mal estan
> als molleiratz,   car se fan gai

>   domnejador   ni drudejan;
>   e·l guizardos qe lor n'eschai
>   ditz el reprocher lo pajes:
>   qi glazi fai,   a glazi es
>   feritz d'eis lo seu colp mortau.
>   . . . .
>   e pos vos [o] aves enqes,
>   drut, moiller e marit—tug tres—
>   sias del pechat comunau. (ll. 15–21, 26–28)⁴

Similarly, Marcabru's championing of marriage demonstrates his divergence from the adulterous norm. Urging men to defend their marriages in "Pois l'inverns d'ogan es anatz," he mocks those who behave like lovers rather than husbands:

>   I cannot help speaking to husbands about
>   Their infamous dereliction;
>   I do not know what authority inspired them
>   To be called lovers;
>   They are like the courtly ass
>   Who wanted to make sport with his master,
>   When he saw him fooling with his dogs.
>
>   Non puosc sofrir qu·als moilleratz
>   Non diga lor forfaitz saubutz;
>   Non sai la cals auctoritatz
>   Lor mostra c'om los apel drutz;
>   Semblan fant de l'ase cortes,
>   C'ab son seignor cuidet bordir,
>   Cant lo vic trepar ab sos ches. (ll. 50–56)

For Marcabru, societal degeneration results from the noble wife's adultery, which dilutes aristocratic bloodlines: a wife who succumbs to the allure of a lover might deliver another man's progeny as the lord's heirs. Although the problem of illegitimacy is addressed in scores of legal documents as well as religious admonitions, most courtly poetry avoids the topic assiduously. Albas follow this trend; and because they exclude time, the world, and, hence, consequences, from their purview, it is not surprising that their characters ignore this issue.

Medieval society viewed the wife's adultery as particularly heinous if it involved a social inferior because it was commonly believed that a father's traits would be passed on to his heir (Bullough et al., 1988, 139–40). Marcabru's verse echoes these concerns:

> Thus are ladies treacherous
> and they know how to trick and lie,
> for they give other men's children
> to their husbands for keeping and feeding;
> from which is born wicked thinking.

> Eyssamens son domnas trichans
> E sabon trichar e mentir,
> Per que fan los autrus enfans
> Als maritz tener e noyrir;
> D'aqui naisso·l malvat [cuiar]. (ll. 22–26)[5]

Hence, when the knight of Marcabru's pastourelle "L'autrier jost'una sebissa" (Dejeanne 1909, xxx, 137–43) insinuates that the vilana he seeks to seduce may be illegitimate, he may believe that such illegitimacy would work wonders for her, infusing her peasant blood with the blue blood of nobility.

Although marriage, if honored, is seen by Marcabru as a virtuous and moral state—"Husbands, the best men in the world,/ You would be, but each of you becomes a lover" ("Moillerat, li meillor del mon/ Foratz, mas chascus vos faitz drutz" ["Al prim comens de/ l'ivernaill," Dejeanne IV, ll. 31–32])—it was primarily a business matter. Prospective husbands in the Middle Ages sought neither beauty nor intelligence but rather an assurance of the continuity of family lineage in their future wives: wives were selected for their family connections, marriage portions, and childbearing ability. Considerations such as beauty, charm, or compatibility rarely entered the picture (Bullough et al. 1988, 139). History records less about what prospective wives were seeking; presumably, they looked for similar advantages from their matches. Marriages of eldest sons and heiresses were of vital family interest because they involved the ultimate disposition of the family property.

Marcabru's diatribes reflect a society (either real or in his imagination) in which adultery on the part of both genders is rife, with promiscuous husbands riddling society with illegitimate children:

> Husbands, by Saint Hilary,
> are confederates in one folly:

> for war has broken out among them
> such that the cuckold has the cuckolded woman
> and the injured cuckold the injured woman,
> and then the "tail" stops complaining.
>
> > (Harvey 1989, 22)

> Moillerat, per saint Ylaire,
> Son d'una foldat confraire,
> Qu'entr'els es guerra moguda
> Tals que cornutz fa cornuda,
> E cogotz copatz copada,
> Puois eis la coa de braire.
>
> > ("Al son desviat, chantaire" ll. 19–24)

Unfaithful husbands reap their just rewards: "The husband who scratches the wife of another man/ knows well that his own wife sins" (Topsfield 1975, 79) ("Maritz qui l'autrui con grata/ Ben pot saber que·l sieus pescha" [Marcabru, "Bel més quan la rana chanta" ll. 49–50]). Bernart Marti, while opposed to promiscuity, allows the domna a lover in addition to her husband:

> A lady is a disloyal lover
> if she gives [her love] to three men:
> > it is against the law
> > that there should be three of them,
> but along with her husband another
> courtly lover I do allow her
> > and if she goes looking for more,
> > she is disloyal
> > and a proven whore.[6]

> Dona es vas drut trefana
> de s'amor pos tres n'apana:
> > estra lei
> > n'i son trie,
> mas ab son marit l'autrei
> un amic cortes prezant
> > E si plus n'i vai sercant
> > es desleiada
> > e puta provada.
>
> > (Marti 1984, 83)

While some poets were writing social commentary from the omniscient point of view (the outsider's), others were creating characters who put forth their own views. Trouvère Etienne de Meaux's song "Trop est mes maris jaloux" exposes the rage of a mal mariée:

> My husband is very jealous,
> Presumptuous, cruel and proud,
> But he will, in time, be a cuckold
> If I find my sweet lover,
> The generous, charming one.
> > My husband I care naught for;
> > Husbands like nothing good.
> > > I tell you:
> > > One should send
> The boring churl packing.
>
> When I look out the window
> He's spying on me all day long;
> He is a real weight on me,
> Because I lose my love on his account.
> He knows perfectly well that I love elsewhere.
> > Now he can go crazy,
> > Because I want to love.
> > > I tell you:
> > > One should send
> The boring churl packing.
>
> Does he think that with his money
> He can put a pretty heart in prison?
> Not at all! He has no power
> To make me entirely his;
> He has failed to win love.
> > No one should have
> > A lover for money.
> > > I tell you:
> > > One should send
> The boring churl packing.

Boldly I will tell him:
Foolish, evil peasant,
I must love without delay
—Take note—another than you;
Now you can be jealous;
    I will leave you,
    I will love another!
        I tell you:
            One should send
The boring churl packing.

For all the wealth in Cîteaux
It is not fitting that a pretty heart
—So says Etienne de Meaux—
Or a fine lady take a husband,
Instead she must have a lover.
    And I will believe him,
    And I will have a lover.
        I tell you:
            One should send
The boring churl packing.

Trop est mes maris jalos,
Sorcuidiez, fel et estouz,
Mes il sera par tens cous
Se je truis mon ami douz,
Li gentil, li savoros.
    Mari ne pris rien.
    Q'il n'aiment nul bien.
        Je·l vos di:
            Dire fi
Doit on du vilain plain d'ennui.

Quant a la fenestre vois,
Il me guete trestoz jorz;
Sachiez q'il vit seur mon pois,
Car por lui pert mes amors.
Il set bien que j'aime aillors;

Or se puet desver,
Car je vueil amer.
  Je·l vos di:
  Dire fi
[Doit on du vilain plain d'ennui].

Cuidë il por son avoir
Metre en prison cuer joli?
Nenil voir! il n'a pouoir
Que soie du tot a lui;
A m'amor a il failli.
  Nus ne doit avoir
  Ami por avoir.
    Ce vos di:
    Dire fi
Doit on [du vilain plain d'ennui].

Hardiement li dirai:
Fol vilain maleüros,
Amer m'estuet sanz delai,
Sachiez, un autre que vos;
Or pöez estre jalos;
  Je vos guerpirai,
  Un autre amerai!
    Ce vos di:
    Dire fi
Doit on [du vilain plain d'ennui].

Por tot l'avoir de Cisteaus
Ne doit avoir cuer joli,
Ce dit Estiene de Miauz,
Jolive dame mari,
Ançois doit avoir ami.
  Et je l'en crerrai
  Et ami avrai.
    Ce vos di:
    Dire fi
Doit on du vilain plain d'ennui.
             (Switten 1988, 152–53)

Sentiments similar to those voiced by this mal mariée appear often in the *chanson de toile*, female-voiced lyrics that are among the oldest in the Old French corpus.

Nonetheless, the fact that far more examples of unhappy than happy marriages exist in literature and legal documents does not prove that marital dissatisfaction or infidelity was the prevailing way of life. Such literary sources do not reveal the full spectrum of medieval attitudes and experiences, but they do indicate that marital discontent was not unheard of; it was a commonplace. The literary witness to adultery offers, according to Boswell, "essential information almost in spite of itself . . . and is a kind of evidence which would rarely if ever occur in purely historical sources" where the majority of instances of adultery "apparently pass unnoticed" (1988, 9, 8). Adultery, found in imaginative writing of every sort, serves as such a primary and convenient plot device—"offering excuses for jealousies, murders, touchingly false suspicions, new groupings of major characters, etc."—that "one imagines it might have been invented for fiction whether it occurred in real life or not. . . . Indeed, most adults probably imagine that adultery is more common in fiction than in real life" (Boswell 1988, 8). But Boswell goes on to claim that the truth is nearly the reverse:

> Most fictional occurrences of adultery are limited to key characters in the story; the rest of the population is presumed—by implicit contrast if not explicit description—to be faithfully married. Moreover, the moral, emotional, legal, and social crises provoked by adultery in nineteenth- and twentieth-century fiction would certainly suggest that it was an event of major traumatic and stressful consequences which most married persons avoided. In real life, however, adultery is not limited to leading characters and can hardly be considered uncommon, whatever its emotional or social consequences. (Even in the 1940's, long before the current sexual revolution, about half of all married men in the United States had intercourse with women other than their wives.)
>
> . . . In any given community a very large amount of extramarital sexuality takes place without giving rise to colorful developments or transformations of character, much less to any record the historian could discover. (7–9)

When we hear the laments of the mal mariée and the alba lady, we may not be hearing the whole story, but we are encountering some combination of fantasy, feeling, and experience.

Fin'amors has often been considered a daydream or fantasy rather than a reality. In their investigation into the origins and meaning of fin'amors, Smith and Snow ask: "Is courtly love not solely literary, but a phenomenon so real as to express psychological truths that may escape the archives and chronicles?" (1980, 5). But even as the expression of a collective literary daydream, the escape that adultery provided was an outlet, according to Bloch, "from the reality of medieval marriage" (1991, 173). Herbert Moller concurs that far from reiterating a real life situation, the troubadours were projecting unconscious emotions, "which in cooperation with a responding public crystallized into a collective [Oedipal] fantasy" (1964, 41). Saville sees adultery in troubadour poetry as "an imaginative projection of the actual authority relationships in society during the period of declining feudalism" (1972, 44; see also Valency 1961, 59–85). According to this view, adulterous love was not so much a sin against morality as a trespass against the husband's property. Most critics accept adultery as a keystone in the literary edifice, regardless of our uncertain knowledge about the place it held in medieval daily life.[7]

Troubadour lyric, especially of the *trobar clus* variety, offers an elitist invitation to sound out hidden meanings. Little is explicit. Even for the more accessible lyrics, "troubadour poetry was always an insider's game" (Burgwinkle 1991, 15). Once the adulterous scenario is put into place, it is no longer necessary that it be continually reiterated in order for the audience to understand the underlying assumptions. The adultery, like any other motif, becomes encoded: "Once one is at all familiar with troubadour song, these other codes are always present as the non-spoken supplement through their association with the rhetorical forms of the song. That is to say that to understand one song, you must in principle know all the songs, or at least a large enough number to allow you to see that troubadour song functions as a highly reflective system within which individual songs resonate of the whole" (Burgwinkle 1991, 17). The kind of analysis that seeks scientific "proof" or legalistic evidence for every critical observation or interpretation evinces a myopic literal-mindedness that fails to read or reflect deeply upon the poetry. It is especially disheartening when scholarship that probes neither poetic meaning nor nuance is wielded to discount the most original and unconventional aspects of artistic endeavor. Such criticism flattens, rationalizes, and documents out of existence the nuanced and coded subtexts of art. If "we do not remember the troubadours because they loved, but because they sang" (Paden 1975, 50), we must also acknowledge that, since the troubadours sang, eros has never been the same.

Whatever the actuality of adultery in medieval culture generally, in the particularized scenario of the alba, an obstacle to love dictates secrecy and dawn parting; that obstacle is most clearly the lady's husband. Why should a couple guard and conceal their love or worry so desperately about the dangers of public exposure? For what reason must love be secret and parting occur so promptly at dawn if not because love is illicit? As Saville asks, "Why must the knight leave in the morning, if not for fear that the husband will return and discover his wife's infidelity? Adultery is the very essence of the *alba*" (1972, 39).

Although the gilos is a central character in the alba, Paden makes no specific reference to the alba in his discussion of the gilos. Yet he notes that in 3 percent of the texts he surveys (fourteen poems), "the troubadour or *trobairitz* appears to speak of extramarital love with a straight face. Half of these poems are from the minor genres and half are *cansos*" (40; here Paden footnotes three albas). The alba is found among the minor genres to which Paden refers. By dismissing the sought-after evidence because it is found in a minor genre, Paden overlooks the light a minor genre sheds on the larger corpus; moreover, his research corroborates the generally held view that the alba is the genre most consistently and blatantly adulterous. Saville notes: "The *alba* is the only form of troubadour lyric that consistently represents the love affair as adulterous" (1972, 39). This is not to say that married love cannot be passionate or that in other genres other kinds of love do not appear, but the alba is not about those other kinds of love. Its concern is with the secrecy, the danger, the fear of exposure—as well as the passion—of a love that cannot be made public.

Most critics view adultery as an essential element in the alba. Their views are predicated upon two elements: the alba plot, in which a night of ecstatic, secret love making is interrupted by dawn; and the references to the lady's husband, either by the word maris or gilos. Whenever he is mentioned in the alba, the gilos looms as a great threat. The gilos is referred to in eight albas, but two poems mention the husband more specifically. In "Cant voi l'aube dou jor venir," it is her "wicked jealous husband" ("mavais maris gilos") whom the lady denounces. In this case, the maris is explicitly the gilos. The lady of Cadenet's "S'anc fui belha ni prezada" staunchly retains her lover despite the boorish, wealthy "vilan" she mentions in her opening strophe. She has been married off to him; she later refers to him as "my wicked husband" ("mos mals maritz"). Even though the term gilos appears nowhere in the lyric, the lady is clearly married to a man she scorns. Her defiance of her spouse is manifest by both her words and her adulterous deeds, as she makes apparent: "and I would die/ had I not my true love by/ to whom to tell my sorrows" ("e murria/ s'ieu fin amic non avia/ cuy disses mo marrimen" [ll. 5–7]). She mentions the taunts and threats of her husband, even though she doesn't refer to him as the gilos:

> Never through threat or bluster
> that my wicked spouse might muster
> shall I fail to stay
> with my love until day.
>
> Ja per guap ni per menassa
> que mos mals maritz me fassa,
> no mudarai qu'ieu non jassa
> ab mon amic tro al dia. (ll. 37–40)

On the other hand, in "En un vergier sotz fuella d'albespi," the lady encourages her lover to "do it all in spite of the gilos" ("Tot o fassam en despieg del gilos" [l. 11]). Dronke, discussing this passage, remarks that the speaker "invites her lover in the tones of a *mal mariée*" (1977, 175), picking up on the unhappiness and resentment that binds the alba lady to the genre in which the feelings of unhappily married women are most vehemently expressed. Dronke doesn't hesitate to identify the scorned gilos as her spouse (176).

Marriage, in the person of the gilos, continually intrudes into the realm of alba love. He poses a major threat to love's continuation in "Reis glorios, verais lums e clardatz" where the watchman worries over the fate of the lover for fear that the gilos will assault him:

> "Fair friend, in singing I call you:
> sleep no longer, for I hear the bird sing
> who goes seeking day through the wood,
> and I fear that the jealous one will attack you,
>   and soon it will be dawn!"

"Bel companho, en chantan vos apel:
Non dormatz plus, qu'ieu aug chantar l'auzel
Que vai queren lo iorn per lo boscatge,
Et ai paor que·l gilos vos assatge,
   Et ades sera l'alba!" (ll. 11–15)

The lady who bids farewell to her lover in the concluding strophe of "Ab la gensor que sia" expresses her fear of the gilos:

"Beloved Lord Steven, go
for I shall remain yours
and if the gilos comes
I have great fear
and great terror
that he will do us villainy."

"Amicx N Esteves via
qu'ieu remanh vostr'amia
que si·l gilos venia
gran paor ai
e gran esmai
que·ns fezes vilania." (ll. 25–30)

Whereas Lord Steven's anger is directed not toward the gilos but the watchman (see discussion and citation earlier in this chapter), the lover of "Gaita be" befriends the watchman, begging him to be on the lookout for the gilos:

"Guard us,   dear watchman of the tower,
from the gilos,   your evil lord,
more hateful to me   than the dawn...."

"Gaitez vos,   gaiteta de la tor,
del gelos   vostre malvays seynor,
enujos   plus gue l'alba...." (15–17)

The gilos of this poem is obviously a powerful and menacing figure.

Some alba ladies, whether or not they fear their husbands, clearly despise them. The lady of "En un vergier sotz fuella d'albespi" who urges her lover to spite the gilos and Cadenet's spirited lady both defy their spouses (cited previously). As these citations demonstrate, love in the alba scenario involves a daring that goes hand in hand with scorn of the gilos.

In sum, the critical assumption of adultery in the alba does not rest solely on references to the gilos but on the idea of secret love that necessitates dawn parting—sometimes (but not always) in conjunction with the defiance or vilification of a character referred to as the gilos when he is not otherwise referred to as maris, the husband. Saville's comments on the importance of the element of adultery in the alba represents the mainline view, which has not been discredited: "All the characteristics of the genre—secrecy, fear of the light, danger, the need to part, the sorrow of the lovers at parting, the role of the watchman himself—depend on the fact that the love is adulterous" (1972, 47).

When we reconstruct the social hierarchy depicted in the alba, one thing becomes clear: the despised gilos is the all-powerful player in the dramatic love triangle even though he is always offstage. He may be physically absent, but his threat is ubiquitous; although silenced in the lyric, his evocation by the watchman or lovers bespeaks a powerful threat. The gilos is lord and master. Without him, the adulterous situation dissolves; for the lovers would not have to disperse at dawn, and the song's raison d'être would likewise disappear. Precisely because Criseyde has no living husband, some readers question her motive for parting from Troilus at dawn after their first night together. Chaucer's literary motive of seizing the opportunity to write a dawn-song seems far more credible than the widowed Criseyde's motive for singing it.

But the curious absence of any equivalent to the gilos in the tageliet, Chaucer's *Troilus,* or variations on the genre such as Shakespeare's *Romeo and Juliet* (where parents take on the role of the gilos) demonstrates that the dawn-song is elastic enough to dramatize an emotional love-parting scene even when the element of adultery is not explicitly mentioned. While the gilos is never openly referred to in the tageliet, critics generally assume that the lady, like her Provençal counterpart, is married to someone else. Once the convention is set into place by the troubadours, it is no longer necessary for the poet to mention the gilos for his presence to remain a factor. In the tageliet, the watchman's warnings of approaching dawn signify the lovers' danger. Although there is no reference to a gilos in Wolfram's "Sîne klâwen," the sharp "talons" of dawn seem to appropriate the gilos's threat (see chapter 5). But interestingly, as the role of the gilos diminishes in the tageliet, the watchman's role expands. The increased importance of the watchman as an integral member of the dramatic cast indicates that love must be guarded and kept secret. The watchman fills the generic propensity to have a third party, an outsider who is either friend or foe, hovering on the periphery of the scene.

Minnesingers of Wolfram von Eschenbach's period had sufficient command of Old Provençal and Old French dawn-songs to be able to write variations on them, as they did on the other Old Provençal genres. Wolfram's anti-tageliet, "Der helden minne ir klage," contrasts married love with the kind of love that gave rise to his four famous tagelieder. Wolfram's tribute to conjugal love presents a liberating contrast to the alba's suppressed love. While the gilos is unmentioned in his tagelieder, Wolfram establishes in both those four lyrics and his anti-tageliet the fact that unmarried love must ever be secret:

> Illicit love's lament
> you ever sang at dawn's ascent,
>   the bitter after the sweet.
>   Whoever has known love and a woman's greeting
>   in such a plight
>   that his love was put to flight,—
>   such warnings as you gave them both,
>   as the morning star grew bright,
>   O watchman, silence! That song cease!
>   Of such sad sorrow hold your peace.

> He who is or was accustomed to
> lay with his lady as lovers do,
>   without concealment from spies
>   need not, when the sun arises
>   struggle to flee with crying eyes
>   he can stay awaiting dawn;
>   he need not be guided out, forlorn
>   for the sake of his dear life.
>   An avowed, sweet married wife,
>   can give love such as this at morn.

Der helden minne ir klage
du sunge ie gên dem tage,
   Daz sûre nach dem sûezen.
swer minne und wîplîch grüezen
     alsô enpfienc,
        daz si sich muosen scheiden,—
     swaz dû dô riete in beiden,
dô ûf gienc
        Der morgensterne, wahtaere, swîc,
dâ von niht <. . . .> sinc.

Swer pflíget oder íe gepflac,
daz er bî líeben wíben lac,
   Den merkaeren unverborgen,
der darf niht durch den morgen
   dannen streben.
     er mac des tages erbeiten.
   man darf in niht ûz leiten
ûf sîn leben.
        Ein offeniu süeze wirtes wîp
kan sölhe minne geben.

Wolfram brilliantly invokes the dawn parting while composing a song that simultaneously nullifies its necessity. In commanding the watchman's silence, the narrator acknowledges that marriage makes the watchman's warnings superfluous. This celebration of married love demonstrates that, even though tagelieder do not make explicit references to the husband or the gilos, they are nonetheless concerned with the same dangerous, illicit love as their Romance counterparts.

Critics have viewed Wolfram's anti-tageliet as his farewell not only to adulterous love but also to his favorite genre; for with adultery eliminated from the alba, the genre itself as a literary form is emptied of significance (Dronke 1977, 179; Saville 1972, 46–48). Because he plays off the genre, Wolfram shows that with the obstacle(s) removed, neither love nor love poetry must cease. Hatto interprets this poetic shift as one that mirrors its author's change of heart, his reassessment of refined love: "From *Parzival*, *Titurel* and *Willehalm* we know that Wolfram had come to reject the illicit implications of Courtly Love, on which his tageliet were of course founded;

while on the other hand he speaks with warmth of love in wedlock and paints entrancing depictions of it. To him in his maturity the marriage bond was but one of a hierarchy of loyalties that embraced the whole feudal world and culminated in God" (Hatto 1965, 454–55n.9). Powerful innovator that he was, Wolfram composed the first dawn-abiding love song for passionate married love, expanding the genre in the process.

Eros in the Socius

> Of medieval genres the lyric is alone in representing a society where numerous men (lovers true and false, the *lauzengeor* and the *gilos*) are all in competition for the favors of one woman. This is not the way courts are presented in romances and epics, and there are grounds for believing them to be more "realistic" in this regard.
> *Sarah Kay,* Subjectivity in Troubador Poetry, *114*

Power, Gender, and Class: The Love Triangle

Realistic or not, the alba presents a triangular love situation in which the lady has two men, and with each her relationship and status are different. Unlike the relationship between husband and wife or between canso domna and her wooer, the alba lady and her lover are equals. Saville and Forster assume that alba lady and lover have the same social standing. Saville notes that "the relationship of the man and woman in the *alba* is one of equality." The lover and the lady, he continues, "are *evidently* on the same social level" (1972, 220; my emphasis). Leonard Forster concurs, observing that the alba is "a splendidly contrived device for dealing with sexual intercourse between lovers of equal—that is, courtly—social status in a discreet manner" (1967, 121). This presupposition provides the foundation for their belief that the alba is a courtly genre: both lovers belong to the courtly—that is, the aristocratic—class. Although I agree that alba lovers are equal, the issue of their equality is more complex than has been recognized, and it is crucially linked to central alba themes. Wherein resides the lovers' equality? Is it based on their sharing the same (aristocratic) social rank; that is, is it assessed and granted by external, communal criteria? Or is it assessed by the way the lovers behave toward one another; that is, is it based on the intrinsic mutuality of their feelings? Does equal social rank necessitate mutuality, or does mutuality of feeling become the equalizing force?

Whether courtliness is to be assessed by external or internal criteria is a prominent troubadour concern that has also been of interest to critics.

Some social historians, such as Kölher, posit that the poets' desire to forge a pathway for themselves into the exclusive aristocratic circle causes them to create or promote a value system that could be independent of lineage and property. The dichotomization of courtliness into internal and external qualities—virtue, integrity, generosity as opposed to the class into which one is born—reflects, among other things, the troubadour's incipient recognition of individuality, of a sense that personal traits are important. Hence, the troubadour presents virtue as ennobling as well as worthy of reward. Without an acknowledgment of individual merit, there can be no criteria other than the external societal one by which to assess courtliness—and no other way to measure equality, either.

But even among members of the same class, equality is not always a given. The noble lady and her husband may both be aristocratic, but there is little equality between them or in the power they wield within or outside of the feudal manor. Kay makes a useful distinction between rank and status, suggesting that rank is automatically conferred by heredity or marriage whereas status is a cultural construct that is negotiable: "The relationship between status and rank is uncertain for women who have the rank of their father until they marry and that of their husband thereafter, but on whom high rank does not necessarily confer enhanced status, because of the widespread tendency to depreciate women and exclude them from situations where men of corresponding rank would exercise power" (1990, 112). Hence, a lady of noble rank can have significantly less status (and power) than a husband who holds a lesser rank. Marriage makes the aristocrat subordinate if she happens to be the female half of the couple.

The relationship between alba lovers, however, differs from that between aristocratic spouses. Whereas the noble wife may be her husband's subordinate, she can be her lover's equal. In a *tenson* with Gui d'Ussel, the trobairitz Maria de Ventadorn describes the difference between the honor a lady owes her lover as opposed to her "lord" (that is, her spouse): "and a lady should honor her lover/ as a friend, but never as a lord" ("e dompna deu a son drut far honor/ cum ad amic, mas non cum a seignor" [Bogin 1976, 100]). Love involves honoring the lover but not subordinating oneself to him.

Historically speaking, medieval marriages were not conceived of as moral or pure. Especially for the aristocracy, marriages of convenience "carried the taint of social necessity" (Kelly-Gadol 1987, 142). Those critics who have called attention to the alba lady's social inferiority to and victimization by her lover (and the male-dominated society they claim he represents) have overlooked the implicit contrast the alba sets up between the lady's relationship with her spouse, to whom she is inferior, and her lover, with whom she is equal. The equality between alba lovers gives the lady a peer rather than a lord; this equality is based not on externally imposed social criteria but rather on the internal, on the fact that each is worthy and their feelings are reciprocal.

The canso lady stands high above her wooer. In all ways she is nobler and worthier; indeed, her superiority is vital to the worth of both. Only if she is superior can the lover's praise of her be meaningful; how else can she be glorified or he ennobled? Love elevates the lover primarily because he adores a lady of superior quality. Arnaut Daniel's canso lover owes his amelioration to his lady: "Each day I am a better man and purer,/ for I serve the noblest lady in the world" ("Tot iorn meillur et esmeri/ car la gensor serv e coli" [ll. 8–9; "En cest sonet coind'e leri," Goldin 1973, 216–19]). Bernart de Ventadorn expresses his devotion in terms of feudal submission:

> Gracious lady, I thank you
> for your gentle love.
> I pledge you with staunch faith and true,
> that never have I loved another so.
> With hands joined, neck bowed and low,
> I submit myself to your command.
>
> Bona domna, merce
> del vostre fin aman.
> Qu'e·us pliu per bona fe
> c'anc re no amei tan.
> Mas jonchas, ab col cle,
> vos m'autrei e·m coman. ("Pois preyatz me,
> senhor," ll. 46–51)

As Burns succinctly describes it:

> The *domna* of the *canso* appears most often as a highly placed, powerful figure before whom the lover/vassal bows in gestures of respect and service, homage and worship:
>
> > "Domna, per vostr'amor
> > jonh las mas et ador"

> ["Lady, for your love
> I join my hands and adore" (Bernart de Ventadorn,
> "Tant ai mo cor ple de joya," ll. 57–58)]
>
> Revered and adored by a coterie of suitors, she occupies *vis à vis* her lover a position of superiority which is as uncontested as the position of inferiority occupied by the medieval wife *vis à vis* her husband. (1984, 257)

Peire Vidal's lover praises his lady as the miraculous source of his virtue, education, courtliness, and song: "And if I can say or do anything/ thanks be to her, for the knowledge/ she gave me and the learning,/ wherefore I am courtly, and can sing" ("E s'ieu sai ren dir ni faire,/ ilh n'aia·l grat, que sciensa/ m'a donat e conoissensa,/ per qu'ieu sui gais e chantaire" [Goldin, *Lyrics of the Troubadours*, 254–55]).

The phenomenon of a man whose beloved characteristically occupies a higher social plane than he in a society where women usually hold lower status than men is considered by some critics to be a "fundamental paradox of Occitan poetry" for which various interpretations have been supplied (Kay 1990, 84). But however it is finally understood, the troubadour's lady ennobles and empowers her admirer, "bringing him good fortune, good looks, and good character" (Burns 1984, 261). By inspiring the singer's eloquence, she secures his social status and fame, as Bernart de Ventadorn boasts: "It is no wonder if I sing/ better than any other troubadour:/ for my heart draws me more toward love,/ and I am better made for his command" ("Non es meravelha s'eu chan/ melhs de nul autre chantador,/ que plus me tra·l cors vas amor/ e melhs sui faihz a so coman" (ll. 1–4; Goldin, *Lyrics*, 126–27). Or as Arnaut Daniel claims in "En cest sonet coind'e leri": "for Love polishes and gilds/ my song, which proceeds from her,/ ruler and guardian of merit" ("q'Amors marves plan'e daura/ mon chantar, que de liei mou/ qui pretz manten e governa" (ll. 5–7; Goldin, *Lyrics of the Troubadours*, 216–17). The lady's superior virtue is obvious regardless of her precise social rank. While she may be subordinate to her husband, she is superior to her wooer in ethical and moral, if not social, terms.

According to Kölher, the troubadours spoke for a lower nobility seeking to integrate themselves into an exclusionary court through the promotion of ethical values common to the nobility. The domna is the chosen vehicle through which the singer can achieve social and economic parity with the nobility. The troubadour scolds the lord (as a gilos), for in jealously guarding his wife, he prevents the access to her through which worthy aspirants can be ennobled (spiritually as well as materially). Although Köhler's theories have been faulted for relying too heavily on a small number of troubadours, his theories fit the alba as well as the canso scenario. Scaglione, too, accepts courtly love as a social-climbing process in which a poor knight's aspiration upward can be aided by appeal to the domna (1991, 94).

For Kay, however, the kind of power that the troubadours attributed to the domna could never be sustained by a real woman in so masculinist a culture. In her view, the domna "is enjoined [by the poet] not to show favour to the powerful, but to embody power herself in her role of lord." Once she possesses such power, she becomes an androgyne, a third, "mixed" gender whose body is female, whose sexuality is passive, and whose social status is masculine (1990, 86, 91, 92). Kay's view of the domna recalls the Athena of Aeschylus's *Eumenides,* who possesses a female body but distances herself from women and considers herself in all other aspects a man. Kay is one of many critics who believe that the troubadour's desire is less for the lady herself than for the enhanced social status that can be acquired through courting her (Kay 1990, 115–16; see also Goldin, *Lyrics of the Troubadours;* Burns 1984; Burgwinkle 1990).

Essentially, the critical question becomes how much power a woman—or even her image in poetry—can possess. For Kay, the lady of the canso bedecked with lordly powers must, by default, be a new gender altogether, an androgyne whose exalted social status is masculine. She cannot represent a real woman because the patriarchal depreciation of the female would legislate against such validation. For Duby and Kölher, she may be a real woman, but her power derives solely from her alliance with her superior spouse; the trappings of that power rather than the lady herself (whom the singer can renounce) are desired.[1] For Paden, the domna is not the troubadour's social superior in the first place: "In only 6 per cent of our texts have we found reason to believe that the poet's lady enjoyed high rank in the literal sense" (1975, 38). But there is no question that the poet's lady enjoyed high regard as a spiritual and moral force.

Whatever her social status, she is graced with the ability to ennoble, as the narrator of Guillaume IX's canso "Mout jauzens me prenc en amar" declares:

> The joy of her can make the sick man well again,
> her wrath can make a well man die,
> a wise man turn to childishness,

a beautiful man behold his beauty change;
the courtliest man can become a churl,
and any churl a courtly man.

Per son joy pot malautz sanar,
e per sa ira sas morir
e savis hom enfolezir
e belhs hom sa beutat mudar
e·l plus cortes vilanejar
e totz vilas encortezir. (ll. 25–30)
             (text and translation from Goldin,
                          Lyrics, 44–45)

Such a *domna* does indeed elevate the singer/lover in the fictive scenario of the courtly lyric as well as in the real court if we accept the historians' hypothesis. The unknowability of the *domna*'s social rank is only one facet of her mystery. But no matter her precise social status or grade of power, she remains the elevated paragon who can miraculously reward those who kneel at her feet.

In the *alba*, however, the distance that divides *canso* lady from her suitor clearly dissolves. Not only do the lovers consider one another friends, companions, and confidants, but they often recount—in a tone of delighted, childlike innocence—their play and joyous laughter. The continual, almost obsessive references to the lovers' side-by-side positions and reclining postures literally portray how close they are but also remind us that they are on an equal plane; their relationship is horizontal rather than hierarchical.

Speaking of his tryst with an unidentified but superlative lady, the lover of "Ab la gensor que sia" begins by describing his position: "By the noblest who might be/ and by the best endowed/ I lay me down the other day" ("Ab la gensor que sia/ et ab la mielhs aibia/ mi colgei l'autre dia" [ll. 1–3]). At the beginning of the second strophe, he again refers to his reclining position: "While I was lying/ and supine, asleep" ("Mentre qu'ieu mi jazia/ e·n sobinas dormia" [ll. 7–8]). Although vague about the mundane details of place, the poem twice specifies the lovers' reclining posture. Twice also in "Gaite de la tor," the lovers' recumbent position is referred to, first by the watchman—"courteous lovers,/ who lie at rest/ in the quiet room" ("cortois ameor,/ qui a sejor/ gisez on chambre coie" [ll. 44–46])—and later by the lover himself: "Too little have I lain/ in the chamber of joy" ("Pou ai geü /En la chambre de joie" [ll. 62–63]). The opening lines of Walther's "Friuntlîchen lac" portray the knight reclining: "Companionably lay/ a splendid knight/ in the arms of a lady" ("Friuntlîchen lac/ ein rîter vil gemeit/ an einer frowen arme" [ll. 1–3]). Later the lady asks her lover to lie there longer: "now just lie awhile: you could never do so well" ("nû lige eht eine wîle: sô getaet dû nie sô wol" [l. 40]).

In many of these examples, the lover's supine posture is mentioned at the very opening of the poem as though it in itself gives a sense of place to the poems. In "Dieus, aydatz," the lover's posture is withheld until the conclusion, when the lady speaks of her lover, "who in my arms/ joyful lies" ("qu'e mon bratz/ jauzen jatz" [ll. 53–54]).

In some albas, the lovers' position is evoked by a phrase, such as "ab son amic" or "pres de mi," indicating the lovers' side-by-side position. "En un vergier sotz fuella d'albespi" introduces the motif of attachment in its opening line: "In a park under the leaves of the hawthorn/ the lady holds her lover at her side" ("En un vergier sotz fuella d'albespi/ tenc la dompna son amic costa si"). In "Cant voi l'aube dou jor venir," the lady also tells us that she misses the presence "at her side" ("encoste mi") of her lover's body. In this context, the word, "costa," which etymologically means "rib," is resonant of the companionable quality of this love; the "breast-to-breast" embrace specificied in the tageliet is reinforced when the lovers' side-by-side position is consistently described by the phrase "bi mir" ("by" or "next to me"). The genre clearly has a stake in portraying its lovers on the same plane and as attached or inseparable.

This horizontal positioning, which coincides with other aspects of the mutuality and equality of alba love, appears with such consistency that it becomes in itself a motif, especially because this phrasing and posturing appear in no other genre. Such posturing is not mentioned in lyrics where the lady speaks about her relationship with her husband, despite the fact that there may be physical intimacy between them. In the alba scenario, the husband is on top.[2] The linguistic formulae I refer to—present in Old Provençal, Old French, and Middle High German versions of the dawn-song—is too prevalent to be fortuitous or insignificant. The poets' continual attention to detailing the lovers' side-by-side position is so prominent it becomes a defining element of the genre. The side-by-side formula is just one of a number of descriptive phrases that reveal the lovers' mutuality.

The equality between the lady and her wooer is not due merely to the fact that no socially imposed distinctions come between them—in other words, that they have always been of the same (aristocratic) stature. Although Saville and Forster assume that the conventional inequality between lady and suitor no longer exists in the alba, it is much more likely, considering that this inequality is a central issue in the canso and the pastourelle, that their equality occurs *as a result* rather than a precondition of their sexual union.

It is abundantly clear that the alba lady, like the canso lady, is a member of the elite. She is designated a domna by the poet, who applies all the conventional signposts of courtliness. But there is nothing in the alba to indicate that her lover possesses equal status. He is not referred to as a lord except in the alba "Ab la gensor que sia," where the lady addresses her lover as "Lord Steven" ("N Esteves"). Otherwise, the limited number of terms used to describe him recognize only that he is a horse-mounted man: he is a "cavalier" or "compagno" in addition to being an "ami"; he is a "ritter" ("rider"), when he is more than "an werden man" or "werder friunt" ("a worthy man or worthy friend"). Yet in the other genres, we find frequent references to "seynor," "don," or "herren." In "Gaita be," the lover refers to the gilos not merely as the watchman's lord but as his "evil lord" ("vostre malvays seynor").

The lover is at least one notch below the lady in status because she is linked to the powerful lord through marriage, whereas her lover is an outsider, a transgressor invading another man's terrain. Legally, he is stealing the lord's property (his wife's body). Thus, the reference to the lover as "sweet stranger" or "guest" ("süezer gast," 30) in Wolfram's "Von der zinnen" may actually be applied to all these knights. But this endearment is euphemistic if not downright ironic: the lover may be the lady's guest but certainly not one invited by her spouse.

In essence, both the lady and her lover are the husband's legal, if not social, inferiors, and neither possesses the lord's power. No matter what her premarital status, when the lady marries, she becomes her husband's subordinate. Hence, in some ways, both alba lady and lover are disenfranchised.

The designation of the alba lover as cavalier, compagno, and ritter is not gratuitous. The lover must be mobile, for his riding or roving has brought him not only within the lady's sphere but to her bower. Such terms also indicate the lover's lack of a fixed, secure place within the established hierarchy.

Even though he is never referred to in albas as jovens, the alba lover might be modeled on the dispossessed youth characterized by Duby and Köhler.[3] Unpropertied himself, such a youth perhaps displaces his jealousy of the lord's property onto the lord in whose service he finds himself employed. Although the lord is called the "jealous one," it is actually the landless youth who has most cause for jealousy. Coveting the lord's material property, he also covets his wife (perhaps as part and symbol of that property). This sociohistorical background gives us cause to feel that the singer's love, rather than being a spontaneous and powerful emotion, may be a calculated attempt to close the economic and political gap between himself and his lord through the lady. But however accurate this historical underpinning may be, there are no references in albas to lead us to interpret alba love as anything but an overwhelmingly passionate experience that equalizes and ennobles lady and lover. We may be more cynical about the ideology that underlies the alba scenario than the poems permit us to be about their explicit meaning.

Why the powerful higher nobility should have countenanced the troubadours' efforts at self-legitimization, especially at the lords' own expense, remains an unanswered but intriguing question. According to Scaglione, "the husband, that is, the lord, accepts this chaste devotion toward his wife and is often reminded not to take on the ridiculous role of gilos. . . . The lords welcomed the ideology and even joined it because it ensured the knights' loyalty, which the lords needed" (1991, 93, 94). But Scaglione's view is predicated upon the singer's chaste devotion rather than the cuckoldry it would have to have been. That the troubadours promoted their self-interest and the interests of those who served the lords, and that the lords made no response that effectively shut down this poetry and its ideology indicates that it served a larger purpose upon which poets, vassals, lords, and their ladies all agreed.

As a rider (ritter), the lover ventures outside his familial boundaries. When he speaks of riding off, the lady frequently expresses a fear that further efforts to see her again may be hindered: "When will you come here to me again?" ("wenne wîlt du wider her zuo mir?" ["Slâfest du, vriedel ziere?"]). In "Ez ist nu tac" the lady laments: "Alas, how will he come hence?/ May the highest peace yet again guide him to my arms!" ("ôwê des, wie kumt ers hin?/ der hôhste vride müeze in noch an mînen arn geleiten"). She concludes the poem by begging her lover: "now come quickly again for true consolation/ alas because of this/ I cannot refrain from sorrow" ("nu kum schiere wider ûf rehten trôst!/ owê dur dáz mác ich strenge sorge niht gelâzen"). When the lover of this poem speaks of riding off, he asks for the lady's love to shield him:

> He spoke: "Now I will ride away.
>   May your womanly goodness have me in its keeping
> and be my shield everywhere today and always"
>
> er sprach: "nu wil ich rîten.
>   dîn wîplîch güete neme mîn war
> und sî mî schílt híute hin und her noch zallen zîten."
>
> (ll. 34–36)

He needs a shield because he is on dangerous ground—literally and figuratively—when he attempts to steal or misappropriate the property of the powerful gilos. Wolfram invokes the traditional chivalric shield in showing the lover's reliance on his lady's virtue as his defense against harm.

The accusations of theft that alba lovers call down on dawn and the watchman are primarily effective rhetorical devices; but they also reveal a concern, perhaps even an obsession, with property and rightful ownership. The Old French "Gaite de la tor" refers to thieves who go in prey and a robber lurking under cover: "Et larron vont en proie. . . . Ne sont pas plusor/ Li robeör;/ N'i a c'un, que je voie,/ Qui gist en la flor/ Soz covertor/ Cui nomer n'oseroie" ("And thieves seek their prey. . . . There are not many/ robbers;/ there is only one that I can see,/ who lies hidden/ under cover of flowers/ and I dare not name him") (ll. 6, 34–39). Ironically, the gilos legally retains physical possession—ownership—of his wife, even though he does not possess her heart, a part of herself she has freely bestowed on her lover. If the lover is a thief stealing the lord's property, the lord, in turn, can be seen as a thief who takes the wife's body as his possession in the first place.

As with the application of status, a distinction between the internal and external becomes an issue. The husband is the gilos because he cares so much for physical possession that he claims ownership of his wife even when there is no corresponding emotional attachment or affection. Gottfried von Strassburg's King Mark claims to love his wife Isolde but lacks the discrimination to differentiate her from her handmaiden Brangane or to distinguish physical possession from love: "To him one woman was as another: he soon found Isolde, too, to be of good deportment. There was nothing to choose between them—he found gold and brass in either" (Hatto 1965, 208). To this kind of husband, women are interchangeable; wives serve as partners for sexual release and as status symbols.

A sensibility that distinguishes possession from passion is one of the gifts that the troubadours transferred from Christianity to the idea of secular love. Christian doctrine gave a new, positive, spiritual meaning to passion: love, "defined as passion for the good, perfects the individual" (Kelly-Gadol 1987, 143). But passion that attached love to sex rather than God represented a threat to Christian doctrine. Experienced as a sacred calling, this kind of love was in tune with Christian feeling even while it violated its doctrine. Chrétien's Lancelot spurns mere sexuality in favor of the fulfillment of a higher, deeper love. As Chrétien makes clear in this dawn-parting passage, Lancelot's love is sacramental as well as sexual: "But to his deep regret, day comes and he rises from his beloved's side. When he did so he was a true martyr: so distressed was he at the parting that when it came he endured terrible martyrdom. His heart is ceaselessly drawn back to where the queen remains; and he has no power to take it away, for it finds in the queen such pleasure that it has no wish to leave her: the body goes but the heart stays behind. . . . As he left, he bowed before the room, behaving just as though he were before an altar, then went away in deep anguish" (Chrétien de Troyes 1987, 247–28). His passion for Guenevere ennobles and purifies him, preventing him from succumbing to many a seductive damsel's invitations. A king such as Mark, who cannot tell his queen from her servant, or Arthur, who lets his queen be abducted in front of his eyes, are foils for a romantic lover such as Lancelot, who responds exclusively to the one woman upon whom he has bestowed his heart: "The knight has only one heart; and that no longer belongs to him, but is entrusted to someone else, so that he cannot lend it out elsewhere. Love, who rules over all hearts, has it remain in just one place. All hearts? No: only those he values. . . . I would not blame him at all if he rejects what Love forbids him and concentrates on what he desires" (Chrétien de Troyes 1987, 201). Such devotion not only makes lovers monogamous but also sanctifies their love.

Refined love enables Lancelot to accomplish superhuman tasks, lifting him above mere earthly concerns and elevating him from typical knight to hero. The canso lady likewise enables the socially inferior lover to ascend to her level, but should she "conceive a passion of her own for her adorer, she would swing right down from her exalted height to a position of equality" (Saville 1972, 221). The alba lady does respond to her lover, and she works an equalizing miracle whereby the lovers achieve the fulfillment and sense of perfection that the canso lover yearns for but cannot have. Alba lovers meet on the plane of sanctified passion. This liberating release is enacted for the first time in the alba, the only troubadour genre in which love is reciprocated and consummated.

It is not chaste devotion but mutuality or complementarity that marks the relation the lady enters into with her ami (Kelly-Gadol 1987, 142). And this intimacy temporarily dissolves the discrepancy in social position between lady and lover not only in albas but also in romances such as Chrétien's *Lancelot*, where the hero is of lesser rank than the Queen, or Chaucer's *Troilus and Criseyde*, where the heroine is far from equal to the princely Troilus. Like the manner of earlier alba ladies, Criseyde's sangfroid thaws once she opens her heart to Troilus; in her alba, she lovingly addresses him as "Myn hertes life, my trist, and my plesaunce" (III, 1422). Troilus, on the other hand, like the alba lover, no longer goes unrewarded by the lady. Before their union can occur, he must be transformed through Love's magic into Love's subject. Troilus, princely leader of men and scorner of Love, becomes Troilus, disciple of Love and worshipper of woman. Criseyde, his erstwhile inferior, is transmuted into his sovereign. In Chaucer's work, this transfer of power is not a good in itself. It weakens, confuses, and ultimately destroys Troilus.

The lover's metamorphosis from ruler to ruled did not occur in the antecedent alba tradition because the courtly cavalier of the alba was not initially his lady's superior; like Lancelot, his relation to his beloved was one of inferiority and vassalage. But love, the great equalizer, transfigures the canso lady's power and icy indifference into the alba lady's warmth and vulnerability. This equalization of the lovers metaphorizes the idea that love is a turning of the self away from the empyrean of isolation and indifference toward the community of delight, of feeling, and therefore of pain. To accept or even treasure the sufferings of love, to believe that the anguish adds valor and value, is one of the innovations that Christianity contributed to the medieval idea of love.

If the real innovation of the canso is, as Singer believes, the idealization of the female (1984, 48), the innovation of the alba is its lovers' equalization. Although Chaucer generally rejects courtly love ideology, his Franklin presents some of its tenets in the introduction to his tale:

> For o thyng, sires, saufly dar I seye,
> That freendes everych oother moot obeye,
> If they wol longe holden compaignye.

> Love wol nat been constreyned by maistrye.
> Whan maistrie comth, the God of Love anon
> Beteth his wynges, and farewel, he is gon!
> Love is a thyng as any spirit free.
> Wommen, of kynde, desiren libertee,
> And nat to been constreyned as a thral;
> And so doon men, if I sooth seyen shal.
>
> (ll. 761–70)

Although Chaucer's Franklin here acknowledges that love can only exist in a relationship of equality and freedom, he problematizes love in applying it to marriage. The kind of equality for which lovers strive comes under continual questioning once they marry. That Dorigen and Arveragus can be lovers as well as spouses is an ideal articulated at the tale's beginning but never realized in the tale. The Franklin's account of the couple's "humble, wise accord"—the understanding they achieve when they marry—is confused and qualified enough to leave the audience doubting exactly what this accord achieves:

> pryvely she fil of his accord
> To take hym for hir housbonde and hir lord,
> Of swich lordshipe as men han over hir wyves.
> And for to lede the more in blisse hir lyves,
> Of his free wyl he swoor hire as a knyght
> That nevere in al his lyf he, day ne nyght,
> Ne sholde upon hym take no maistrie
> Agayn hir wyl, ne kithe hire jalousie,
> But hire obeye, and folwe hir wyl in al,
> As any lovere to his lady shal,
> Save that the name of soveraynetee,
> That wolde he have for shame of his degree.
> . . . .
> Heere may men seen an humble, wys accord;
> Thus hath she take hir servant and hir lord—
> Servant in love, and lord in mariage.
> Thanne was he bothe in lordshipe and servage.
> Servage? Nay but in lordshipe above,
> Sith he hath bothe his lady and his love;
> His lady, certes, and his wyf also,
> The which that lawe of love acordeth to.
>
> (ll. 741–52, 791–98)

Each pledges obedience and submission to the other: if Dorigen takes Arveragus for her lord (qualified by the Franklin's ironic aside: "Of swich lordshipe as men han over hir wyves"), Arveragus promises to obey and follow Dorigen's will "in al." But Dorigen's dominance is immediately belied by the acknowledgment that, for honor's sake, Arveragus should bear the "name of sovereignty."

The Franklin may find this "humble" agreement "wise," but we see during the course of the tale that Dorigen's wifely sovereignty is a myth; her ostensible equality erodes as she is gradually reduced to a pawn traded between men. By the tale's end, she is forced into considering the only solution she knows to her plight: martyrdom. She finds, however, that she must obey her husband after all: Arveragus decides that, because "trouthe is the hyeste thyng that man may kepe" (l. 1479), Dorigen must keep her word; he then forbids her "up peyne of deeth" (l. 1480) to breathe a word of this disgrace to anyone. Although Dorigen is sent off to sacrifice herself in what can only be understood as rape, Arveragus bursts into self-pitying tears lamenting the loss of his honor. As Chaucer designs the plot, Dorigen has forfeited her bid for wifely equality through her own (playful/foolish) words. But fin'amors, even in so chastening a story as "The Franklin's Tale," is still put forth as a volitional, equalizing relationship; it is marriage that creates inequality and obligation.

The fact that the alba allows the knight to achieve momentary fulfillment through union with his lady makes the genre the most socially subversive of the lyric forms. The clash of social classes that is an overt theme in the pastourelle and canso seems to evaporate in the alba. This absence, however, belies the genre's obsession with the issue. The crucial difference between the alba lovers and their counterparts in the canso and pastourelle is not that both lady and lover were born into the aristocracy but that the lady reciprocates rather than disdains, ignores, or resists her wooer's attentions. Passionate mutual love renders class distinctions insignificant. Alba love unifies but also elevates lovers to a plane that transcends mundane concerns such as class. In the alba, the reciprocity so vital to the meaning of passionate love as we have come to understand it today emerges as a literary theme for the first time.

The alba's disdain of socially prescribed class distance is subversive. In contrast with the other genres, the alba implicitly defies the status quo, inverting or redefining societal values so completely that a desirable, aristocratic lady—the symbol of the elite class—perceives a socially inferior male as more refined, more worthy of love, more courtly than the reigning, politically powerful seynor; and she deliberately and vociferously prefers such a lover to her spouse. This preference is what the canso singer seeks from his beloved, but because she does not respond, it is never acted out in that genre.

Furthermore, the alba poet allows the adulterous couple to enjoy their illicit union while eluding discovery and societal censure. The lady's preference makes it clear that wealth and worth are unrelated. She favors her less economically advantaged interloper because he possesses qualities she values, qualities attainable by a man of any economic status: fine appearance, discretion and restraint, eloquence, gentleness, trustworthiness, respect, and fine manners. These inner qualities vie with the external ones of wealth and inheritance in the courtly arena. Given the choice, the alba lady selects the man who demonstrates intrinsic worth over the man whose value is bestowed upon him from the outside. Despite an inferior social position, the lover can still be an embodiment of courtliness. He is called "cortes" and a "fin'amics"; he possesses many "virtues." The tageliet knight, like the Romance alba "companho," is passionate, patient, understanding, sensitive, daring, considerate, and calm. In "Ez ist nu tac," the lady characterizes her lover as a wooer whose soft words and sweet kisses "tutored by rare excellence" (as Hatto nicely translates it; 1965, 449) have won her respect as well as her heart. She fell in love, she tells him, because of

> your mouth, which many a greeting
>   bade me and also your sweet kiss,
>   as your excellent goodness taught it,
>   and that companion of yours, loyalty.
>
> dînen munt, der manigen gruoz
>   mir bôt únde ouch dîn kus,
>   alse ín dîn ûzerwelte güete lêrte,
>   und dín geséllè dîn triuwe. (ll. 42–45)

To the alba lady, this is the sort of man who has real class.

For alba lovers, whatever pleases is desirable, beautiful, and good. Worth is assessed by attractiveness and etiquette. The source of their appeal for one another is their capacity to provide pleasure and affection. To present oneself as "pleasing," shown in good bearing, refined manners, and eloquence, demonstrates a sensitivity to the desires of others, a lack of selfishness.

The lady has freely chosen an outsider beneath her husband's, and possibly her own, social position. The cortoisie referred to in the alba, like the gentilesse praised by Chaucer's Alice of Bath, is based not on an inheritance from birth but on deliberate, courtly bearing. When the lover of the alba "Gaita be" says, "for I am rich and I have what I most desire" ("qu'eu sui ricx /e so qu'eu plus voilh ai" [Rimbaut de Vaqueiras, l. 9]), he means not that he possesses calculable wealth but that he feels fulfilled by his lady's love. His feelings are more palpable than any tangible wealth. Raimbaut de Vaqueiras's narrator expresses a similar sentiment in the canso "No m'agrad'iverns ni pascors": "And so, what's all this wealth and conquest worth to me?/ I thought I was far wealthier/ When I was loved and a faithful lover" (Goldin, *Lyrics,* 270–71) ("Doncs, qe·m val conquistz ni ricors?/ qu'eu ja·m tenia per plus rics/ qand er' amatz e fis amics [Raimbaut de Vaqueiras xxii, ll. 37–39]). Emotional fulfillment enriches courtly lovers, to whom nothing else seems real. This theme is aptly picked up by the narrator of Donne's "The Sunne Rising," who declares that compared to his love: "All honor's mimique; All wealth alchimie" (l. 24).

Cadenet's alba lady presents her lover as the embodiment of refinement and courtesy in contrast to her spouse, whom she calls vulgar, "un vilan." Surprising as we might find such a designation for the feudal lord who rules over a court and castle, the husband in the alba is unrefined and uncourtly. He is a vilan because, like a rustic, he is unaware of how to behave decorously; but like a lord, he can afford not to care. Although he lacks subtlety, refinement, amicability, and discretion (traits of the courtly man), perhaps his material superiority makes these traits unnecessary; he need not cultivate manners or concern himself with providing pleasure for others. Consequently, his wife perceives him as unattractive, displeasing, selfish—a bore/boor. Ironically, in the inverted alba world, the aristocratic husband becomes the outcast, the social misfit, vilified and mocked among courtly lovers. In two albas, the gilos is not merely the intruding outsider; he is evil. For the lord to become courtly, his behavior, attitudes, even gestures would have to accord with a new standard, one he has had no part in designing.

The disenfranchised lady and her lover-knight, perhaps like their poet, substitute a new attainable kind of status for the older established hierarchy that bars them from equality with the lady's lord if not from each other. Scaglione claims that, in time, with succeeding generations of troubadours, this acquisition of status is actually obtained: "Reputation and honor (*pretz* and *honor*) no longer depended on property but on public recognition of this ideal of inner perfection. The critique of power and property, noble or bourgeois as the poets might be, was founded on this perception of a superior nobility of spirit" (1991, 95). In consummating their love, lady and lover are not only equalized; they are lifted to a plane where they can act out what they and their poets envision as a more honorable, more moral, and ultimately more spiritual choice.

Fin'amors: Conflicting Loyalties; Divided Selves

> To conduct one's amours in such a way as will saddle oneself with exposure would be impolitic.
> Wolfram von Eschenbach, "Von der zinnen" (Hatto 1965, 453)

The alba lady's circumstances lead her into opposition with the hegemonic forces that keep her apart from her love. More than any of the lyric genres, the alba violates the status quo because it hinges upon the opposition between the personal and the public. The conflict between law and personal desire may be a prevalent underlying theme of courtly literature in general, but the alba is the one lyric genre in which this conflict quietly grows great.[4]

The alba lady must choose between a rapturous, gratifying, and self-centered realm of mutual love, freely offered and nurtured, and a mundane, mercenary, loveless (and therefore base) marital bond. Although confined by existing social constrictions, the lovers rebel against them. For the lovers of Gace Brulé's "Cant voi l'aube dou jor venir," society is an enemy:

> "I cannot see you by day
> For I greatly fear it would be seen,
> And, indeed, in truth I say
> That the envious ones guard against it.
> Now I hate nothing as much as day,
> Love, which sends you far away."

> "Je ne vos puis de jor veoir,
> Car trop redout l'apercevoir,
> Et se vos di trestout por voir
> K'en agait sont li enuious.
> Or ne hais riens [tant com le jour,
> Amins, ke me depairt de vos]."

(ll. 7–12)

The community strives to enforce obedience to its laws; maintaining social order demands from citizens not only self-control but the subordination of personal desire to public good. Because the basis of marriage is a legal contract, the relationship became subject to laws of property and vested rights. But once it became supervised by the Church, moral laws were imposed upon it as well. Romantic liaisons outside of marriage are subversive—they violate the all-embracing code.

The lady of Cadenet's alba "S'anc fui belha ni prezada" gives us the closest glimpse of any alba lady's unhappy marital situation. She speaks of having been given to a boorish husband "solely because of his great wealth" ("a un vilan sui donada/ tot per sa gran manentia" [ll. 3–4]). She presents herself as a pawn in someone else's game. (The use of the passive construction in the first strophe of her song bears this out, as discussed in chapter 1.) Cadenet's lady concludes that love outside the strictures of marriage compensates for the loneliness of her married life: "and I would die/ had I not a noble lover by/ to whom to tell my sorrows" ("e murria/ s'ieu fin amic non avia/ cuy disses mo marrimen" [ll. 5–7]). Because this lady's eloquent outcry is created by a male poet, we cannot simply assume that she speaks for actual medieval women or that her reaction to her unhappiness reiterates real behavior. Nonetheless, her plight may reflect a real one (even if unspoken or unacted upon) for many medieval women. The female narrator of a canso by the Contessa de Dia, the earliest and most prominent of the trobairitz (female troubadours), sang to her beloved:[5]

> If only I could lie with you an hour
> and kiss you lovingly—
> know this, I'd give almost anything
> To have you in my husband's place.
>
> e que jagues ab vos un ser
> e qu'ie·us des un bais amoros;
> sapchatz, gran talan n'auria
> qu'ie·us tengues en luoc del marit.
>   (ll. 19–22, "Estat ai en greu cossirier";
>   Bogin 1976, 88–89)

Despite her complaints and those of many a mal mariée, a medieval wife's body legally belonged to her spouse: "It is true that woman was not legally 'a free and lawful person,' that she had no lot or share then, or indeed until the twentieth century, in what may be called public as distinct from private rights and duties" (Power 1975, 388–89). St. Paul's oft-quoted admonition to wives served as a convenient medieval justification for female subordination: "Wives, submit yourselves unto your own husbands, as unto the Lord. For the husband is the head of the wife, even as Christ is the head of the church: and he is the saviour of the body" (Ephesians 5:22–23). The alba lovers' resistance to monogamous marriage and the society that enforces it puts them in opposition with such institutional views.

The alba offers an implicit commentary upon the conflicting claims of romance and community. Alba lovers acknowledge that society is aligned with the husband and assiduously guard their guilty secret. The lover of "Gaita be" bids his lady adieu for fear of being caught:

Lady, adieu!   no longer may I stay;
despite my dearest wish   I must race away.
   So forlorn am I   that the coming day,
   forces me to rise   and send me up and on my way;
       to betray
     us wishes the dawn
   the dawn, yes the dawn!

Domn', adeu!   que non puis mais estar;
malgrat meu   m'en coven ad anar.
   Mais tan greu   m'es de l'alba,
   que tan leu   la vei levar;
       enganar
     nos vol l'alba,
   l'alba, oi l'alba! (21–27)

The narrator of an early anonymous tageliet, "Ich sich den morgensterne brehen!" declares: "When one loves in secret how well it is that love should have a care!" ("swer tovgenlichen minnet, wie tugentlich daz stat,/ da friuntschaft hûte hat!").[6] Spies, gossips, and slanderers litter the alba landscape, poised to report any wifeiy indiscretions to the husband. The lovers' resentment of the husband and those associated with him—the members of the larger, uninitiated, and therefore hostile world—is nurtured by the unsympathetic stance the lovers attribute to representatives of the socius. Exposure of the illicit love affair would bring alba lovers disgrace at the very least; at the worst, it might bring death.

During the twelfth century, there was a spectrum of attitudes, laws, and punishments for adultery. Although the Church demanded monogamy of a married couple and in most countries adultery carried the same penalties for men and women, monogamy was differently defined for man and woman (Shahar 1983, 19; see also Bullough et al. 1988, 18): "A man's extramarital relations were not everywhere invariably considered adulterous, whereas such behaviour in a woman was invariably considered adulterous.... In some regions a married woman who had intercourse with another man, whether married or a bachelor, was considered an adulteress, while a married man was regarded as an adulterer only if he had relations with a married woman (a relationship with a spinster or widow was defined only as fornication)" (Shahar 1983, 107).

Church courts granted more separations on the grounds of the wife's adultery than the husband's. To Ivo of Chartres, adultery constituted "the second most serious offense after heresy" and was punishable by excommunication, prohibition of future marriage between adulterer and paramour, whipping, public humiliation, and exile. If an innocent husband failed to take action against his adulterous wife, he was considered to condone the offense and might himself be punished (Brundage 1987, 208–9). Ecclesiastical courts punished adultery with "penitence by fasting, prayer and temporary celibacy, or fines, and even a period in the stocks" (Shahar 1983, 106).

Secular courts often tried and punished adulterers, although there was no uniformity in the punishments imposed. Adulterous wives were known to have their noses cut off, be banished from their homes, kept under house arrest, placed in jail, or receive public lashings: "In the towns of southern France, an adulterous couple was forced to run through the streets naked and hitched together in humiliating fashion, and was lashed as they ran" (Shahar 1983, 108; see also 18–19). And private revenge for adultery was not always prohibited or controlled, especially among the nobility. Although there are records of aristocratic husbands' avenging themselves against both the adulterous lady and her lover, "there are no records of cases among the nobility where a wife took revenge on an adulterous husband" (Shahar 1983, 107). The Church condemned adultery for both sexes but in actuality was unable to impose the penalties on adulterous men (Gaunt 1990, 59).

The watchman of Wolfram's "Sîne klâwen" warns the loving lady to "save honor and life" by parting from her lover:

> "He must hence at once,
> without delay!

> Now give him leave, sweet lady.
> Let him love you
>   later so secretly,
>   that he will save honor and life."

"Er muoz et hinnen
    balde und ân sûmen sich.
        nu gip im urloup, süezez wîp.
lâze in minnen
    her nâch sô verholn dich,
        daz er bahalte êre unde den lîp."
                                    (ll. 21–26)

The lover of Walther's "Friuntlîchen lac" speaks to the issue of his beloved's honor: "Lady, it is time:/ bid me, let me depart./ Indeed it is for your honor that I desire to go" ("Frouwe, ez ist zît:/ gebiut mir, lâ mich varn./ jâ tuon ichz dur dîn êre, daz ich von hinnen ger" [ll. 41–43]). Both lovers may have to worry about preserving their lives, but the idea of honor—reputation in the outside world—seems a concern only for the woman.

The martial imagery of certain albas makes the lovers' conflict with the world more concrete. In "Gaite de la tor," the lover speaks of the dangerous "dawn that combats me" as though dawn were in league with the rest of the world against lovers ("Trop m'a neü/ L'aube qui me guerroie" [ll. 64–65]). In "Gaita be," the lover accuses dawn of intending to steal his joy:

> a new joy
> dawn steals from me,
> the dawn, yes the dawn!
>
> joc novel
> mi tol l'alba,
> l'alba, oi l'alba! (5–7)

and of wishing to deceive him:

> to cheat
> us wishes the dawn
> the dawn, yes the dawn!

> enganar
> nos vol l'alba,
> l'alba, oi l'alba!(26–28)

Ironically, however, both the theft and deception are, from the legal point of view, acts committed by the lover. These lines brilliantly portray his perspective—the psychological and emotional torment of being deprived of one's love—but they subliminally reveal the opposing worldly perspective in which the lover is the transgressor. The lover of the poem also expresses fear of the gilos and dawn:

> Watch for us   dear watchman of the tower
> for the gilos,   your evil lord,
>   more envious   even than the dawn
>   for yonder   we speak of love.
>   But we know
>   to fear the dawn
>   the dawn, yes the dawn!

> Gaitaz vos,   gaiteta de la tor,
> del gelos,   vostre malvays seynor,
>   enuios   plus que l'alba
>   que za jos   parlam d'amor.
>   Mas paor
>   nos fai l'alba,
>   l'alba, oi l'alba! (15–21)

The threat of the *lausengiers,* those liars and slanderers who infiltrate the courtly corpus creating mischief for courtly lovers and their poets, pervades the alba. (In other genres, the lausengiers are viewed by the lyric narrator as envious rivals, flatterers of the lady; often they are stand-ins for rival poets.) In the Old French dawn-song "Cant voi l'aube dou jor venir" the lady reveals her awareness of the "envious ones" ("li enuious" [l. 10]) who are on the watch. Despite such "slanderers" ("medixans" [l. 27]) and "wicked jealous husbands" ("mavais maris jalous" [l. 28]), she urges all true lovers to "sing this song" celebrating adulterous love: "Or pri a tous les vrais amans/Ceste chanson voixent chantant" (ll. 25–26). In the anonymous "Est il jors?" the lady suggests they forget the "mesdixans" (ill-speakers), those despised love spies: "Let us forget the slanderers,/

And lie here a little longer" ("Faixons mesdixans crever,/ E gixons un poc ancores" [ll. 7–8]). The watchman of "Eras diray ço que·us dey dir" warns that the lover "against the misdeed must guard himself henceforth" ("que del fortfayt/ se guard d'uymay" [ll. 13–14]) and exhorts: "Away and rise, Knight/ Warrior, lest the lausengiers/ attack you at dawn!" ("Via sus, cavalhiers/ guerrers, que lausangiers/ no·us assauton en l'alba!" [ll. 17–19]). Although the most fearsome and despised adversary is the gilos, all these threats of violence add tension and excitement to the atmosphere.

Alba lovers—and the poets who fashion them—create a new morality based on freely chosen, mutually fulfilling love that coincides with the typical definition of fin'amors set forth by Marie de Champagne (the twelfth-century proponent of courtly love) and her courts of love, a love that presides over the canso as well as the alba: "We declare and we hold as firmly established that love cannot exert its powers between two people who are married to each other. For lovers give each other everything freely, under no compulsion of necessity, but married people are in duty bound to give in to each other's desires and deny themselves to each other in nothing" (quoted in Capellanus, 106–7). The courts of Eleanor of Aquitaine (granddaughter and heir of Duke William IX of Aquitaine, the first troubadour) in France, of her second husband, Henry II of England, and of her daughters, Marie, Countess of Champagne, and Alix, Countess of Blois, are credited with initiating and promoting the cultural transformation in which fin'amors was born. Fin'amors is "a refined erotic love between man and woman that was considered something good in itself, referred to as 'true love,' 'pure love' or 'fine love' by poets" (Moore 1972, 90)—what Gaston Paris referred to as "courtly love" ("amour courtois"). Troubadour fin'amors is less a well-defined set of ideas than a spectrum of sympathetic attitudes toward romantic love.

Choosing an illicit relationship based on mutual love is seen by the lovers and their sympathizers as morally superior to passively submitting to an obligatory monogamous marital arrangement, especially in light of the spouse's duty to be sexually available to the other partner regardless of inclination: "While Augustine and his contemporaries cautioned against intercourse for pleasure, they also reminded their married hearers that they were obliged to give their spouses sex upon demand. The marital debt was a right that either party could claim. The partner from whom it was demanded must accede to the spouse's request, and doing so was no sin. . . . Equality of the sexes in marriage meant equality in the marriage bed, but not outside of it" (Brundage 1987, 93). Given the inferior status of women and the legitimated abuses against them, can there be any doubt that, in practice, the woman was most often the partner on the receiving end of unsought demands (Chaucer's fictive Wife of Bath notwithstanding)? Despite the proviso (cited previously) that a number of family members could beat the lady of the house, medieval art, literature, and history portray the violence between husband and wife with greater frequency than any other violence between male and female. In iconographic and literary representations, women are depicted scolding and beating their husbands; a common image was Phyllis astride Aristotle beating him with a switch. But there are no historical records to indicate that men were actually at physical risk in their marriages or that these conventions were something other than aspects of the era's pervasive antifeminism. After all, it was the husband who was explicitly permitted to beat his wife: "Many women feared their husbands, and some were even beaten by them. Law and custom permitted a man, whatever his class, to bring his superior physical strength to bear against the woman who was supposed to be his helpmate" (Shahar 1983, 138).[7]

If sex within marriage—the purpose of which was procreation, not pleasure—was a documented duty and not a choice, it was debased, according to Marie de Champagne and her coterie. By definition, the institution of marriage precludes an ideal, ennobling love—that is, love that is freely willed, freely given, and freely received—because the obligatory bond it forges between spouses intrinsically prevents the free bestowal of love.

Insofar as marriage is an institution of property and possession, it prohibits love and thus sanctions a form of prostitution: "The love viewed in courtly imagination as the source of all beauty in life and manners because freely given by the lady became after marriage not a free gift (which only a superior can award) but a duty of obedience from one who has sunk from lady into mere woman" (Kelly-Gadol 1987, 32). This devaluation of a lady once she married is reflected in the opening lines of Cadenet's alba, where the lady laments:

> "If ever I was fair or prized
> I am turned from high to low,
> for to a boor I am bestowed
> all for the sake of his great wealth"

> "S'anc fui belha ni prezada,
> ar sui d'aut en bas tornada,
> qu'a un vilan sui donada
> tot per sa gran manentia" (ll. 1–4)

Indeed, historical evidence supports this lady's contention that marriage diminishes her worth: "We find that under English common law the unmarried woman or widow—the *femme sole*—was, as far as all private, as distinct from public, rights and duties are concerned, on a par with men. She could hold land, even by military tenure, and do homage for it; she could make a will or a contract, could sue or be sued. On the other hand, when she married, her rights, for the duration of the marriage, slipped out of her hands. The lands of which she was tenant-in-fee at the time of her marriage, or which she might acquire later, forthwith became her husband's for the duration of the marriage" (Power 1975, 38). Although the impossibility of romantic love in marriage is a prevalent theme in the literature of the late eleventh and twelfth centuries, it was by no means a sentiment universally accepted.

Like Cadenet's lady, all alba lovers follow their inner promptings, implicitly rebelling against the unjust and immoral but legally sanctioned marriage. In requiring the confinement of love to a relationship that is subject to legalities rather than feelings, the society reveals itself to be corrupt, authoritarian, cold, and cruel and sets up a double code of morality. Such a society may be said to outlaw love altogether: if love is not the basis of marriage, neither is love allowed to flourish in any other licit ways. That romantic love is not allowed open expression, that lovers' irrepressible passions are outlawed by society, compels the lovers to question the morality of social convention and law. Pursuit of personal fulfillment becomes a law unto itself. The lovers are convinced, without misgivings, of their own innocence and morality.

But romantic love, by favoring individual attachment over social obligations, is disruptive and antisocial. Society discourages passionate love: it threatens the stability and disrupts the integrity of the tightly knit and well-organized community. Anarchic eros thwarts the best-laid parental marriage plans. While Chrétien de Troyes may have endeavored in romances such as *Erec* to work out a solution to the painful dilemma caused by the irreconcilability between romantic love and public life, even he, many critics suspect, ultimately gave up. Gottfried von Strassburg tackles the issue in his *Tristan* by openly admitting the incompatibility between eros and society. Love, he declares, only flourishes in the wild, away from the public sphere: "Love and her concerns are not assigned to the streets nor yet to the open country. She is hidden away in the wilds" (Hatto 1965, 265).

If, to the Christian ascetic, sexual love lured one to hell, to the secular lord, fin'amors was threatening because it not only deflated the importance of marriage (through which his wealth and power were transferred) but also placed doubt on the legitimacy of his heirs. Although a nobleman could easily find women outside of marriage to satisfy sexual desires, the wife who did so might secretly substitute another man's offspring for her husband's.

The fact that such romantic love "had nothing whatsoever to do with propagation" clearly manifests its opposition to Christian marriage (Shahar 1983, 81). Its single-minded passion fosters an implicit rejection of established authority. This courtly ideology manifests new political, philosophical, and sociological tendencies. The literary revision of gender relations—in which a couple sequesters itself from the socius—opposes both the feudal and ecclesiastical orders (Bloch 1983, 70–82; 1977, 258).

Describing the marriage of the Englishwoman Margaret de Rivers, chronicler Matthew Paris easily answers the rhetorical questions he poses:

> The law married them, love and the marriage bed,
> But what kind of law? What kind of love?
> What kind of marriage?
> A law that was no law, a love that was hate
> A marriage that was separation.
> 						(Shahar 1983, 138)

So great is the rift between society and the lovers that the latter can exist only in contradistinction to and defiance of society's sanctions. The conflict between lovers and society may be inevitable even when love is not adulterous, as Freud was to note: "On the one hand love comes into opposition to the interests of civilization; on the other, civilization threatens love with substantial restrictions.... We derive the antithesis between civilization and sexuality from the circumstance that sexual love is a relationship between two individuals in which a third can only be superfluous or disturbing, whereas civilization depends on relationships between a considerable number of individuals. When a love-relationship is at its height there is no room left for any interest in the environment; a pair of lovers are sufficient to themselves" (1961, 50, 55). How much more intense must be the exclusivity of an adulterous passion that is outlawed from the start and pursued despite inherent dangers? Setting their union against society, alba lovers form their own "society of two."

Although the adulterous nature of love in the canso often impedes the physical consummation of love (thus guaranteeing the canso love's ideal and chaste quality, according to some critics), the contrary is true for the alba, which celebrates consummation despite all impediments. The love exemplified in the alba condemns marriage without deprecating sex or vilifying women. The critics who claim that courtly love itself is chaste have overlooked the emphatically sexual love of the courtly alba. Adultery, in opposing Christian morality and law, isolates the alban love affair from all other systems: "it is made to constitute a value system in itself" (Saville 1972, 40). Love, no longer frustrated as in the canso, flourishes for a time.

The lovers' separation from their community is evident in the isolated settings of their trysts as well as the expressed need for secrecy and concealment. In most albas, the poet emphasizes how alone together the lovers are. In "En un vergier sotz fuella d'albespi," lady and lover seclude themselves "in a park beneath the leaves of a hawthorn"; two other private settings, meadow and garden, are mentioned in the song. The lovers have left behind the courtly realm, the public world. The isolated sense of self evinced in alba settings concomitantly entails alienation from others. The sounds of nature may surround the lovers; occasional infiltrations of the watchman's voice are the only human sounds. For those lovers who secrete themselves in the lady's chamber, silence becomes the law of love. In this setting, too, the lovers attempt to isolate themselves by barring entrance to their realm. Their separation from the court is always volitional, but it implies alienation and demonstrates that the affair has become a world unto itself.

The lovers may be alienated from their society and may violate its legal injunctions, but they do not believe that they are morally or spiritually culpable. Their frequently sounded invocations to God—addresses all the more significant because they occur only rarely in other troubadour genres—illustrate the lovers' piety and sense of righteousness. Although they can hope to hide their illicit affair from human eyes, the lovers cannot conceal it from God's, and their prayers reveal that they have no wish to. While Saville justly observes that "it is taken for granted that there is nothing outrageous in asking for God's help in adultery or in associating God's beneficent government of the universe with the successful achievement or repetition of a night of sexual love," his explanatory paraphrase of the lovers' prayers to God misses the point: "what the poets are saying is 'May God help me to enjoy the illicit pleasures of the wicked, fallen, sinful, flesh-dominated world, and may He shower his blessing on me and my acts.'—in short, 'May God help me to go to the Devil!'" (1972, 98). The lovers' prayers are more innocent and sincere than Saville believes, even if we ultimately interpret their moralistic attitude as a rationalization for enjoying illicit pleasures. The lovers believe they have right, and therefore God, on their side.

The watchman calls on God at the opening of "Reis glorios, verais lums e clardatz" "to be a faithful aid" to his companion, as does the watchman of "Dieus, aidatz" ("God, help us") who repeats the plea of his opening words in the song's refrain. The "Reis glorios" watchman also calls on "the son of Holy Mary" ("lo filh Santa Maria") toward the end of his song as his anxiety over his companion's fate grows greater, pleading for his friend's safe return. The lover of "Ab la gensor que sia" asks God (referred to, as in "Reis glorios," as "lo filhs Sancta Maria"), to curse the watchman, as does the lady of "L'abe c'apiert au jor," who implores God to give anyone who parts them "ill recompense." The lady of "En un vergier sotz fuella d'albespi" calls out to God in her refrain—"Oh God, oh God, the dawn! How quickly it comes!" ("Oy Dieus, oy Dieus, de l'alba!/ Tan tost ve!")—but also addresses a strophe-length prayer to Him, begging for the prolongation of night and protection from discovery. Like this lady, the lover of "Gaite de la tor" prays to God to "turn day into night." The lady of "L'abe c'apiert au jor" invokes St. James similarly for protection and prolongation of night. In "Cant voi l'aube dou jor venir," God is again invoked as a protector—"God have you in his keeping"—and for remembrance: "I beg you in God's name, do not forget me" ("A Deu soit vos cors comandeis./ Por Deu vos pri, ne m'oblieis!" [ll. 20–21]). The knight of "Us cavaliers si jazia" asks his lady to remember him "for God's sake" ("Per Dieu, no m'oblidetz mia" [l. 33]). The lady of "Ez ist nu tac" begs God's help in returning the lover to her arms ("der hôhste vride müeze in noch an mînen arn geleiten" [l. 12]); the lady of "Friuntlîchen lac" begs God to protect her lover once he departs ("von dem ich habe die sêle, der müeze dich bewarn" [l. 48]). The watchman of "Eras diray ço que·us dey dir," who sings of the oath he made "in the name of my God" to sound a dawn-warning to the lovers, resembles the watchman of "Reis glorios, verais lums e clardatz" who reminds his companion that he stands guard solely because he was begged to do so.

These oaths and invocations demonstrate a faith not only in divine power, but in divine sympathy for lovers. Lazar observes: "Considérée du point de vue de l'Eglise, la fin'amors est une conception immorale, anti-religieuse, perverse et dégradante. Malgré les affirmations de Jeanroy, Scheludko, Wechssler, Casella et de nombreux autres médiévistes, la lyrique provençal ne doit rien à une quelconque influence chrétienne. . . . Chaque foi que les troubadours mentionnent le nom de Dieu, des Saints et de la Vierge, c'est à obtenir de celle-ci la joie d'amour et la récompense promise. Dieu est avec les amants. Il n'est pas avec les maris bernés. Il fait triompher le droit de la fin'amors contre la loi et l'ethique religieuse" (1964, 11) [Considered from the Church's point of view, fin'amors is an immoral concept, anti-religious, perverse and decadent. Despite the affirmations of Jeanroy, Scheludko, Wechssler, Casella and a number of other medievalists, the Provençal lyric owes nothing whatsoever to Christian influence. . . . Each time that the troubadours mention the name of God, the Saints and the Virgin, it is to obtain from them the joy of love and the promised reward. God is with the lovers. He is not with the mocked husbands. He makes the rule of fin'amors triumph over law and the ethics of religion]. Believing that God is on their side, the lovers feel only righteous indignation at attempts by the gilos and others to impede them. But believing that God sympathizes makes the lovers more anti-establishment than anti-Christian. Their forgiving and loving divinity has an encompassing vision that transcends mundane law and understands that the lovers do what is morally right in a corrupt society.

This movement toward an individual and private relationship with God can also be detected in the medieval cult of the Virgin. Mary, rather than a priest or the Pope, becomes the intercessor between human and Christ. And the alba watchman, a dramatic character whose model may have been the actual watchman on the walls, is transformed into a character whose importance grows with the enlargement of his mediatory role. This shift toward gentler, more sympathetic, and unconventional intervention parallels the movement in secular life toward a romantic relationship whose intercessor is a sympathizer, friend, friendly watchman, handmaiden, saint, Mary, or God rather than a civic or religious authority (as for a marriage).

God is on the lovers' side, perhaps because Christianity fostered a similar passion and exaltation. Love, whether sacred or romantic, is suffered as a destiny and submitted to. Once "converted" by passion, lovers are directed and dominated by it; they martyr themselves for it. Courtly lovers, like mystics, seek the ecstasy that devotion to their love brings. Fin'amors departs from Christian teaching because, rather than being purged of sexuality, its impetus and goal is sexual union (whether or not that union is achieved).

Once the Church took to regulating sexual activity, it was tolerated as a mundane and practical necessity in marriage, serving the purpose of procreation. Even adultery, as long as it had nothing to do with romantic passion, was less of a threat to the status quo. The early Church, however, disparaged marriage, regarding it as a state that existed solely for natural necessity and therefore as inferior to celibacy, the ideal religious state that transcended such "necessity." Early Christian doctrine held that virginity was the highest form of human virtue. Sexuality polluted, and women were the carriers of the disease. The ferocity with which St. Paul denounced sexuality had no parallel among either the Hebrews or the Greeks, but his attitude set the tone for future Christian intellectual and practical traditions. For Tertullian, who asserted that sexual abstinence was the most effective way to achieve clarity of soul, woman was the Devil's gateway (*Tertulliani Opera,* "De exhortatione castitatis," X). St. Jerome, following Paul and Tertullian, inverted Paul's concession that "it is better to marry than to burn" (I Corinthians 7:9) by praising a pre-Virgilian version of Dido who, after building a funeral pyre in memory of her deceased husband, threw herself on it, preferring to burn rather than (re)marry (*Against Jovinianus*).

The Christian obsession with virginity, especially for women, was so great in the Middle Ages that a female virgin who was raped, even if she was a nun, was condemned to forfeit salvation. St. Jerome warns that "although God can do all things, He cannot raise up a virgin after she has fallen. He has power, indeed, to free her from the penalty, but He has no power to crown one who has been corrupted" ("Letter to Eustochium," I:135, quoted in Schulenburg 1986, 11).[8] Physical intactness, *integritas,* was an aspect of female perfection (a woman's wholeness) as well as a sign that a woman had succeeded in transcending her sexual nature. Hence, a consecrated virgin "was no longer a woman; she had become a 'sacred vessel dedicated to the Lord'" (Eusebius; quoted in Brown 1988, 260). Such women received the highest patristic compliment: they became "male" or "virile."[9] Lack of virginity, no matter how it occurred, polluted the whole woman. To the end of preserving female virginity, even suicide was justified.[10]

Although marriage was accepted as a divine institution created for the regeneration of the species, its acceptance was a reluctant concession to the uncontrollable desires of fallen humanity, a refuge for souls too weak to bear the higher discipline of celibacy: "The Church fathers never hesitated to remind their readers that marriage at best was a painful affair, with the trials of pregnancy, the pains of childbirth, the anxieties of parenthood, and the distractions brought about by wives, children, and family life" (Bullough et al. 1988, 97). Like Jerome, St. Augustine believed that nonprocreative sex was immoral even in marriage; but for Augustine, "procreative sex counteracted and redeemed the intrinsic wickedness of marital sex; marital sex moderated venereal desire by diverting it to the task of procreation" (Brundage 1987, 90; see also Bullough et al. 1988, 99). Although St. Augustine's attitude toward marriage was, relatively speaking, more moderate, he, like his Church brethren, upheld a double standard for the sexes in which the male was entitled to sexual freedom that was denied to the female.

Despite its initial dim view of marriage, the Church gradually undertook to regulate it. From a mere concession to human frailty, marriage was transformed by the eighth-century Church into a sacrament. Over time, the Church instituted relevant norms, laws, and customs. By the year 1000, the Church established a systematic theology and canon law of marriage and claimed the right to adjudicate marriage cases within its courts rather than civil courts. In the eleventh and twelfth centuries, theologians succeeded in substituting canon law for existing secular marriage laws (Herlihy 1985, 78–80). Gratian's *Concordia Discordantium Canonum* (otherwise known as the *Decretum*), completed before 1140, was a fully developed, legal code that provided a written Church doctrine on marriage. Before that time, "marriage was essentially a lay matter. Wedding ceremonies were domestic occasions: a priest might bless the union, but the central ritual was an agreement between two families and the handing over of a woman by one man (or group of men) to another man (or group of men)" (Gaunt 1990, 56). Consequently, the civil marriage bond, formerly outside Church supervision, became a sacrament and by the twelfth century was completely subordinated to Church control. The new rules, among other things, governed sexuality with the apparent aim of separating marriage as far as possible from sex. Married couples were allowed to have sex as long as permissible times and places were limited and couples obeyed strict rules about how they conducted themselves—in sum, as long as they refrained from enjoying it (Gaunt 1990, 58; see also Brundage 1987, 93). Monogamy within marriage was, of course, a cardinal rule.

As long as sexual activity did not involve a competing love that would draw parishoners' allegiance from the Church, it could be accepted as inevitable and forgivable. So while sex was grudgingly excused as necessary for procreation, passionate love between the sexes was a greater threat, distracting the soul from the proper object of its desire: "To love a woman for her own sake was to be faithless to the Father" (Valency 1961, 19).

Fin'amors, portrayed in courtly literature as a devout calling, applied devotion that was rightly God's to another human. Love, experienced as a sacred vocation, was in accord with Christian feeling even while it violated Christian doctrine. In seeking ecstasy in another human rather than in God, the courtly lover defied religious dogma. If "men and women could justifiably love each other with passion," they would discover a supreme joy not to be found elsewhere in life, a fulfillment that could fully satisfy and even sanctify (Singer 1984, 32). Christian love is hard put to rival that. Chrétien's Lancelot, like a mystic, seeks complete fulfillment in union with his beloved. Mere sexuality is spurned in favor of fidelity to his higher love. Chrétien, whether or not he is parodying courtly love or mocking its disciple in this romance, portrays Lancelot as love's mystic. The knight literally loses himself in mystical contemplation of Guenevere: "He becomes oblivious of himself, unaware of whether or not he exists, not remembering his name, not knowing if he is armed or not or where he is going or where he comes from; he remembers no single being save one, and on her account he has put the others from his mind. He is so intent on her alone that he neither sees nor hears anything" (Chrétien de Troyes 1987, 194). He venerates the golden hairs left behind in Guenevere's comb, thus demonstrating how love for Guenevere replaces his faith in St. Martin and St. James: "Never will the eye of man see anything receive such reverence; for he begins to adore them, putting them fully a hundred thousand times to his eyes and mouth, to his brow and his face, with every show of joy. They are his great treasure and delight. He places them against his breast, between his shirt and flesh, next to his heart. He would not exchange them for a cartload of emeralds or carbuncles. Now he is confident that he will never suffer from boils or any other illness. He scorns potions of crushed pearl, pleurisy cures or theriac, or even the protection of Saint Martin and Saint James, having no need of their help, such is the faith he places in those hairs" (204–5). And he genuflects when he leaves her at dawn. His love, sacramental as well as sexual, makes the Christian saints irrelevant. Despite its adulterous nature, Lancelot's reverence and passion for Guenevere ennoble and purify him even though they may make him laughable to Love's atheists. So, too, are religious mystics mocked. Love makes him utterly faithful, enabling not only his easy rejection of the invitations from seductive damsels during his quest but his discarding of any "higher" good. Ultimately love makes Lancelot the chosen hero, empowering him to accomplish deeds unachievable by any other knight.

It was its exaltation and sacramentalization of love (rather than its adultery) that made fin'amors a threat to the Church; the sanctifying passion of love violated Church doctrine. Passion should be reserved for God; passion for one's spouse was considered inappropriate, even sinful; passion for anyone else was even more depraved. People were free to worship God, not one another. A man too passionately in love with his wife is uxorious or, worse, an adulterer. According to St. Jerome, "nothing is filthier than to have sex with your wife as you might do with another woman" (*Against Jovinianus* I:49). Such sentiments spill over into romances such as Chrétien's *Erec* where the newly married and enamored hero causes a scandal by extending his honeymoon so long that he is considered recreant, neglectful of his public duties.

In literature, courtly lovers, like religious mystics, sought ecstasy; heroic discipline, ascetic fortitude, and single-mindedness were self-imposed. Such lovers could not be reined in by conventional means: love and its demands removed them from the mundane, the expected, the routine. It set them apart as an elite, superior to societal conventions (Kelly-Gadol 1987, 143).

In their invocations and prayers to God, alba lovers are as sincere as any medieval sinner. But their love is all the more radical, subversive, and threatening because it never issues into a love of divinity. On the contrary, "fin'amors serves as an *imitation* of religious or philosophic love, which it uses as a theoretical model to be duplicated among human beings" (Singer 1984, 47–48; emphasis in original). Rather than subordinating human love to the love of God, fin'amors encourages self-sufficiency. Consequently, the troubadours themselves were seen by the religious establishment as idolatrous and heretical because the kind of love of which they sang substituted salvation by another human for the salvation that only God could provide.

Fin'amors elevates sexuality to an ethical and aesthetic attainment, "a splendid ideal worth striving for, a holy oneness between man and woman that has no relation to the institution of marriage" (Singer 1984, 22–23). By keeping love detached from marriage, fin'amors allowed women to express sexual desire: "We dare not oppose the opinion of the Countess [Marie] of Champagne who ruled that love can exert no power between husband and wife," wrote Andreas Capellanus (1990, 175). This kind of antimatrimonial stance gave women the same freedom that men—married or single—had to pursue sexual attachments: "In opting for a free and reciprocal heterosexual relation outside marriage, the poets and theorists of courtly love ignored the almost universal demand of patriarchal society for female chastity, in the sense of the woman's strict bondage to the marital bed. . . . Marriage, as a relation arranged by others, carried the taint of social necessity for the aristocracy" (Kelly-Gadol 1987, 142). A number of historians and critics have reasoned that evolving ideas of romantic love were a reaction to changes in the institution of marriage in the Middle Ages. Brundage conjectures that idealized romantic love was born at the same time that rigid rules of marriage advocated by Church reformers began to be accepted: "Early twelfth-century poetry enunciated attitudes about sexual behavior and personal feelings that were foreign to beliefs current, say, a century and a half earlier. The poetic typology of romance took shape in opposition to and as an escape from, a bleak marriage ideology that canonists and theologians championed" (1987, 184). Singer likewise sees the sexual courtesy and individual choice of romantic love as a counter to the largely impersonal economic and political considerations that controlled most people's lives: "Courtly love . . . revealed the importance of choice and personal preference in the creation of authentic love between men and women" (1984, 29–30). Duby also argues that the emergence of romantic love bears a cause-effect relationship to the radical upheaval in society's view of marriage.

While scholars may argue over the benefits for real women of such an ethical and aesthetic system, fin'amors may be viewed as an innovation that clearly ennobled men: "The troubadours celebrate the lover rather than the lady" (Gaunt 1990, 68). While there is no doubt that fin'amors elevated the lover and idealized love, its benefits for the female beloved (and for women more generally) have been much more difficult to gauge. If Singer sees fin'amors as favoring the personal over the communal, Benton sees it as a blatant denial of the individuality and worth of women: "Courtesy was created by men for their own satisfaction, and it emphasized woman's role as an object, sexual or otherwise. Since they did not encourage a genuine respect for women as individuals, the conventions of medieval chivalry, like the conventions of chivalry in the southern United States, did not advance woman toward legal or social emancipation. When men ignored chivalry, women were better off" (1973, 35). Gravdal views courtly love as a literary discourse promoted by a male-dominated martial society whose concern was not women or love but furthering patriarchal aristocratic power (1985, 363). For Blumstein, the courtly code's "implicit patriarchal assumptions" make the idealized portrayal of the lady "a *covert* form of misogyny" (1977, 2). The troubadour, according to Cholakian, creates levels of interpretation that simultaneously convey "the established *fin'amors* code of masculine submission and an underlying disdain of the female who is 'idealized'" (1990, 181). Burgwinkle similarly views the courtly lady as a powerful literary device that provides a standard against which masculinity can be measured: "What has often been referred to as woman's finest hour in literature and as a lost Eden of female power is no more than a poetic device which allowed the poet to display his tricks and which only coincidentally referred to women. Woman as synecdoche for patron, court and land is no different from Woman as Liberty, or Woman as personification of any other virtue or vice" (1990, 75).

The promulgation of the lady as the symbol of courtly society's most important values is now viewed by some as a function of women's loss of power, "which liberates 'woman' as a sign of something else" (Bruckner 1992, 869). Some historians and literary critics argue that the two movements that seem to empower women and elevate their status—the cult of the Virgin and courtly love—were not only developed by the misogynist Church and the male-centered aristocracy respectively but coincide with an actual decrease in women's rights and political power (Erler and Kowaleski 1988, 12; Rose 1986, xvi–xv). The increasing subjugation of women at this time, marked by a loss of status and legal rights throughout later medieval society, has been well documented.[11]

The troubadours' "paradoxical portrait of the 'lady' who is admired and the 'woman' who is feared" (Burns 1984, 254) has left so indelible an impression on subsequent generations that a number of recent critics attribute present-day repression of women to the promotion of masculine desire in twelfth-century fin'amors: "the domna of troubadour lyric eventually leads to the 'lady on the pedestal' of nineteenth-century Victorian society and its inheritors today" (Bruckner 1992, 869). And a number of recent critics attack what they now see as the negative impact of a courtly code still in full force today: "A transformation has also taken place in the critical reception of the woman as love object in male-authored *canso*. . . .

Rightly seeing a historical continuity between twelfth-century promotion of masculine desire ('courtly love'), and the present-day repression of women, feminist writers have good reason to annex the troubadours to their current political aims, and in unmasking the sexism in the medieval lyric, to denounce it in contemporary society" (Kay 1990, 85).[12]

In the alba, the lady achieves a gratifying control over the emotional side of her life, but the larger circumstances in which she is placed seem otherwise beyond her command. Staking out a space of her own, she declares personal needs important enough to act on; her poet, in dramatizing if not inventing this attitude, considers this an important and interesting subject to explore. In the alba, there is no sense that the male lover is elevated at his lady's cost; that is, the alba male is hardly accorded greater respect or drawn with more individuality than its lady.

Alba lovers depict their union as just and deserving of their audience's sympathy. In fact, they present their love as an alternate model—a moral one—that favors the primacy and intensity of feeling over obedience to obsolete, immoral custom. This model replaces an unfair and inequitable condition, the marriage of convenience, with a relationship that appears more honest, volitional, and just.

Hence, despite its antisociability and the risks of pursuing the illicit affair, this kind of love is attractive, compelling, and not without its own justification and rewards. In the alba, two ethics—one based on private passion and personal fulfillment, the other on personal sacrifice and community identification—meet head on. The sexual autonomy that underpins alba love is a personal manifestation of a larger political autonomy that encourages the freedom to determine for oneself which public strictures to obey, and this in itself is a great threat to hegemony.

On the personal level, the alba poet exalts passion over security, conventionality, and conformity. He paints his lovers as brave, gallant, and clever in their determination to forsake what they (and presumably he) regard as the inferior life of mundane marriage, for his praise of the lovers manifests a sympathy for them. But as a consequence of their choice, alba lovers suffer severely. They renounce comfort and safety and live with the continual threat of discovery. Although they succeed in uniting without discovery or censure, their meeting is necessarily short-lived. The brevity of the encounter engenders their pain, but their anguish augments our sense of their dignity.

In acting on emotions that differentiate them from the rest of the community, the lovers achieve a heightened sense of self. As Freud noted, such a sense of self concomitantly entails alienation from others: "Two people coming together for the purpose of sexual satisfaction, in so far as they seek for solitude, are making a demonstration against the herd instinct, the group feeling. The more they are in love, the more completely they suffice for each other" (1960, 93). The lovers' energies are directed inward, toward each other, rather than outward, toward the society and the preservation of communal order. Secrecy and discretion become essential because they provide the only rapprochement possible between the lovers and their society. The lovers must safeguard their love from discovery. Private and public diverge but are kept separately, because secretly, intact. As long as there is no contact between public and private, no collision ensues, and each phase of the lovers' bisected lives can be distinctly maintained and managed.

The lovers' actions subvert law, for they allow—indeed, encourage—a division of allegiance. Law, although outwardly obeyed, is continually questioned. The clandestine, illicit union quietly undermines the status quo by denying the legal and moral authority of the social order. The lovers' rejection of law never evolves into open rebellion but causes the lovers to acquire a bifocal vision and estranges the passions of their hearts from the scruples of their minds. It necessitates dishonesty and dissembling. This lack of commitment to community promotes societal decay from within.

The alba lovers' separation from their community engenders new allegiances. Their keen awareness of their inner selves is augmented by societal antagonism to their desires and needs. A crucial part of their being is expected to remain hidden, unheeded, suppressed. The lovers suddenly see themselves as different, separate. They befriend the local watchman whenever possible, who becomes an accomplice. The lovers' affirmation of personal feeling over social rule impels a recognition and acceptance of their individuality. Not only do they question social hegemony, but in defiance of law they unite, experience perfect pleasure, and are not apprehended or punished for their transgression despite the risks they take.

That the alba couple, at odds with both lay and ecclesiastical establishments, is allowed to experience fulfillment and joy reveals that this particular courtly model celebrates a liberating kind of love. While freedom to love is explored quietly and solely on the personal level, the desire for more encompassing artistic, gender, and political freedoms is implicitly voiced in the alba couple's outcry against unfulfilling and obstructive communal and conventional values.

II
Eros and Identity

4

Eros and Dawning Identity

> O night! whose sable veil was wont to be
> More friend to lovers than the noisefull day:
> Wherefore, oh, wherefore dost thou fly from me,
> And carry with thee all my joys away?
> Anon., *"At Parting," in* Seventeenth Century Lyrics
> from the Original Texts

Nocturnal Wonders: (K)Night Calls

For alba lovers, night is love's refuge, its "derke wede" cloaking their activities. Criseyde's paean to night sums up the protective and nurturing role that alba lovers ascribe to night:

> O blake nyght, as folk in bokes rede,
> That shapen art by God this world to hide
> At certeyn tymes wyth thi derke wede,
> That vnder that men myghte in reste abide,
> Wel oughten bestes pleyne, and folk the chide,
> That there as day wyth labour wolde vs breste,
> That thow thus fleest, and deynest vs nought reste.
> (III, ll. 1429–35)

Dreading change, alba lovers cling to their fleeting present of happiness and fulfillment. The lady of "Est il jors?" emphasizes her present joy, concluding: "Oh God! how sweet it is now to talk of love!" (Hatto 1965, 375) ("Deus! keil parleir d'amours fait ores!" [l. 9]).

When night is ascendant, the lovers long for permanent merging. Fearful about the future, they desire time to stop so that their present may be perpetuated, and they plead for immunity to the changes that time metes out. Nocturnal darkness comes to symbolize a utopian stasis. As realm of the unseen, night veils and sustains lovers, providing a sanctum within its shadows.

Within the symbolic tradition that extends back to ancient Greece, night is a time of potentiality and germination, "related to the passive principle, the feminine and the unconscious. Hesiod gave it the name of 'mother of the gods,' for the Greeks believed that night and darkness preceded the creation of all things.... Hence, night—like water—is expressive of fertility, potentiality and germination . . . ; for it is an anticipatory state in that, though not yet day, it is the promise of daylight" (Circlot 1962, 218). Night also "engenders consciousness itself, the return to one's foetal intimacy" (Aziza et al. 1978, 142; trans. Cholakian 1990, 40n.49).

Alba lovers are most alive at this time when the rest of the world sleeps. The lady of "Entre moi et mon amin" recounts her joyful rendezvous, "Tuesday/ All night by the moon" ("mairdi/ Toute lai nuit a la lune" [ll. 3–4]). Moonlight plays a significant role in Heinrich von Morungen's beautiful "Owê, sol aber mir iemer mê." In gazing at his lady, the lover becomes so enchanted that, rapt in an almost hallucinatory vision, he loses all sense of time:

> "Alas,—
> shall never more for me
>   shine through the night
> whiter even than the snow,
>   her body so beautiful?
>   It tricked these eyes of mine:
>   I thought it must have been
>   the light of the moon shine.
>   Then it dawned."

> "Owê,—
> Sol aber mir iemer mê
>   geliuhten dur die naht
> noch wîzer danne ein snê
>   ir lîp vil wol geslaht?
>   Der trouc diu ougen mîn.
>   ich wânde, ez solde sîn
>   des liehten mânen schîn.
>   Dô tagte ez." (ll. 1–9)

Although the action occurs at night, this light-filled stanza, notes Dronke, "plays on the theme of reality and illusion in the three kinds of light—moonlight, daylight, and the radiance of the beloved's body" (1977, 181). The lady's luminous body—whiter than snow, as bright as moonlight—fooled the lover's dazzled eyes into believing that her body reflected the moonlight and therefore that night was still ascendant; in fact, her body had a radiance all its own. In comparing his lady to the gleaming snow and brilliant moonlight, the lover demonstrates her eclipsing of these natural beauties. That she outshines natural light lends her a haunting, supernatural beauty, the kind often associated with the moon. At night, the moon and snow are stunningly bright, their sheen in keen contrast with the dark sky. In her lover's eyes, the lady outmarvels the enchanting moon. She surpasses natural splendor, instilling the scene with a sense of wonder that is jarringly shattered by dawn's light. Both snow and moon are diminished by the sun, one melting in its heat, the other paling in its light. So, too, is love's spell broken by daylight. Beginning on a note of loss and ending at the break of dawn, the lyric encircles and encapsulates the lovers' heartbreak.

But one of night's effects upon lovers, as Heinrich's speaker makes plain, is to abrogate their sense of time. As any watchman knows—for this is his raison d'étre—night's darkness obscures the perception of time's passage. In the dark, lovers seek temporary obliviousness to night's passing. They often dream up fantastical resolutions to express the impossible wish (in rhetorical figures known as *adynata*) for the prolongation or perpetuation of night. The lady of "Entre moi et mon amin" tells us "how glad we should have been/ had that night lasted one hundred" ("adonc vocexiens nous lai/ ke celle nut durest sant" [ll. 18–19]). Voicing much the same sentiment, the lady of "L'abe c'apiert au jor" prays for the extension of one night into thirty:

> May it now please St. James
> That no one might see or blame us
> > And that the night last for thirty,
> > So that each has his desire!
>
> Pleüst ore a saint Jaike
> Ke nuns ne nos puist veoir ne reprandre
> > Et la nuit durast trante,
> > S'avroit chascuns son desir! (ll. 6–9)

Such a wish recalls the Greek myth in which Jove extends to twice its length the fabled night he spends with Alcmene, during which Hercules is conceived. The Jove/Alcmene episode is mentioned in a Greek dawn-poem by Meleager (c. 140–70 B.C.):

> Loveless dawn, why do you rise so swiftly over my bedroom,
> where till this moment I felt the warmth of dear Demo's skin?
> If only you'd reverse your swift course and be Hesperos,
> you who shed the sweet light that is so bitter to me!
> Indeed once before you went backwards: for Jove and Alcmena—
> it's not as if you didn't know how to turn roundabout!
>
> (Dronke 1977, 169)

Chaucer's Criseyde is the only medieval alba character to allude explicitly to this myth: "O nyght, allas, why nyltow ouere vs houe,/ As longe as whan Almena lay by Ioue?" (III, 1427–28). Criseyde alludes, however, not to Meleager's dawn-poem but to the passage in Ovid's *Amores* I:13 in which the narrator castigates Aurora for her too-swift ascent: "The very father of the gods, that he should not see you so often/ United two nights for his pleasure" ("ipse deum genitor, ne te tam saepe videret,/ commisit noctes in sua vota duas" [ll. 45–46]).

Grandsen calls attention to Ovid's "deflationary treatment of myth"; in his view, Ovid presents Jove as having "altered the cosmos for [his] own sexual gratification" rather than for something important (1979, 160). But how deflated is Jove's power to control the cosmos when it is juxtaposed with the lamenting lover's inability to do likewise only for pleasure's sake? The contrast serves, it seems to me, to highlight the limitations imposed on strictly human love; the speaker's acceptance of his powerlessness is succinctly conveyed through his allusion to its opposite—Jove's cosmic might. It is not Jove's power but the lover's that Ovid deflates. Chaucer's Criseyde mourns her similar impotence. No matter how reluctant they are to accept the futility of the wish for perpetual night, alba lovers, like Ovid's, must eventually accept day's advent.

The lady of "En un vergier sotz fuella d'albespi" prays God to ensure that the night "not fail"; that is, that its obscuring darkness never fade:

> May it please God that the night not fail
> nor my lover part far from me,
> nor the watchman see neither day nor dawn!
> Oh God, oh God, the dawn! How quickly it comes!

Plagues a Dieu ja la nueitz no falhis,
ni·l mieus amicx lonc de mi no·s partis,
ni la gayta jorn ni alba no vis!
Oy Dieus, oy Dieus, de l'alba! Tan tost ve! (ll. 5–8)

Because the verb "falhir" can also mean "to be false to" and "to be at fault," the lady's prayer is double-edged, suggesting night's capacity for betraying illicit lovers, i.e., "May it please God that the night not betray us." Adding the watchman to her prayer, the lady transforms him into either an all too fallible human (who misses what he should see, letting everyone sleep) or so potent a figure that, like Jove himself, he can forestall day's arrival. The watchman of Cadenet's alba claims similar powers but for the opposite reason, asserting that were he guarding a castle where false love reigned, he would hide the day as long as he could in order to expedite its exposure:

> If I were watching in a castle where
> false lovers made repair
> false I'd be, not to hide
> day as long as I could abide;
>   for I would never fear
> to part lovers insincere.
>
> S'ieu e nulh castelh guaitava
> ni fals'amors y renhava,
> fals si'ieu, si no celava
> lo jorn aitan quan poiria;
>   car volria
> partir falsa drudaria. (ll. 19–24)

Criseyde implores an anthropomorphized night to bind itself "so faste ay to oure hemysperie . . . that nevere more under the ground thow wynde!" (III, 1439–40), calling on night to maintain its ascendancy so that the buried day gathers no strength for resurgence.

   The alba lady is not alone in expressing such thoughts; the male lover of "Us cavaliers si jazia" also conjures a prolongation of night:

> My sweetheart dear, if only
> dawn and day would never be,

> a great boon would set us free,
> at least in the place where
> true lovers hold each other near
>
> Doussa res, s'esser podia
> que ja mais alba ni dia
> no fos, grans merces seria;
> al meyns al luec on estai
> fis amicx ab so que·l plai (11–15)

The lover of "Gaite de la tor" likewise prays for perpetual night:

> If only the Lord might hear
> A faithful lover's prayer
> And make the night from day
>> How gladly I would stay;
>>> Of my sorrow and my pain
> Nothing at all would remain.
>
> Se salve l'onor
> Au criator
> Estoit, tot tens voudroie
>> Nuit feïst del jor;
>>> Ja mais dolor
> Ne pesance n'avroie. (ll. 67–72)

The preponderance of wishes and adynata as well as invocations and prayers to God demonstrate the lovers' fantasy that reality will accommodate itself to their desires. God is called upon for help or prayed to as the Lord or the son of Holy Mary in the majority of Romance albas. In the Old French "L'abe c'apiert au jor" St. James is also invoked.

The watchman of "S'anc fui belha ni prezada" favors the longest and darkest nights that best conceal true lovers, even though during them he suffers most:

> Well am I pleased by long night's dark
> in wintertime, when it's most stark,
> and never shall I fail, even for the cold,
> to be a loyal watchman bold
>> always

> Be·m plai longua nueg escura
> el temps d'ivern, on plus dura,
> e no·m lais ges per freidura
> qu'ieu leials guaita no sia
>   tota via. (ll. 28–32)

The trusty watchman is as out of tune with society as are the alba lovers he means to protect.

In this generic context, Giraut de Bornelh's atypical invocation of the holy spirit as "true light and splendor" in "Reis glorios, verais lums e clardatz" is all the more striking. Rather than favoring night's perpetuation or shunning daylight, Giraut's watchman calls on the forces of light, praying for his companion's return and an end to darkness as well as love. Only a watchman-outsider could ever express such sentiments, but Giraut's gayta is the only one who does. Indeed, he is so dominant and forceful a character that he takes over the song. Through the words of his watchman, the poet infuses "Reis glorios, verais lums e clardatz" with the language of sacred dawn-hymns, conflating the signifying meaning of profane and spiritual dawns. This has an enlarging effect, for the secular love song grows ever more resonant of ultimate and transcendent destinies. (See the discussion of "Reis glorios, verais lums e clardatz" later in this chapter.)

The lack of specified settings in most albas helps to isolate the lovers. The world of love in the alba is self-created, emerging from the lovers' emotions, desires, and imaginations. Sir Walter Scott, a writer especially attuned to his medieval heritage, picked up the idea of romantic love as autonomous and heavenly: "Love rules the court, the camp, the grove,/ And men below, and saints above;/ For love is heaven, and heaven is love" (*The Lay of the Last Minstrel* 1923, III:2). But in Scott's much later conception, love reigns and is ubiquitous. In albas, love is limited in place as well as time; sometimes the lovers are in the lady's chamber, but often we are given no indication at all about where they are secluded. Only in the disconnected realm in which albas are set can illicit love be autonomous.

Such a deliberate expulsion of the world from the purview of the poems indicates how isolated the lovers' meetings are. In either of the two groups into which the alba can be divided, "the alba in a castle with a watchman, and the alba in a wood with birds" (Saville 1972, 150), the lovers keep apart from the public sphere, reposing either in a tranquil, simple green-world—a park, garden, meadow, or flower garden ("en un vergier," "yns el jardi," "aval els pratz," "en un boix," "jos la flor")—or in the lady's chamber ("en chambre coie," "en la chambre de joie" ["Gaite de la tor"]). These pastoral settings evoke a private idyllic haven where the lovers leave behind their daily drudgeries.

The culmination of this motif may be seen in Gottfried's *Tristan,* where the heights of love are attained in the "cave of lovers," the Minnegrotto, hidden in the wilds of a savage mountainside: "the country that leads to [Love's] refuge makes hard and arduous going.... The tracks up and down are so obstructed with rocks for us poor sufferers that, unless we keep well to the path, if we make one false step we shall never get back alive. But whosoever is so blessed as to reach and enter that solitude will have used his efforts to most excellent purpose, for he will find his heart's delight there. Whatever the ear yearns to hear, whatever gratifies the eye, this wilderness is full of it. He would hate to be elsewhere" (Hatto 1965, 265–66). Once the exiled Tristan and Isolde make their careful way to the Minnegrotto, they leave intrigue and society behind and, for the first time, live in complete harmony. They have no need for anything external. But while Tristan and Isolde discover a lovers' paradise in a desolate wasteland, the alba lovers' disregard of place serves to make it insignificant. The only important place is *time*—more precisely, nighttime. The lovers have found harbor so safe that the outside world remains unaware of their activities and vice versa. Union seems to overcome time's threat.

The lover desires to protect and possess the beloved. The lady of "En un vergier sotz fuella d'albespi" holds her lover at her side": "tenc la dompna son amic costa si" (l. 2). Walther's tageliet opens with an image of embrace that isolates the lady's arms: "In love lay/ a splendid knight/ in the arms of a lady ("Friuntlîchen lac/ ein rîter vil gemeit/ an einer frowen arme" [ll. 1–3]). Walther speaks of the lady's protective arms rather than the knight's. (The English pun on "arms" would neatly refer both to her physical body and his warrior function.) So, too, the lady of "Dieus, aydatz" specifies her embracing arms ("mon bratz") as the locus of action, in contrast to the rhyming "armed ones" ("armatz") who threaten disruption:

> Never believe
> That for the armed ones
> I shall leave off the games
>   With my friend
>   Who, in my arms,
>   Joyful, lies.

> Non crezatz
> Per armatz
> Que jogars
> De mon amic lais,
> Qu'e mon bratz
> Jauzen jatz. (ll. 49–54)

The lady's arms provide shelter and joy. Rather than indicate the lover's knightly, protective function, the other "arms" (armatz) in this lyric refer to the danger posed by enemies—the gilos and his spies. The Janus-face of the dawn is refigured in these double images of arms that simultaneously evoke the protective and perilous aspects of alba love. The lady's arms are not only embracing and protective but possessive, especially in their capacity to enclose and contain.

The lover of Heinrich's tageliet tells us that his beloved "embraced me all around" ("und mich al umbevie" [l. 26]). The lady of Wolfram's "Ez ist nu tac" embraces her man: "The good woman, her friend's body fast embraced:/ who was sleeping there" ("Daz guote wîp ir vriundes lîp vast umbevie:/ der was entslâfen dô" [ll. 13–14]). After glimpsing dawn, her lover likewise clasps her to his breast: "an sîne bruste dructe er sie" (l. 17). This same lady evinces a desire to protect, possess, and perhaps even absorb her beloved when she tells us: "I in my eyes would gladly encastle him/ if I could keep him thus" ("ich in mînen ougen gerne burge,/ möht ich in alsô behalten" [ll. 8–9]). Wolfram's isolating of her eyes is striking. The speaker's wish to possess her lover with her eyes evokes Medusa and her monstrous capacity to paralyze through the agency of sight. In her capacity to freeze the Other, Medusa asserts a power that is a form of possession.[1] The lady's phrasing of her desire as an impossible wish reveals an awareness of her impotence. What makes the wish for perpetual embrace (or capture?) poignant is the recognition of its necessary failure. The lady's eyes yearn to absorb the identity of the Other; her lover would be subsumed into her gaze, her subjectivity, her "eye/I."

The desire to "encastle" is also significant because the real noblewoman upon whom the alba lady's character is based, confined within her husband's property, is presumably the one literally subject to encastlement. Medieval aristocratic women, including the lord's wife, were strictly guarded:

> Women were held to be the principal, and insidious, source of domestic danger. They administered poison, cast spells, sowed dis-

> cord, and caused weakness, disease, and death. . . . Hence women of noble birth were kept under close surveillance and tightly disciplined. The cornerstone of the system of values that governed behavior in the noble household was a precept derived from Scripture: women, being the weaker sex and more prone to sin, had to be held in check. The first duty of the head of household was to watch over, punish, and if necessary kill his wife, sisters, and daughters, as well as the widows and orphans of his brothers, cousins, and vassals. Since females were dangerous, patriarchal power over them was reinforced. They were kept under lock and key in the most isolated part of the house: the *chambre des dames* was not a place for seduction or amusement but a kind of prison, in which women were incarcerated because men feared them. (Duby 1987, 77)

Desiring to keep her beloved as she herself is kept, Wolfram's Lady wishes to appropriate her spouse's power. The merged allusions to Medusa and the lady's husband suggest the power potential of both sexes. The lady acknowledges the limitations of her power (as opposed to her husband's) by her displacement of the idea of possession from her husband to herself. But in her recognition that she cannot keep her lover thus imprisoned, she also reveals the difference between true, "free" alba love and the bondage of coercive marriage.

The indefiniteness about place or the absence of references to it emphasizes the importance of the here and now to render the love union autonomous. The word "now" is often also used to convey the confrontation with reality—the recognition of dawn's advent—rather than the avoidance of it. The watchman of "Reis glorios, verais lums e clardatz" worries that his friend, who is within the lady's chamber, is no longer interested in his own welfare, concluding, "now neither my song nor my friendship pleases you" ("aras no·us platz mos chans ni ma paria" [l. 29]). The German word for now, "nu," is repeated three times in the first five lines of "Ez ist nu tac" ("It is now day"). This same phrase, which begins the poem, reappears in "Sîne klâwen" when the watchman reminds the lady, "ez ist nu tac" (l. 23). A similar phrase, "owê, nu ist ez tac," comes up in Heinrich's tageliet as well (l. 13). In "Slâfest du, vriedel ziere?" the word "nu" is also used: "nu rüefestû, kint, wâfen" ("now, dear, you give the alarm" [l. 6]). In contrast, the speaker of "Gaite de la tor" commands, "or soit teü" ("Now be silent" [l. 29]). In "Ich sich den morgensterne brehen," the lover is advised: "nu, helt, la dich niht gerne sehen" ("now, knight, do not willingly let yourself be seen" [l. 2]). And in the refrain of "Cant voi l'aube dou jor venir," the lady reiterates the sentiment: "now I hate nothing as much as day" ("or ne hais rien tant com le jour" [l. 5]).

The theme of love's intimacy and the lovers' wish to shut out the world was exploited by John Donne centuries after the first albas were sung. By the time Donne picked up the form, its popularity had come and gone. His masterful handling of the genre gives it a significant and powerful place in the English lyric corpus. "The Sunne Rising" demonstrates precisely how alba lovers feel their world contracted into a universe of two:

> She'is all States, and all Princes, I
> Nothing else is.
> Princes doe but play us; compar'd to this,
> All honor's mimique; All wealth alchimie.
> Thou sunne art halfe as happy'as wee,
> In that the world's contracted thus;
> Thine age askes ease, and since thy duties bee
> To warme the world, that's done in warming us.
> Shine here to us, and thou are every where;
> This bed thy centre is, these walls, thy spheare.
>
> (ll. 21–30)

Donne's inversion of the alba—with the lover ultimately inviting rather than rejecting the sun's light into his chamber—captures the feelings expressed by medieval alba lovers. The idea, so brilliantly realized by Donne, that the world exists of and for the lovers alone, is the medieval alba lovers' supreme fantasy. That the medieval fantasy becomes a Renaissance "reality" highlights a significant contrast between the medieval and Renaissance concepts of human potential. In the Middle Ages, human power was thought to extend only as far as man or woman's own limited autonomy. By the Renaissance, the conception of human potential had so greatly expanded that it claimed to subsume the surrounding physical world under its control. Marlowe's Dr. Faustus, a figure hovering uncomfortably between the medieval world of Faith and Renaissance attraction to the occult, learns to wield forces beyond the human but pays with his soul for doing so. With expanding possibilities come consequences all the more terrifying. If human potential grows, so, too, does the potential for evil. Increased freedom and mobility allow not only more opportunities for error but also for errors of greater catastrophic extent.

"The Sunne Rising" violates the alba poets' and our own sense of reality yet utterly fulfills the genre's potential. Ironically, alba poets may be more realistic than their Renaissance counterparts, despite the vaunted Renaissance preference for realism and verisimilitude. The narrator's view that love is immune to time is expressed in the first and last lines of the opening stanza:

>   Busie old foole, unruly Sunne,
>   Why dost thou thus,
>   Through windowes, and through curtaines call on us?
>   Must to thy motions lovers seasons run? . . .
>   Love, all alike, no season knowes, nor clyme,
>   Nor houres, days, moneths, which are the rags of time.
>   (ll. 1–4, 9–10)

In his bold denial of the sun's (hence, time's) power to affect love, Donne's narrator succeeds in sealing off the world of love (an act desired, but never accomplished, by alba lovers) so that the sun runs to lovers' motions rather than vice versa. Although Chaucer's Troilus vilifies day and insults the sun, he never goes so far as to challenge the sun's ultimate ascendancy or the reality of cosmic law. Indeed, Troilus's resentment and anger, his frustration, demonstrate his acceptance of that law. Donne's speaker's annoyance at the sun and his detailing of the sun's duties—

>   Sawcy pedantique wretch, goe chide
>   Late schoole boyes, and sowre prentices,
>   Goe tell Court-huntsmen, that the King will ride,
>   Call countrey ants to harvest offices (ll. 5–8)

—are steps in the process by which he deflates the sun's power. He simultaneously proves that physical reality can be conquered by the emotional reality that there is nothing more real than love. If the speaker welcomes the sun into his room at the poem's end—"Shine here to us, and thou art every where"—it is because having diminished its threat, his anger and annoyance dissolve. It is the lover who feels so powerful, rather than the sun (which is obeying Nature's orders), who is in charge.

If the lustrous body of Heinrich von Morungen's lady miraculously outshines moonlight, the brilliant eyes of Donne's lady eclipse the sun itself ("If her eyes have not blinded thine/ Look" [ll. 15–16]). And the speaker likewise could eclipse the sun by a mere blink:

> Thy beames, so reverend and strong
> Why shouldst thou thinke?
> I could eclipse and cloud them with a winke,
> But that I would not lose her sight so long.
> (ll. 11–14)

From his perspective (which is the only one that counts), his power is greater than the sun's. By the poem's conclusion, the once remote realm of alba love becomes the center of everything: "This bed thy center is, these walls, thy spheare."

The lover of Donne's "The Good-Morrow," who celebrates a new dawn in which his soul has been awakened through love, likewise proclaims: "For love, all love of other sights controules,/ And makes one little roome, an every where" (ll. 10–11). In both "The Good-Morrow" and "The Sunne Rising," Donne's lover so extends his love that it becomes, by the poems' conclusions, coextensive with the universe. The sun's power shrinks accordingly, eventually becoming subservient to the speaker's will. Thus, Donne incorporates all the inherent and inherited conventions of the alba while exploding its potential in an inversion both grand and grandiose. His poetry takes on a unique, substantial, logical reality of its own. But for medieval as well as Renaissance alba poets, poetry is the place where love magically extends and empowers itself, providing the stasis during which time can seem timeless.

In all his dawn-poems, Donne employs alba conventions only to overturn them. In "Breake of Day," he uses a female voice rare in his lyrics but not in the alba sources he parodies. Like the lover of "The Sunne Rising," she deflates the sun's power, claiming that love transcends the laws of the physical world:

> 'Tis true, 'tis day; what though it be?
> O wilt thou therefore rise from me?
> Why should we rise because 'tis light?
> Did we lie downe because 'twas night?
> Love which in spite of darknesse brought us hither,
> Should in despight of light keepe us together. (ll. 1–6)

She continues, using Troilus's imagery of daylight as a voyeuristic spy, in her description of light:[2]

> Light hath no tongue, but is all eye;
> If it could speake as well as spie,
> This were the worst, that it could say,
> That being well, I faine would stay,
> And that I lov'd my heart and honor so,
> That I would not from him, that had them, goe.
>
> (ll. 7–12)

Chaucer's Criseyde, on the other hand, fears the ruin that exposure would bring her:

> That I was born, allas, what is me wo,
> That day of vs moot make disseuerance;
> *f*or tyme it is to ryse and hennes go,
> Or ellis I am lost for euere mo. (III, 1423–26)

But rather than destroying love by betraying their secret to the world, the light of which Donne's narrator speaks exposes only the honor and loyalty of true lovers. They prove their love by showing that it outlasts the night. Then again, these lovers, like Troilus and Criseyde, have less to hide than the typical adulterous alba couple, as the final stanza makes plain:

> Must business thee from hence remove?
> Oh, that's the worst disease of love,
> The poore, the foule, the false, love can
> Admit, but not the busied man.
> He which hath businesse, and makes love, doth doe
> Such wrong, as when a marryed man doth wooe.
>
> (ll. 13–18)

For Donne's couple, honor is measured between lovers, not externally bestowed by society. Love is available to people of all kinds; only businessmen are excluded because it is not to love but to material interests that they dedicate themselves. For such people, time is money, and it never can stand still.

But time stands still for alba lovers for the duration of their song. The exclusion of place in the poems leaves nothing but time. Time is literally of the essence. There are no competing factors of interest. The fulfillment the lovers experience together is so great that they have no need for the rest of the world.

The lack of sequential narrative structure in most Romance dawn-songs leads to an experience of atemporality that the audience can share. The order of the strophes seems literally inconsequential, even interchangeable. Rather than being ordered by events that move in a logical or chronological sequence, the poems are framed by a permanent stasis. The refrain, too, serves to frame the poem in a timeless reiteration of dawn's advent. All action is simultaneous: love is forever present; past love is preserved, memorialized.

For alba lovers, freedom is attained, but only temporarily, as they attempt to suspend their awareness of reality. When the lady is with her spouse, she has all the time in the world; but ironically she is deprived of the emotional and psychological space that would make such time valuable.

Although they may sometimes align themselves with birds or nature, alba lovers generally seek escape from nature, wishing to transcend both it and its handmaiden, time. They wish, in effect, to escape flux and decay—mortality. They create their own anti- or supranatural world immune to time. In their aspiration to transcend the natural, they continually implore God or His stand-in, the watchman, to abrogate the cosmic cycle. Although the lovers attempt to obfuscate or evade the passage of time, they realize their failure to do so as it dawns.

The lovers can sustain their idyllic freedom only temporarily, ignoring the passage of time in an attempt to control the present. As Sayce notes, one consistent dawn-song feature "is the refusal to recognize the signs of day ("Sîne klâwen," 27–30) . . . or the attempt to shut it out ("Den morgenblic," 12–14)" (1967, 256). Thus, the lovers can feel for a while like dwellers in paradise with no contingent cares, for they have occluded every reminder of objective reality.

The action of Giraut de Bornelh's "Reis glorios, verais lums e clardatz" consists of the watchman's relentless but apparently futile efforts to rouse the lover's consciousness of such signs.[3] "Reis glorios, verais lums e clardatz" juxtaposes a lovers' paradise against the watchman's Heaven. The lovers' haven, a "time of timelessness," is hidden in a secret earthly setting. Like Gottfried's Minnegrotto, it is a realm so remote that the watchman's cries barely penetrate it:

Glorious king, true light and brightness,
Powerful God, Lord, if you please,
to my companion be a faithful aid,
for I have not seen him since the night has come,
    and soon it will be dawn!

Fair friend, are you asleep or awake?
Sleep no longer, softly rise,
for in the East I see the star grown bigger
which brings day; I have known it well,
    and soon it will be dawn!

Fair friend, in singing I call you:
sleep no longer, for I hear the bird sing
who goes seeking day through the wood,
and I fear that the jealous one will attack you,
    and soon it will be dawn!

Fair friend, go to the window,
and look at the signs in the sky;
you will know if I am your faithful messenger:
if you do not, yours will be the harm,
    and soon it will be dawn!

Fair friend, since parting from you,
I have not slept nor budged from my knees,
But prayed to God, the son of Holy Mary,
To give you back to me in loyal companionship,
    and soon it will be dawn!

Fair friend, outside on the steps
you begged me not to fall asleep,
but to watch all night till day;
now neither my song nor my friendship pleases you
    and soon it will be dawn!

Reis glorios, verais lums e clardatz,
Dieus poderos, senher, si a vos platz,

Al mieu companh siatz fizels aiuda;
Qu'ieu non lo vi pos la nuechs fon venguda,
   Et ades sera l'alba!

Bel companho, si dormetz o velhatz?
Non dormatz plus, suau vos ressidatz;
Qu'en orient vey l'estela creguda
C'amena·l iorn, qu'eu l'ai conoguda,
   Et ades sera l'alba!

Bel companho, en chantan vos apel:
Non dormatz plus, qu'ieu aug chantar l'auzel
Que vai queren lo iorn per lo boscatge
Et ai paor que·l gilos vos assatge,
   Et ades sera l'alba!

Bel companho, yssetz al fenestrel
E regardatz las ensenhas del cel;
Conoisseretz s'ie·us suj fizels messatge.
Si non o faitz, vostres n'er lo dampnatge,
   Et ades sera l'alba!

Bel companho, pos me parti de vos,
Eu no·m dormi ni·m moc de genolhos,
Ans preiei Deu, lo filh Santa Maria,
Que·us me rendes per lejal companhia,
   Et ades sera l'alba.

Bel companho, la foras als peiros
Mi preyavatz qu'ieu no fos dormilhos,
Enans velhes tota nuech tro al dia;
Aras no·us platz mos chans ni ma paria,
   Et ades sera l'alba!

In lieu of the characteristic love-parting scene, Giraut's poem depicts a faithful watchman's increasing anxiety as he attempts to wake his comrade and prevent the catastrophe of exposure. If we characterize the poem as a love song at all, its evocation of love occurs only via the lovers' silence, which indicates that the watchman's eloquence is sorely inadequate to effect a disruption of his friend's romantic idyll. The watchman's revelation of his thoughts forces the audience familiar with the genre to imagine the contrary responses of the lovers, which is usually the substance of the song. The lovers' unheard protests become the voices of Night, just as his own becomes the voice of Day.

"Reis glorios, verais lums e clardatz" conveys the intensity of feeling between the unseen and unheard lovers.[4] The more desperately the watchman pleads, the more poignant the situation grows; the lovers remain sequestered and mute. Wilhelm aptly comments that the lover's response "is fully evident in the interior dialectic of the poem: his friend's lonely vigil implies the lovers' sensual satisfaction" (1965, 200).

Far from asking God, as other alba narrators do, to perpetuate night, postpone dawn, or in any other way alter the cosmos, this watchman accepts even while he fears the natural order of things. Saville suggests that the watchman prays to God to forestall His imminence and violate His purpose: God is invoked "to aid the speaker's friend in the safe achievement of an adulterous sexual union!" and "to aid the doings of night. . . . A tension between what God is and what He is asked to do is thus immediately established" (1972, 94). For Saville, this tension is announced in the opening lines: "The suggestion of a symbolic identity between the God who is prayed to and the dawn which is feared leads to the inference that the friend is praying to God, the origin of the Christian moral code, to help the lovers by *not* being imminent, as the dawn is—that is, to help the lovers by effacing Himself and His moral judgments" (95). But although God is implored to rescue the lover, this request does not contradict divine function, for the watchman is invoking God in His role as intercessor and savior, as He who rescues man from harm as well as sin.

The watchman's anxiety over his friend's fate is countered by a deep faith: he believes so fervently in God's grace that he implores divine aid no matter how great his friend's sin. The watchman, acting as intercessor between God and the lover, asks God to perform the same function he does, to be a "faithful aid" to his companion, who has vanished within the mysterious and perilous realm of the lady's chamber. Giraut makes the relationship between the watchman and God so central to the poem that, as Spence notes, "we are asked to read the poem as both a dawn-hymn and an erotic *alba*" (1981, 214).

In requesting God to be a faithful aid ("siatz fizels aiuda"), the watchman asks Him to fulfill a social function, as he himself does. The watchman's references in his salutation to "reis" and "senher," titles that apply not only to God but secular rulers, demonstrate his awareness of the communal order, the importance of social hierarchy and roles, and the loyalty that cements together levels of society. The world depicted in the watchman's opening lines is ruled by God, dominated by secular kings, populated by lords and vassals, and, most vitally, held together by companhos, faithful friends and allies.

A hierarchy is established, stemming from God through the watchman to the lover. If the watchman begs God to perform the same service he has been executing, he also implies that in some sense he performs a divine office. He uses the same word, "fizels," in the third line of strophes 1 and 4, and in the same metrical position on that line, in reference to both God's aid and his own watch. In strophe 1 he asks that God "to my companion be a faithful aid"; in strophe 4 he states, "you will know whether I am a faithful messenger" ("Al mieu companh siatz fizels aiuda" [str. 1]; "conoisseretz s'ie·us suj fizels messatge" [str. 4]). The watchman thereby tightly links God's aid to his own message. Additionally, the words "verais" in reference to God and "lejal" (which appears in a similar though not identical metrical position as the two "fizels") reiterate the theme of faithfulness.

The watchman calls on God in His manifestation as light with the words "lums" and "clardatz." Whereas for alba lovers dawn's light is love's destroyer, for Giraut's watchman, God's light, though much more potent and splendid, is praised and desired. The watchman's desperate desire for illumination evokes a darkness so profound that only God's splendor, of which day's light is but a pale reflection, can penetrate it and protect the lover. The watchman has become anxious, not because he has grown tired and weary of his chore (Saïz 1976, 39) but because he suspects that only God's intervention can restore the lover's senses and rescue him from the grave danger in which he has placed himself.

But the watchman can only aid the lover by trying to shake him from his lethargy, by exhorting him to help himself. The watchman grows increasingly desperate, frightened, and saddened by the lover's unresponsiveness, his exhortations becoming increasingly more urgent. The pastoral beauty evoked by the singing bird's seeking day in strophe 3 is shattered by the sudden intrusion of the gilos, and danger is brought swiftly to the foreground. Rather than just to wake, the watchman presses the lover to "go" and "look."

The watchman perceives the irony, if not injustice, of his discomfort; after all, it was the lover who first begged him to stand guard. Yet like the watchman of Wolfram's "Sîne klâwen," Giraut's gayta expects that the more faithful he is to his pledge, the more displeasing he will be to the one for whom he made it in the first place.

Strophe 5 focuses on the watchman's feeling of paralysis. Having neither slept nor moved from prayer, the watchman stayed awake and aware. His efforts—the prayer and song that plead for action—represent his belief in the efficacy of words to persuade to action. But he gradually transfers to God the responsibility for stirring the lover because he fears that the lover has receded so far into the lady's domain—that is, into a sphere of powerlessness and captivity, however delightful—that he cannot rouse himself. Realizing the limitations of his power, the watchman gives over to God the responsibility for retrieving the lover.

The watchman realizes that no matter how much—or what kind of—love exists between individuals, there is a limit to what one can do for another. This realization acknowledges the inexorable boundary between individuals and the real autonomy, or free will, of every person. So, too, can God have foreknowledge of events yet be unable to help individuals avoid catastrophe no matter how well or often He exhorts people to beware. Although the watchman prays fervently, his pleas are of no avail if the lover himself remains unaware of his own peril. The watchman warns the lover about the consequences of ignoring the message—that is, his song. Although he watches and worries, he cannot physically intervene and rescue the lover from the dangers that are marshaling to beset him.

The use of the words "lejal companhia" in the context of Mary, God, and prayer and the fact that all the nouns in strophe 5 are linked to the sacred add to the sense of the sanctity of friendship that pervades the poem. Many of the words refer to relationships: "Reis," "Dieus," "Senher," "aiuda" (strophe 1); "companho" (strophes 1–6); "gilos" (strophe 3); "messatge" (strophe 4); "Deu," "filh," "Santa Maria," "compania" (strophe 5); "paria" (strophe 6). The watchman pleads with the lover, not to gain the lover's "sympathy and understanding" but to prove how selflessly he has acted (Saïz 1976, 42). The pious and deferential tone that pervades the entire lyric manifests the speaker's sincerity and fidelity.

Remarkably for a love poem, there are no references to romantic love or women: the only woman mentioned in the poem is "Santa Maria." Lamenting like any alba lady, however, the watchman reminisces about parting from the lover, recalling their last meeting: "pos mi parti de vos" ("since I parted from you"). Like the typical alba lady, the watchman anxiously awaits the return of the lover, fearful lest his escape be hindered. The watchman affirms his loyalty by evincing how faithfully he has done the lover's bidding, how he has suffered for it with little hope of reward. Like the unrequited courtly lover, this watchman has faithfully served an unresponsive master, requesting nothing in return. Wilhelm interprets the lover's silence as confirmation of two of the watchman's perceptions: that he has displeased the lover and that the lover rejects both his song and friendship (1965, 200). In fact, however, we are simply left with the watchman's fear of rejection rather than any indication that this rejection is actual.

The real lament presented in "Reis glorios, verais lums e clardatz" is not occasioned by the loss of love between the illicit lovers, which, however poignant, occurs off-scene, but by the debilitating effect of romantic love on the bond between comrades. Saïz astutely observes that the watchman "seems to be offering his friend a choice between true comradeship and an adulterous love affair" (1976, 142). Hence, even more striking than the lovers' silent evocation of love is the poem's subtle inversion of the typical alba. Because it centers on the watchman's emotional self-portrait of his loyal and self-sacrificing service on behalf of his friend, the lyric more explicitly concerns the bond between male companions than between lovers. As such, although the lyric ostensibly centers on heterosexual romantic love, the greater concern is actually with the value of social relationships between men—what Eve Sedgwick refers to as "homosocial desire." Love for a woman is viewed in "Reis glorios" as an inconvenient and dangerous distraction from more essential and rewarding matters. The forlorn plea of the watchman who urges, unavailingly, the swift, safe return of his comrade has a haunting resonance that conveys his own loneliness even while it foreshadows the sorrow of the soon-to-be separated couple.

The friendship between comrades, like the relationship between the lovers, is time-bound; the relationship between the watchman and his God, however, is not. This relationship sustains him throughout his vigil and can never be severed by others. The pervasive infusion of sacred into the poem and the watchman's continued anxiety over the lover's safety demonstrate neither incompatibility between illicit love and Christian doctrine nor an obliviousness to such incompatibility (Saville 1972, 101). Rather they show the watchman's faith in the magnanimous splendor of God's grace and His ability to bridge the chasm that separates man from Him. Saville suggests that in the first six strophes of "Reis glorios, verais lums e clardatz" "the essential ideological incompatibility between adulterous love and Christian God is blithely ignored" (216). He further observes that "the lover, who speaks in the last strophe of Giraut de Bornelh's *alba* is setting himself up in opposition to God, in terms of the narrative and perhaps in terms of the light symbolism as well. His inner world. . . . is declared to be superior to God's grace and perhaps to God Himself" (105). But although the lover rejects dawn and the gilos in this final and possibly inauthentic strophe (see note 4), he never declares his world superior; never, even in the mouths of the most outspoken and angry of adulterous lovers does the alba poet diminish sacred love or put it into diametrical opposition with secular love. "Reis glorios, verais lums e clardatz" is the lyric that effects the closest overlapping of divine and secular love. Such an overlapping may insinuate a logical irreconcilability between the two forms of love; but this perspective, which is the extradiagetic audience's rather than the watchman's or lovers', remains—like so much else in the lyric—elusive.

If overtones of the Last Judgment pervade "Reis glorios, verais lums e clardatz" (Wilhelm 1965, 199; Spence 1981, 216; Simonelli 1974, 196–207), then what becomes clear is that the watchman is worried about not merely the lover's safe escape from the lady's chamber but his ultimate destiny—the salvation of his soul. Wilhelm posits that "the watchman's last outcry about the coming dawn sounds like a last judgment being pronounced on the lovers' souls" and that the lover is, in effect, "condemn[ing] his own soul to any hell that awaits him" (1965, 199, 200). The ominous atmosphere that pervades the lyric along with the watchman's continued and increasingly frustrated calls to awareness contributes to the audience's sense of the awaiting peril. That the elaborate and somber melody for the lyric came originally from an Old Provençal hymn to the Virgin only adds to our sense of the seriousness and sanctity of the song. (Its music was later used for a lament about the martyrdom of St. Agnes in a fourteenth century Old Provençal play.) In this loaded context, the gilos takes on connotations beyond that of the cuckolded husband: he is revenge itself, a force of judgment poised to overwhelm the lover unless he quickly comes to his senses and removes himself from jeopardy. The gilos is no longer the scorned spouse, or even the Devil (Simonelli 1974, 14), but the jealous God angered by the lovers' blatant sinfulness.

Because it is sung by the sympathetic outsider, "Reis glorios, verais lums e clardatz" reveals a dual perspective that contrasts the allegiances of lovers with those of the rest of society. The lovers' viewpoint, implied in their silence (and the watchman's fears for them), proclaims that no yawning peril will dictate the curtailment of their union. The watchman's concerns disclose a wider, more objective, or merely different perspective in which a greater force (God) and a definite Christian destiny (damnation) do exist. Hence, grave consequences must ensue from the lovers' illicit meeting. The audience, left to determine which of these competing forces is the more compelling and powerful, feels the anguish of the conflict.

Love's Timeless Utopia: Regressive Fantasies

> O night, to me more blissful and bright
> Than the most blissful and brightest of days;
> Night deigned by the first and rarest of minds
> To be praised, not merely by me;
> You of my joys have been
> Sole minister faithfully; you all the bitternesses
> Of my life have turned sweet and dear,
> By giving into my arms he who has captured my heart.
> Only one more gift could have been mine,
> That of lucky Alcmena, for whom so long
> Beyond the usual time Aurora delayed her return.
> Yet as it is I shall never be able to praise you,
> Enough, shining night, so that the words
> Would be equal to the song.
> Gaspara Stampa, "Notte d'amore," Rime (1554)

In their desire for stasis, alba lovers often attempt to create a space of timelessness, the kind that an infant perhaps experiences before he or she is old enough to apprehend the passage of hours and days. Psychoanalysts tell us that "nearly every child experiences paradise in infancy, a state referred to in psychoanalysis as the symbiotic phase which precedes the separation from the mother" (Mahler 1975, 85–86).

That lovers act childlike, if not childish, is one of the alba poets' insights into the nature of love. The irrational childlike state to which alba lovers regress returns to them a long lost infantile freedom. Safe with each other, they reexperience the joy of uninhibited play. When Freud examined the phenomenon of love through the study of infantile sexuality, he observed that love engenders "an infantile mode of feeling or an early ego state" (Bergmann 1971, 24).[5] Alba lovers, who yearn for a nocturnal stasis, seem to regress to a childlike state of playfulness, naturalness, instinctuality, and merging. Their innocence is one of the most appealing aspects of the genre. Within their protective space, the lovers freely laugh and sport. As presented in the alba, sexual activity has an uninhibited joy. There is "a new game" ("un joc novel") in both "En un vergier sotz fuella d'albespi," where the lady invites her lover—"Let's play a new game" ("Fassam un joc novel")—and in "Gaita be," where the treasured "joc novel" is stolen by dawn. The lovers' enjoyment is increased by the fact that this particular game is played against the lady's husband, the gilos—and one of the game's childish aims is to trick him.

The lady of "Entre moi et mon amin" recalls a tryst during which she and her lover were "playing" ("juwant"). Similarly, the lover of "Ab la gensor que sia" recounts a rendezvous in which he and his lady were "playing, laughing" ("jogan rizen"). Earnshaw's theory that one of the functions served by the lyric female voice is to play the "perpetual adolescent, engaged in battle with the grown-up world" is supported particularly well by the alba lady, especially in her love of play (1988, 121). But the alba male shares in her rebellion against patriarchal strictures.

The female narrator of the final strophe of "Dieus, aydatz" says that she will not be frightened into ending the games that she and her lover play:

> Never believe
> That for the armed ones
> I shall leave off the games
> With my friend
> Who, in my arms,
> Joyful, lies.
>
> Non crezatz
> Per armatz
> Que jogars
> De mon amic lays
> Qu'e mon bratz
> Jauzen jatz. (ll. 49–54)

The joys of love are frequently asserted. The watchman of "S'anc fui belha ni prezada" speaks of the "fine lover" who "takes joy from his worthy lady" ("fins drutz, quan jauzimen/ de domna valen" [ll. 34–35]). The lovers' joy and playfulness reveal the liberating self-expressiveness that accompanies romantic love even while they allude to the sexual satisfaction implicit in the word "joi."

The numerous references to play, sport, and laughter in the alba display the lovers' freedom from the tyranny of time and conventional adult behavior. Love relaxes binding strictures; the gilos takes on the role of authoritarian overseer who threatens the lovers' full self-expression and playfulness. In serving as a patriarch, he renders the lovers childish by comparison. These references may imply that the lovers have regressed to a state of childishness, relinquishing their worldly responsibilities for the emphasis on carefree pleasure and release may be seen as infantile.

In presenting an idyllic vision of perfect, self-fulfilling love, alba poets implicitly call for an integration of play, self-expression, and creativity within the social structure of their real world. Paradoxically, the passion that compels alba lovers to merge also encourages an exploration and expression of their individual selves. Alba love first individualizes by alienating the lover from the community, but the resulting self-exploration goes further. The desire for self-expression may be shared by their poet, may even be the impetus for the song's composition. Hanning notes that the courtly poet, aware that he was "writing for a self-consciously elite society," was original in "redefining the poetic act as the fresh application of intelligence and sensitivity—of *ingenium,* or *engin,* to use twelfth-century terms—to large preoccupations of the moment, under the guise of tales and adventure" (1984, 11–12). The alba poet, so sympathetic to the illicit lovers about whom he writes, must have craved the same liberty to vent feelings and express aspirations—as much in his verse as in life—that he grants his lovers.

The lovers throw themselves into carefree play in the face of dire consequences. But their play does not diminish their worth or stature in the poet's eyes; the adjectives describing the "fine" lover and "worthy" lady of numerous albas serve to establish the lovers' personal dignity. Childlike qualities emerge in other ways. The lover in the charming tageliet "Slâfest du, vriedel ziere?" addresses his beloved as "kint":

> "Are you asleep, beloved dear?
> They will wake us too early.
>> A little bird so fair,
>> Is perched on a twig of the linden-tree."

> "I was sleeping so softly:
> Now, child, your alarm wakes me.
>> Joy without sorrow there cannot be.
>> Your bidding, my dear friend, I'll do faithfully."

The lady began to moan
"You ride off and leave me alone.
    When will you return here to me again?
    Alas, my joy you take and I remain."

"Slâfest du, vriedel ziere?
man wecket uns leider schiere;
    ein vogellîn sô wol getân
    daz ist der linden an daz zwî gegân."

"Ich was vil sanfte entslâfen,
nu rüefestû, kint, wâfen.
    liep âne léit mách niht sîn.
    swaz dû gebiutest, daz leiste ich, vriundîn mîn."

Diu vrouwe begunde weinen:
"du rîtest hínnen und lâst mich eine.
    wenne wîlt du wider her zuo mir?
    owê, du vüerest mîne vröide sant dir!"

The word "kint," for Dronke, holds the key to the entire poem: "The girl, who speaks in the first stanza is still almost a child, chattering with excited curiosity. She does not yet know for herself what a leave-taking means. . . . In the last stanza she is not *kint* but *frouwe*. Suddenly she realizes what loneliness will be hers, and her words, which from an experienced lover would sound banal, are moving because it is she who says them, discovering through them the universal feelings of women in love" (1977, 177–78). This transition from "kint" to "frouwe," however, also entails a concomitant shift in speaker from the lover to the omniscient narrator. In the objective narrator's eyes, the lady appears a grown woman; in her lover's eyes, however, she is more endearing and particularized. Her maturation from child to woman may be due to her pain, as Dronke proposes, but it may just as likely be the result of the two different male perspectives, the lover's and narrator's. The diminutive this lover uses, "vriundîn mîn" (similarly employed by Walther in "Friuntlîchen lac," where the lady is "friundinne"), like "kint," is a term of affection, similar to a pet name used in childhood.

    The lovers' impotent rage and disappointment may also seem immature. There is certainly something childish and unrealistic about their blaming and threatening the watchman and dawn in their frustration. Dawn, personified as thief, is accused of stealing the beloved or trying to cheat the lovers of precious time. "Gaita be" opens with the lover's exclamation that day is uncalled for and dawn steals his joy:

> Watch well, dear watchman of the castle,
> for the one who is best and most beautiful
>   I have by me   until dawn,
>   And day comes   and I do not call it.
>   new joy
>   the dawn steals from me,
>   the dawn, yes the dawn!

> Gaita be gaiteta del chastel
> quan la re que plus m'es bon e bel
>   ai a me   trosqu'a l'alba.
>   E·l jornz ve   e non l'apel;
>   joc novel
>   mi tol l'alba
>   l'alba, oi l'alba! (ll. 1–7)

The alba concludes with the claim that dawn wishes to deceive them: "To cheat/ Us wishes the dawn, the dawn, yes, the dawn!" ("Enganar/ Nos vol l'alba, l'alba, oi l'alba!" [ll. 26–28]). The lover of "Gaite de la tor" sees dawn as the warrior enemy: "Too much it has harmed me/ The dawn which combats me" ("Trop m'a meü/ L'aube qui me guerroie" [ll. 65–66]). So does the lady of "Cant voi l'aube dou jor venir," who reiterates her hatred of dawn continually in the refrain: "Now I hate nothing so much as day,/ Love, which parts me from you" ("Or ne hais riens tant com le jour,/ Amins, ke me depait de vos" [ll. 5–6]).

In castigating the watchman or dawn, alba lovers display a delusion or fantasy that a human (either themselves or their watchman) can control the cosmos. Yet their rage also reveals a frustrated acceptance of their impotence. Their displacement of the desire to alter the order of things onto the watchman graces him with the superhuman powers they know they lack. The lovers childishly desire reality to be as they wish it, but jarring day intrudes unsought: "And day comes and I do not call it" ("E·l jornz ve e non l'apel" ["Gaita be," l. 4]). Unlike the heroic lover of many courtly romances, the alba hero, although a knight, is incapable of vanquishing all the obstacles that hinder union with his beloved.

Fusion, Androgyny, Inseparability

Sweet one, I'm on my way.
I am yours, wherever I may be.
By God, never forget me,
For here the heart of my body stays,
and from you my thoughts shall never stray.

Sweet one, if I did not see you,
soon believe that I would die,
for my great desire would undo me;
wherefore I shall soon be nigh,
for without you, what life have I?
Bertran D'Alamanon or Gaucelm Faidit [?], "Us cavaliers si jazia"

The inseparability of alba lovers is a medieval variation on an ancient theme. The idea of love as merging receives early expression in the well-known myth that Aristophanes recounts in Plato's *Symposium*, which presents the origin of both hetero- and homosexual love as the search for one's missing other half. According to this myth, there were originally three sexes; the third was a combination of male and female: "The hermaphrodite was a distinct sex in form as well as in name, with the characteristics of both male and female" (*Symposium*, 59). The dual-sexed creature, lodged in a single body, was four-legged and two-headed. But Zeus proposed that the creature be bisected to simultaneously weaken and multiply the species. As a result, "each half yearned for the half from which it had been severed. When they met they threw their arms round one another and embraced, in their longing to grow together again, and they perished of hunger and general neglect of their concerns, because they would not do anything apart" (*Symposium*, 60–61). When the two parts came together, entwining in mutual embraces and longing to merge, love was born.

The innate love that humans feel for one another "restores us to our ancient state by attempting to weld two beings into one and to heal the wounds which humanity suffered" (*Symposium*, 62). We are half of what we once were, and each of us perpetually searches for his or her corresponding tally. Once the other half is found, the couple refuses to be separated even for a moment: every couple has the urge to be one instead of two: "The reason is that this was our primitive condition when we were wholes, and love is simply the name for the desire and pursuit of the whole" (*Symposium*, 63–64).

Plato's Aristophanes speaks of two lovers becoming one flesh, of healing the incomplete human state. For philosopher Irving Singer (who emphasizes that Aristophanes is not to be viewed as spokesman for Plato's preferred concept of love), this myth exemplifies the idealist conception of love, which involves a loss of individuality or a reversion "to a profounder oneness that preceded it" (1984, 6). These lovers are immersed in something bigger and grander than themselves as separate entities, "something that negates and even destroys the boundaries of routine existence" (1984, 6). Such a lover belongs no longer to the world of separate selves, and he or she often loses all concern for former responsibilities: "He may lie, he may steal, he may kill—there is nothing a Tristan or Iseult will not do in order to preserve their sense of oneness. In merging with the beloved, lovers in the idealist tradition believe that they have transcended the restraints of ordinary life, even though they cannot escape them entirely" (Singer 1984, 6–7). From the psychoanalytic viewpoint, this fable captures the symbiotic element of love, "the sense of yearning and missing that both precedes and accompanies falling in love" (Bergmann 1987, 45; 1971, 20–21).

If the Greek idealist feels incomplete without a partner or desires the complete submergence of self in the beloved, for Ovid, the merging of the sexes into one being creates not the empowered double-creature of Greek myth but the half-man Hermaphroditus. The water nymph, Salmacis, falls desperately in love with the indifferent Hermaphroditus, son of Hermes and Aphrodite (two deities associated with sexual union). She coils herself around him, praying that the gods unite them. Her prayer is answered when their bodies merge, and they become a single being with male and female characteristics:

> "O gods, do grant my plea: may no day dawn
> that sunders him from me, or me from him."
> Her plea is heard; the gods consent; they merge
> the twining bodies; and the two become
> one body with a single face and form.
> As when one grafts a twig around a bough
> and wraps the bark around them, he will see
> those branches, growing to maturity,
> unite: so were these bodies that had joined

> no longer two but one—although biform:
> one could have called that shape a woman or
> a boy: for it seemed neither and seemed both.
> (*Metamorphoses*, 124)

In Ovid's myth, the female, whose mad desire overwhelms the resistant and struggling Hermaphroditus, is contented by the arrangement; but Hermaphroditus feels emasculated, destroyed:

> And when he saw just what the pool had done,
> how he who was a man had now become
> a half-man—one whose limbs had lost the force
> they had before he plunged—as he stretched out
> his hands, Hermaphroditus, though deprived
> of manly voice, now cried: "Do grant this gift,
> dear father and dear mother, to the son
> who carries both your names: whoever comes
> into this pool as man, may he emerge
> a half-man; at these waters' touch, may he
> be weakened, softened." And they heard his plea;
> moved by their biform son, his parents poured
> into the pool a potion that endowed
> those waters with a pestilential power.
> (*Metamorphoses*, 124)

In Aristophanes' myth two beings joyfully become one, the culmination of a healing quest for self-completion; but in Ovid's Hermaphroditus legend, similar merging is considerably one-sided: the domination by one half entails the subjugation and diminution of the other. From the viewpoint of the myth that Ovid recounts, the male half is weakened, polluted by union with the female. Identity as well as body is altered.

Heilbrun's distinction between androgyny and hermaphroditism highlights a difference between the Platonic and Ovidian myths. Androgyny is the mutually binding union that makes two lovers feel complete, hermaphroditism the biological anomaly where one being possesses sexual traits of both sexes. Heilbrun warns that the terms have often been (mis)used interchangeably so that "androgyny, an ideal, [is] confused with hermaphroditism, an anomalous physical condition" (1973, xii). Hermaphroditism dissipates and makes the whole being incomplete whereas androgyny empowers and makes a partial being whole.

From its inception, the idea of the passionate merging of male and female encompasses the idea of androgyny. These classical antecedents are illuminating but not because alba poets were necessarily alluding to the concepts of androgyny formulated by these myths, although Plato's ideas were widely known in the Middle Ages.[6] Alba poets clearly portray the same phenomenon: the intense desire for physical merging that accompanies romantic love is an emotional one that far exceeds the desire for mere sexual union.

This desire is beautifully expressed in the kinds of merging implicit in the alban image of dawn. We have already seen that alba lovers extricate themselves from stereotypical gender roles. In their freedom of exploration, their rebellion from hierarchical dictates, and their intimacy with one another, they seem to transcend gender, taking on the aspects of androgyny that have since ancient times been associated with love.

Dante's reversal of the Platonic myth in his portrayal of Paolo and Francesca highlights the difference between his treatment of romantic love and that of both his classical and medieval antecedents. The love experience, as Dante depicts it in troubadour fashion, is as illicit and intense as that portrayed by the earlier troubadours:

> Love, that can quickly seize the gentle heart,
> took hold of him because of the fair body
> taken from me—how that was done still wounds me.
> Love, that releases no beloved from loving,
> took hold of me so strongly through his beauty
> that, as you see, it has not left me yet.
> (*Divine Comedy*, Book V, 42, ll. 100–105)

> Amor, ch'al cor gentil ratto s'apprende,
> prese costui de la bella persona
> che mi fu tolta; e 'l modo ancor m'offende.
> Amor, ch'a nullo amato amar perdona,
> mi prese del costui piacer sì forte,
> che, come vedi, ancor non m'abbandona.
> (V, 43, 100–105)

But the consequences of illicit love prove grave and final when Dante's lovers' souls, "that stained the world with blood" ("noi che tignemmo il mondo di sanguigno" [V, 42, 90]), are condemned to eternal union. The perpetual union that was for Aristophanes a yearning finally fulfilled and for Ovid a pollution has for Dante become an everlasting hell. If love makes Hermaphroditus less than a man, it renders Paolo silent (Poggioli 1957, 354–55); Francesca speaks for both while Paolo, silent, weeps: "And while one spirit said these words to me,/ the other wept" ("Mentre che l'uno spirto questo disse,/ l'altro piangëa" ([*Divine Comedy,* Book V, 44, ll. 139–40; V, 45, ll. 139–40]).[7]

The contrasting *Symposium* and *Inferno* versions of merging are linked through the alba vision of love, for Paolo and Francesca's sin results not from love alone but from the illicit kind of love that the alba celebrates. For Dante's couple, alban love becomes the vehicle of lust, bloodshed, death, and damnation. Dante employs the Paolo and Francesca tale to criticize the romantic obsession that overwhelms propriety and control, like Lancelot's love for Guenevere. Such love is lethal, as Francesca says: "Love led the two of us unto one death" ("Amor conduisse moi ad una morte" [V, 42, 106; V, 43, 106]). For Dante, obsessive, overpowering love is not the joyful coalescing of two bodies into one but the violent transformation of the living into the dead. Paolo and Francesca's short-lived earthly union engenders an afterlife in which they are forever bound.

Genesis intimates that of all animals only man came into being without a mate, a manifestation of his primordial loneliness and separateness. Once God realizes that "it is not good for man to be alone" (Genesis 2.18), he corrects this oversight by creating a helpmate for Adam. Taken from Adam's rib, Eve was originally a corporeal part of him. Several Jewish Midrashim tell of a literal sawing or splitting in half of a bisexual Adam. According to the *Bereshit rabba* (8.1), a legend recounted by Maimonides in the twelfth century, "Adam and Eve were made back to back, joined at the shoulders; then God divided them with an axe stroke, cutting them in two" (Delcourt 1961, 74).

The biblical myth makes Adam the progenitor, the source of the woman, inverting the biological process in which the female gives birth. Because this myth "flies flagrantly in the face of everyday experience that man comes out of woman and not vice versa," on psychoanalytic grounds "we may assume that the myth grew out of man's envy of woman to bear children, an envy that has been demonstrated clinically" (Bergmann 1987, 85–86). Man's desire for female generative power is openly expressed by male artists and writers when they speak of giving birth to their creations. It was expressed at least as far back as ancient Greece. (Zeus assumes the power to give birth to not only Athena but Zagreus and Dionysus as well.)

The biblical myth of Eve's creation from Adam's rib justifies the ascendancy of the male over the female in the Judeo-Christian tradition. Futher, Adam gives birth painlessly, in his sleep, whereas after the Fall, woman gives birth as a punishment and suffers great pain in childbirth.

Both Old and New Testaments ordain a fleshly union between man and woman similar to the symbiotic attachment Aristophanes describes in Plato's *Symposium*, but the biblical texts reserve this union for spouses only: "Therefore shall a man leave his father and his mother, and shall cleave unto his wife and they shall be one flesh" (Genesis 2:24). Jesus' restatement is almost identical: "For this cause shall a man leave father and mother and shall cleave to his wife; and they shall be one flesh. Therefore they are no more twain but one flesh" (Matthew 9:5). If the Ovidian myth illustrates male terror of female passion and domination, the biblical rule that the male half—being the elder and progenitor of the female—should govern allowed religious authorities to give vent to their similar fear. That this command was drawn upon by religious and civil authorities to inculcate and institutionalize male subjugation of women is one of the great and enduring injustices of human history. And once the Church made marriage a sacrament, the ceremony "clearly marked the precedence of the husband" (Duby 1987, 130).

Among Church fathers, Peter Lombard is rare in drawing a more positive picture of gender relations. He proclaims: "God did not make woman from Adam's head, for she was not intended to be his ruler, nor from his feet, for she was not intended to be his slave, but from his side, for she was intended to be his companion and his friend" (Power 1975, 34). The breast-to-breast and rib-to-rib position of alba lovers recalls this companionable aspect of love rather than the hierarchical one.

In general, however, women's equality is barely acknowledged by Church fathers, who recognize that women are in spirit equal to men but usually relegate this fact to the background. The Church fathers emphasize keeping women in their place here on earth: "while women were recognized as 'joint heirs of the grace of life,' they were also called the 'weaker vessel who were to remain in subjugation to their menfolk' (I Peter, 3, 1–7). . . . Man was the image and glory of God. Women on the other hand were 'the glory of man. For the man is not of the woman: but the woman of the man. Neither was the man created for the woman; but woman for the man' [I Corinthians II: 4–9]" (Bullough et al. 1988, 86).

My point here is not that male fear and envy of women or the socially and legally sanctioned bond between spouses became justifications for the oppression of women—subjects well beyond the scope of this study and addressed in numerous recent publications on women's history.[8] My point is, rather, that the symbiotic magnetism between lovers was a subject deeply fascinating to alba poets and, although not original with them, was perceptively, lucidly, and sympathetically portrayed by them. Like their classical forebears, alba poets observe that erotic love (whether marital, nonmarital, or illicit) engenders a profound desire for fusion that goes beyond sex. Through the lovers' actions and words, the poets present characters who transcend traditional gender roles and stereotypes. Alba love alters both their daily circumstances and their inner lives.

Alba poets portray the lovers' fusion as intense and vital; hence, our compassion for alba lovers as they suffer a shattering dawn parting is justified and deepened. Although alba poets' portrayal of erotic love echoes ancient proclivities, alba love is nonetheless distinctly of its time because the exploration of the urge for fusion in love is bound up with a contemporaneous discovery of the individual (see chapter 5).

Love's symbiosis and omnipotence achieve their medieval apotheosis in the tale of Tristan and Isolde, where a love potion binds the lovers so intimately that they cannot survive independently; death is chosen over separation. Heilbrun views their union as "a metaphor for the androgynous condition, the need of a merging of the masculine and feminine with equal passion" (1973, 24). For Gottfried von Strassburg, such a union is sublime: "Man was there with Woman, Woman there with Man. What else should they be needing? They had what they were meant to have, they had reached the goal of their desire" (Hatto 1965, 263). In psychoanalytic terms, the symbiosis created by this kind of love (the *Liebestod*) represents a dangerous emotional state.

Alba lovers express the deprivation they will feel without the beloved, but their song ends in their separation, not death. In Walther's tageliet, the lover swears that he will not be long parted from his lady:

> That must thus happen
> that only if I cannot help it,
> would I remain away from you, my lady, for an entire day.

> Das muoz alsô geschehen
> daz ich es niene mac,
> sol ich dich, frowe, mîden   eines tages lanc.
>
> (ll. 25–27)

Forced separation, if only for a day—the span of light/time that must necessarily sunder alba lovers—is excruciating. But alba lovers speak metaphorically. Like Tristan and Isolde, they articulate a feeling of symbiosis that they metaphorize as a merging of their individual boundaries. But when this feeling is experienced as entirely real, "we are no longer dealing with mature love but with a dangerous regression to the symbiotic phase. Because love revives emotions that once belonged to the symbiotic phase, it is often feared as endangering the boundary of the self" (Bergmann 1971, 32).

Modern psychological studies of early childhood have developed the concept of symbiosis between mother and child as an important dimension of healthy growth. Post-Freudian theorists, drawing on Freud's concept of primary narcissism, have come to understand the critical need of the infant for oneness with the mother, which is a necessary condition if an individual is to separate successfully, achieving individuation and a fully formed sense of self (Zweben-Howland 1993, 3). The capacity of an adult to form and sustain a mature love relationship depends on both the relationship with the parent of the opposite sex and on the complex network of interaction between the infant and his earliest caretaker. Margaret Mahler, who has made systematic and minute examinations of the mother-child interaction, uses the term symbiosis to describe "that state of undifferentiation, of fusion with the mother, in which the 'I' is not yet differentiated from the 'not-I' and in which inside and outside are only gradually coming to be sensed as different" (Mahler 1975, 45). The defining characteristic of symbiosis, according to Mahler, is the omnipotent delusion of fusion with the mother, more specifically, "the delusion of a common boundary between two physically separate individuals" (44, 45).[9]

Psychiatrist John Bowlby's landmark analysis of attachment, separation, and loss further explores the psychodynamics of affectional bonds and, like Mahler's, concentrates exclusively on the mother-child attachment. The emotion of love is regarded as a means of coping with mother-child separation: for theorists like Fromm and Reik, love is not only the striving to regain oneness with the mother, which Freud emphasized, but also a healthy means of coping with the necessary separation from her (Singer 1984, 5). In their 1987 study, Hazen and Shaver claim to be the first to explore the possibility that psychoanalytic theories on infant attachment offer "a valuable perspective on adult romantic love" (511). Because love is "in the service of refinding lost childhood bliss in favor of undoing the boundary that separates the self from the other," understanding the mother-child bond may tell us about the development of the adult human capacity to love (Bergmann 1987, 142).

Albas give the idea of attachment and merging some of its most gripping and evocative portrayals. Love's symbiosis is apparent in the alba lover's claim that his very existence depends upon his beloved's presence; separation leaves the lovers feeling incomplete and desolate. In "Us cavaliers si jazia," the lover's need for visual contact is so overwhelming that it threatens his life:

> Sweet one, if I did not see you,
> soon believe that I would die
> for my great desire would undo me;
> wherefore I shall soon be nigh,
> for without you what life have I?

> Doussa res, s'ieu no·us vezia,
> breumens crezatz que morria
> que·l grans dezirs m'auciria,
> per qu'ieu tost retornarai,
> que ses vos vida non ai. (ll. 41–45)

Desire has become so potent that it is externalized and autonomized, dominating all other aspects of being. The lover of "Est il jors?" similarly exclaims: "it would wound me to death/ if anyone should curtail the time so short" ("Bien m'avroit navreit a mort/ Ke si tost l'amoinroit ores" [ll. 3–4]).

Ironically, the "Us cavaliers" lover's focus on vision ("if I did not see you") indirectly evokes dawn's light, which, in this case, precipitates the disaster of separation rather than the togetherness for which the lover yearns. But perhaps the lovers see each other by their own rather than dawn's light(s); the shining limbs of Wolfram's lovers in "Den morgenblic" and the glimmering body of Heinrich von Morungen's lady give off a radiance of their own.

Symbiosis in the alba leads neither to the death Tristan and Isolde cannot avoid nor the damnation of which Dante warns. In albas, God is on the lovers' side. Despite the wrenching grief that separation brings, alba love allows for parting, and the lovers, presumably, escape undetected. Love's brevity sends them sorrowing back to their lonely former lives, but back they go.

First Light
Mask and Masquerade

> Thus love instructs honest minds to practice perfidy, though they
> ought not to know what goes to make a fraud of this sort.
> *(Gottfried von Strassburg,* Tristan, *205)*

Like other fictional characters, alba lovers have an identity in their fictive context that is socially determined. Specifically, the alba lady's social identity is dictated by her legal status as the wife of a lord and a member of the aristocracy, a role neither meager nor meaningless. The alba lady's lover is a knight; the references to him as cavalier or ritter indicate that he is a member of the "professional estate [of horse-mounted men] tied to actual exercise of the military arts and to official recognition by ritual dubbing" (Scaglione 1991, 18). His chivalric role enables the courtly audience to recognize him as one of their own (Saville 1972, 37–38). Both lovers have social roles regardless of whether reference is made to their social rank in any individual lyric.

The alba, unlike other lyric genres, is predicated upon the dilemma that the lover's social identity has come into conflict with his or her personal desire. When the lady's marital status, if not her social standing, prohibits union with the man her heart has chosen, a gap is created between her social role and personal needs. Although the alba domna and her cavalier live in a world of communal expectations dictated by social rank, those roles are ignored once the couple unites; by the time the alba comes to be sung, both the knight's and the lady's social functions are rendered irrelevant. Although vital to their social identities, the knight's role as warrior and the lady's as wife are immaterial to their love. But if identity in the communal world that characterizes courtly life is so deeply determined by social role, what identity is left for the illicit lovers?

Psychoanalyst Erik Erikson's theory of identity formation in adolescents provides a useful formulation for our understanding of the identity conflict in the alba. Adolescents experience a dual (individual and social) identity similar to that implicit in the alba characters' plight. In describing the parameters of identity, Erikson details a process "'located' *in the core of the individual* and yet also *in the core of his communal culture,* a process which establishes, in fact, the identity of those two identities" (1968, 22; emphasis in original). In other words, adolescents form their sense of self by synthesizing communal and personal identities. For fictive alba lovers, personal identity emerges as a result of their dissatisfaction with their social identity. Social role alone has become inadequate, unfulfilling, dishonest. But alba lovers, unlike Erikson's modern adolescents, cannot synthesize communal and individual identities; in their medieval world, the two are in conflict. The ensuing collision between individual and communal identity is manifest in the lyrics' imagery of dismemberment, analyzed in the conclusion of this book.

Dissatisfaction with their social identity causes the lovers to reassess themselves. Their poet sometimes presents them as feeling out of tune with the rhythms of normal life or nature, like the lady of "Den morgenblic":

> . . . she spoke: "Alas, dawn,
> the wild and tame rejoice in you,
> and gladly meet the morn, but for me alone. What shall I do?
> For now he may no longer stay here, mine,
> my friend: you hunt him with your shine!

> . . . sî sprach: "ôwê tac!
> Wilde und zam daz vrewet sich dîn
> und siht dich gérne, wán ich eine. wie sol iz mir ergên?
> nu enmac niht langer hie bî mir bestên
> min vriunt. den jaget von mir dîn schîn." (ll. 6–10)

Alba lovers feel alienated from the daytime world and its natural and social imperatives; they feel isolated, alone.

The lovers offer an unembarrassed portrait of subjective response that reveals their conflict with the world. Their opposition to social structures generates or coincides with their dawning self-consciousness. The marked difference that illicit lovers discern between themselves and others underscores their individuality. Albas that present the dramatic, unmediated speeches of their characters give the audience a glimpse into the lovers' inner lives. Despite the adultery—which alba lovers usually downplay or disregard—the audience is moved to compassion for the lovers in their dilemma; through their song, we identify with their heightened emotions.

The illicit nature of the relationship contributes to the intimacy between the lovers. They defy custom and law only if their love is overwhelming and irresistible, for the risks they take could cost their lives. Intimacy finds additional impetus in the lovers' united hostility toward the lady's jealous husband, and the required secrecy augments their dependence on one another, for they must trust each other only and utterly. Andreas Capellanus, in many ways a problematic source for understanding fin'amors, is consistent with its basic ideology when he warns: "The man who wants to keep his love affair for a long time untroubled should above all things be careful not to let it be known to any outsider, but should keep it hidden from everybody; because when a number of people begin to get wind of such an affair, it ceases to develop naturally and even loses what progress it has already made" (1990, 151). He later notes that love usually does not last long after it has been made public "but begins to fail just as soon as it is revealed" (1990, 153).[1]

Secrecy fosters the personal devotion that is an essential feature of the love relationship. The description of a much admired domna that concludes "En un vergier sotz fuella d'albespi" reveals that, although many regard the lady, none can discern the loyal but secret love concealed within her loveliness: "The lady is pleasant and pleasing/ for her beauty many regard her,/ and she holds her heart loyally on loving" ("La dompna es agradans e plazens,/ per sa beutat la gardon mantas gens,/ et a son cor en amar leyalmens" [ll. 21–23]). Surface composure may mask an emotional state perceptible only to the initiated (other fins amants) and sympathizers in the listening audience. Like Tristan and Isolde or Lancelot and Guenevere, the lovers show one face to the world, concealing their true feelings. When King Arthur's court reacts with utter amazement—"as if he had just dropped from the heavens"—at Lancelot's unexpected return after a two-year absence, Chrétien comments on Guenevere's predicament:

> And the queen: is she not there amid all this rejoicing?—Indeed she is, and right in the forefront. . . . Never before had she been so jubilant as she is now on his return.—Would she not have gone up to him?—Indeed she has: she is so close to him that the body virtually came within an ace of following her heart.—Where, then, is her heart?—It was kissing and making much of Lancelot.—Why,

then, was her body hiding? Why is her joy not complete? Is it, then, mingled with anger or hatred?—Certainly not in the least; but it is possible that the king or some of the others there, who have their eyes on everything, would have quickly become aware of the whole situation if she had been prepared to follow the promptings of her heart under the public gaze. And had Reason not rid her of this foolish thought and mad impulse, they would have seen just what her feelings were, and that would have been the height of folly. So Reason shuts away and shackles her foolish heart and rash thoughts and has to some extent brought her to her senses and postponed the outcome until he sees and spies out a favourable and more private occasion where they might fare better than they would at present. (Chrétien de Troyes 1987, 276–77)

Secret lovers live a lie; like dawn, they are Janus-faced. The lovers' need to mask evinces the alba poet's recognition that to be a lover in the communal world is an uncomfortable and dangerous, if compelling, proposition. Ironically, deceptive behavior toward the outside world is the only means by which illicit lovers can avoid a worse kind of self-betrayal. Gottfried von Strassburg remarks wryly about love's capacity to transform innocents into skillful dissemblers: "Thus love instructs honest minds to practice perfidy, though they ought not to know what goes to make a fraud of this sort" (von Strassburg 1967, 205).

In following their hearts rather than their obligations, alba lovers choose self over society. The opposition that they anticipate to their pursuit of personal fulfillment, however, leads to a split between inner emotion and social behavior. Masking the truth is required. Although the lover is torn over which impulse to follow, neither impulse can be completely fulfilling. As a result, the conflict between self and society does not remain solely on the periphery of the alba; it is recapitulated within the lovers themselves because the division they make between their emotional world and social duty leads to self-alienation.

The troubadours, by focusing on this phenomenon, shape into song a vision of love in the social world. When Freud much later characterized this phenomenon, he documented it not from literature (one of his customary sources) but from his own social milieu. He described the social life he knew as creating a "double morality" in which erotic love is disconnected from society. Such a society cannot attain to "love of truth, honesty, and humanity" except to a certain narrowly limited degree and must incline its members to concealment of the truth, false optimism, euphemism, self-deception, and the deception of others" (Freud, 1959, 182). Dissimulation and secrecy are practices necessary for maintaining this double morality. But as a result of internalizing the conflict, the lovers' sense of self is fractured.

Ferrante analyzes the fictions, prevarications, false oaths, and other subterfuges to which female characters in medieval literature often resort in their efforts to "exercise real power over their own or others' lives" (213). But such behavior, as she acknowledges, is not the preserve of female characters alone. There are admirable characters of both sexes who must resort to deception when they become entangled in illicit love affairs. Often such characters emerge as great romance heroes or heroines. Chrétien's Lancelot, like Tristan, dissembles and swears ambiguous oaths. In Béroul's *Tristan,* the lovers are advised to dissimulate when they return from their forest exile to life in the court; for, according to the hermit Ogrin, "to remove shame and cover up the wrong/ One must lie a little" ("Por honte oster et mal covrir/ Doit on un poi par bel mentir" [1962, ll. 2353–54]). Sargent-Baur notes: "Thus does the hermit Ogrin, with more policy than principle, counsel Tristan and Iseut—not that they greatly require such encouragement. To efface shame and conceal evil through the skillful lie, so that they may continue to enjoy their illicit *amours*, is a perennial concern of the lovers" (1984, 393–421). Isolde, too, manipulates her ordeal so that she can swear to a truth that her judges naively interpret one way, her more knowing lover another. Such behavior, the invariable concern of all alba lovers, reveals the chasm between the promptings of the heart and society's demands. This revelation leads to an exploration of the self in relation to the beloved, on the one hand, and to the rest of the world, on the other.

The alba's concern with individual feeling, self-expression, and personal choice coincides with the emergence of a sense of individuality in medieval culture between the eleventh and twelfth centuries.[2] This period saw "the flowering of the vernacular languages, the rise of romance, the emergence of the first universities, the sudden expansion of town life and the Church's growing commitment to the life of this world. It was a period marked not only by a general reawakening of intellectual activity, but particularly by an interest in the individual as he relates to himself, his God, and his world" (Georgiana 1981, 1).

As the idea of individuality became central to twelfth-century European society, a new consciousness of the self and recognition of the importance and distinctiveness of the individual as apart from the group emerged. Individual perceptions, a sense of individual reality, and an appreciation of the dignity and worth of individual people were developing (Cantor 1973, 203). An elaboration of the chivalric code in literature, paralleling the loyalty and courage encouraged in social conduct by nobility and government, focused on individual prowess and achievement in battle as well as courage and fidelity to an honorable code of conduct. The interest in the heroic individual likewise engendered an interest in his personal character and relationships.[3]

Courtly romance—with its complex of character formations, delicate use of irony, psychological realism, and examination of interpersonal relations—is, in Hanning's view, fertile terrain for the development of a vocabulary for individuality. Hanning focuses on the courtly romance as a form that provided a liberating ethic of personal fulfillment and offered authors an opportunity to meditate on the "implications of individuality . . . implications which twelfth-century theologians and philosophers were beginning to confront, but were not yet able, for lack of technical and conceptual vocabulary, fully to describe and categorize" (1977, 3).

Romance characters struggle to establish their identities in unconventional and personal ways. In the stories surrounding the most admired and beloved romance heroes, such as Tristan, Gawain, and Lancelot, a pattern emerges in which the hero must journey into the wilderness to prove himself or develop his potential. Despite the fact that the successful hero brings back a lesson or prize in which the whole community can share, romances demonstrate how difficult it is for personal needs to be met within the parameters of existing social convention (Zweben-Howland 1993, 1), a difficulty likewise inherent in the alba lovers' plight.

The emergence of vernacular lyric, a poetry of self-expression, is one of the period's most distinctive and important literary innovations (Morris 1973, 69). It also manifests a more introspective attitude. Personal self-expression became bound up in the idea of romantic love: "The Western concept of love (in its heterosexual and humanistic aspects) was—if not 'invented' or 'discovered'—at least developed in the twelfth century as never before" (Singer 1984, 35–36). The analysis of "the affections" and of the various stages of love were newly embarked upon. The interest in self-discovery was related to the new conviction that human relationships were of real value; furthermore, there was an inclination "to find in personal relationships the summit of human experience and source of good" (Morris 1973, 118, 158–59).

The interest in the individual led to an investigation of the self's capacity to experience intimacy with another. Some twelfth-century poets found the legend of Narcissus and the symbol of the mirror useful literary vehicles by which to reflect "the birth of self-consciousness through love" (Goldin 1967, 21–22). The idea of romantic love is linked to the attempt at self-understanding, for the beloved lady of the canso holds up a mirror in which the lover can see himself more clearly.

The alba's exploration of individuality reflects the era's impetus toward a new sense of self, as most vernacular lyrics do. But the genre focuses on issues of intimacy and identity that arise in no other genre, for the alba acts out the human struggle toward individuality, especially as we experience passionate love. Alba poets' insight that love transforms identity is reflected in the newly charged significance they give to the image of dawn. A dualistic image in which aspects of night and day, dark and light can be intertwined or extricated from one another, dawn stands as a visible representation of both the fusion and separation of alba lovers. Dawn and its metaphorical movement (from night to day) mime the actions and psychological experiences of alba lovers. At dawn, night and day are intertwined. Just as lovers in intimate embrace are unindividuated, so, too, night and day are undelineated at dawn. The love unit, though comprised of two sexes, is neither; it is a fusion of both—all-encompassing, androgynous, totalizing. But while dawn images the culmination of two into one, it also represents the fracturing of the union, as night—the time of love—begins to fade into day—the time of separation.

When not dismissing the dawn symbolism of the alba altogether, critics have simplified or trivialized its significance. Early critics attributed the poets' choice of dawn to the alba plot: secret lovers must part at dawn because day's light will otherwise expose them. Saville highlights and dismisses the importance of dawn simultaneously: "The dawn—or more properly, the sun—in the alba carries with it a number of functions and associations. It is, first of all, a great natural force" (1972, 56). Saville contrasts the alban dawn's symbolic function with Christian associations of light and dark in order to show how alba poets invert traditional Christian meanings (61, 88–90). W. T. H. Jackson, accepting the alba's setting as conventional, dismisses it without investigating its significance: "The alba, by definition, must be set at dawn and by convention it is set in a castle room or even on the battlements. These are not true temporal or spatial definitions. . . . The time and space are set in order to endow a definite situation with its own conventions. . . . As John [*sic*] Saville has shown, it is the contrast between the attributes associated in literature with light and darkness that are important, not the fact that events take place at dawn" (1980, 17). The night/dark and day/light symbolism of the alban dawn are undoubtedly significant, as Saville shows (1972, 61, 88–90). Classical and Christian symbols of night and day have obvious resonance for alba poets. But dawn itself—not just night and day—accrues new meanings in the poets' hands. Saville's view that the alba's dark/light contrast clashes with conventional Christian dichotomies, while accurate as far as it goes, ignores the symbol's most essential and intriguing aspects. The troubadours made the dawn symbol of the alba into a subtle, perceptive, and original exploration of the emotional and psychological dynamics of the romantic love they envisioned. That an entire genre was written around these dynamics make them of general literary interest for the first time.

These psychodynamics appear with a vengeance in the tagelieder of Wolfram von Eschenbach, who lavishes great attention on just how entwined alba lovers can be. In "Ez ist nu tac" he presents lovers so close they achieve new heights of intimacy:

So nobly together did these friends fit,
that never had two been so tightly knit,
   wherefore still now Love retains the renown.
      If three suns (instead of one) had been shining,
         even their light could never glance through such entwining.

Si hâten beide sich bewegen,
ez enwárt sô nâhen nie gelegen,
   des noch diu minne hât den prîs:
      ob der sunnen drî mit blicke waeren,
         sine möhten zwischen sî geliuhten. (ll. 29–33)

The magnified brilliance of Wolfram's poetically tripled suns discloses no visible space between the lovers. They are so inextricable that they appear physically attached—even under the scrutiny of the voyeuristic narrator who apparently is bent on making fine distinctions (and whose interest in such matters merits greater critical investigation than it has so far received). The lovers appear fused, as one; individual silhouettes cannot be discerned. Their intimate union eclipses the object—the one real sun—that will eventually sunder it. Ironically, the actual sun will be the immediate cause as well as the revealer of their disengagement.

In "Den morgenblic," Wolfram again focuses on the lovers' physical closeness. He tells us: "the lady pressed her lover fast to herself" and "her tears moistened both their cheeks" ("diu vríundîn den vriunt vast an sich dwanc./ ir ougen diu beguzzen/ ir beider wangel" [ll. 14–16]). As in the previous song, love's intimacy is impelled by leave taking. The narrator concludes with this extraordinary portrait, which, like the earlier one, invokes the poetic imagination:

> The sad man swiftly took his leave like this:
>   their smooth bright skins
>   came nearer, thus the day shone in.
>   crying eyes—a sweet woman's kiss!
>   thus they could then intertwine
>   their lips, their breasts, their arms, their white thighs.
>
> Der trûric man nam urloup balde alsus:
>   ir liehten vel, diu slehten,
>   kômen nâher, swie der tac erschein.
>   weindiu ougen—süezer vrouwen kus!
>   sus kunden sî dô vlehten
>   ir munde, ir bruste, ir arme, ir blankiu bein. (ll. 21–26)

In this portrait, at once vivid and full of motion, Wolfram conveys the frantic intensity, the restless tumult, the profusion and interpenetration of body parts, the complex and swift intertwinings. The lovers are moving so quickly that they seem disembodied, yet their embrace is so intimate that they appear as a single creature. As in "Ez ist nu tac," their fusion is so complete that body parts cannot be identified with either individual. They seem part of a greater being; as the lady previously describes it, they are one body with two beating hearts: "Two hearts and one body have we./ Utterly unbroken will our troth with one another be" ("Zwei herze und ein lîp hân wir./ gar ungescheiden unser triuwe mit ein ander vert" [ll. 17–18]). The lady depicts herself and her lover as two halves of the one being that makes each of them whole: the lovers have become a couple. They are incomplete, unfulfilled, without each other.

Love in the alba generates a sense of self in which the lover feels bound to the beloved—a self-definition that now incorporates the other as part of the self. Union seems to obliterate the boundaries of the self altogether. Freud's characterization of love's power to erode, confuse, or eviscerate personal boundaries describes in more prosaic terms the same phenomenon the alba captures: "At the height of being in love the boundary between ego and object threatens to melt away. Against all evidence of his sense, a man who is in love declares that 'I' and 'you' are one, and is prepared to behave as if it were a fact" (1961, 13). The idea of the fusion of night and day implicit in the symbol of dawn not only reinforces the idea of the lovers' fusion but also crystallizes the point of convergence, providing a temporal locus wherein a myriad of potential actions can be momentarily scrutinized—held up, so to speak, to the dawning light.

Alba poets obsessively depict the physical closeness between the lovers, references that are especially striking in view of the fact that albas are so nondescriptive, their settings so generalized and often vague. Narrators (whether an objective narrator, the watchman, or one of the lovers) stress the lovers' newfound intimacy as physical attachment. The portrait of lady and her lover laterally conjoined that opens "En un vergier sotz fuella d'albespi" sets generic expectations: "the lady holds her lover at her side" ("tenc la dompna son amic costa si"). The lady of "Cant voi l'aube dou jor venir" laments that she misses the presence "at my side" ("encoste mi") of her lover's body. The "breast-to-breast" embrace referred to in the tageliet echoes the Romance poets' use of the word "costa," which etymologically means "rib." These references to specific body parts emphasize the physicality, corporeality, and intimacy of the attachment. Because these body parts are already doubled (that is, an individual has two breasts, a ribcage two symmetrical halves), the poet magnifies not only how the lovers mirror each other but also how fused they are. Attachment is so essential a component that it becomes a motif in itself.

If, as Duby observes, "it is almost a commonplace to say that the couple as we know it was invented in twelfth-century France," that concept derives much of its refinement from the alba (1987, 144). While Wolfram surpasses his rivals in his brave and blunt exposure of specific intimacies of love, all albas share an interest in this subject. Modern psychoanalytic research has articulated the couple dynamic in its more scientific manner. Psychologist Van der Waals notes that couples manage to modify their respective narcissistic needs so that they become compatible with the relationship: "the couple itself in time becomes a narcissistic unit" (quoted in Bergmann 1987, 246). This narcissistic unit is all the more poignantly memorialized in the alba because its life span is only as long as night. When the watchman of "S'anc fui belha ni prezada" remarks, "I am well pleased by the long dark blackness/ of wintertime, when night lasts longest" ("Be·m plai longua nueg escura/ el temps d'ivern, on plus dura" [ll. 28–29]), he shows his compassion for the lovers. His understanding is further manifest in his conclusion to the poem: "Never have I seen a joyful/ lover pleased at dawn" ("Anc no vi jauzen/ drut que·l plagues l'alba" [ll. 46–47]). Reentry into the daylight world of social realities extinguishes the perfect union that alba lovers wring, however briefly, from time.

Janus-Faced Dawn and the Dualisms of Love: Pivot and Potentiality

> His claws through the clouds he draws,
> with great might aloft he soars,
> I see him growing silver-grey,
> as if about to dawn
> —the Day!
> *Wolfram von Eschenbach, "Sîne klâwen"*

Events occur at dawn in the alba because dawn itself is a loaded symbol. It symbolizes a time of utopian stasis in which night and day are held in balance while it simultaneously signals light, the future, and movement. Although night and day cannot be individuated from one another at dawn, day will gradually break free of night. The Elizabethan dramatist Arthur Broke expresses this succinctly in his *Romeus*, a predecessor of Shakespeare's *Romeo and Juliet*. He graphically portrays Romeus's view of this particular cosmic moment/movement: "As yet he saw no day, ne could he call it night,/ With equall force decreasing darke fought with increasing light" (ll. 1713–14). Despite the "equall force" of night and day, the outcome of the struggle is presaged by the words "decreasing darke" and "increasing light." Night and day, like the secret lovers, must unravel "in time."

Dawn is the threshold that reveals the ragged end of darkness, the first tint of light in the night sky. In Ovid's *Metamorphoses*, Aurora is the gatekeeper who upholds the double portals of night and day, delineating night's terminus from day's advent ("quod teneat lucis, teneat confinia noctis" [VII, 706]). The portal she upholds, like the gate that Chaucer's narrator in *Parlement of Foulys* describes (and through which he is subsequently pushed by Africanus), spans two realms. Through Aurora's gateway night flows into day. The dawn threshold pinpoints the temporal juncture at which night and day are equal in strength. Dawn literally marks time, apportioning it into its two component parts. As a gatekeeper, Aurora represents the border, a permanent gate, a static marker. The dawn-song obeys the lovers' demand for stasis because it actually presents a moment of stasis—a tableau wherein all potential conflicts are held at bay. It offers a paradoxical moment of timelessness. Pierre Bec and Sarah Spence comment on dawn's timelessness; but in viewing the alba's unresolved dramatic tension as "timeless like the ambivalent dawn itself" (1984, 118), Spence associates timelessness with an ambivalence we do not find in the alba. Ambivalence or irresolution plays little part. Just as each dawn resolves itself ineluctably into day, the lovers necessarily resolve to separate despite their reluctance.

Because of the lovers' desire for stasis, the alba captures the pivotal moment in a process of transition. It encompasses so many possibilities that it generates an aesthetic of potentiality. The alba freezes an inherently untenable situation; it pinions the surcharged moment at its greatest intensity. The poet allows the lovers and their audience to experience headlong the conflict of two incommensurables: desire and necessity. The song extends the fleeting moment. The act of articulating the song consumes a span of time, transforming the finite, climactic instant into an entire lyric—one that not only consumes time in its recitation but may also be repeated, prolonging that instant into the future. The refrain serves this purpose of repetition within the lyric, and the verse's musical rhythm gives the poem a time all its own.

In signaling simultaneously both union and separation, dawn becomes a viable symbol for the plight of illicit lovers, who, in order to continue their relationship over time, must disrupt its continuity. A bidirectional movement occurs in the poems: verbally, the lovers move toward parting; physically, as the passages from Wolfram's tagelieder show, they often draw closer together in a renewal of their intimacy.

Wolfram's tagelieder exemplify this phenomenon in an explicitly sexual way. Ironically, for all his intense focus on parting, his poems evoke sexual intimacy more graphically than any others in the genre. The concluding strophe of "Den morgenblic" leaves us with the image of the intimacy impelled by leave taking:

The sad man swiftly took his leave like this:
   their smooth bright skins
      came nearer, thus the day shone in.

crying eyes—a sweet woman's kiss!
  thus they could then intertwine
    their lips, their breasts, their arms, their white thighs.
      Whichever painter were to portray it
        companionably as they lay, that would indeed have
          been enough.
        Although their love bore them many sorrows,
      They cultivated love without any hate.

Der trûric man nam urloup balde alsus:
  ir liehten vel, diu slehten
    kômen nâher, swie der tac erschein.
weindiu ougen—süezer vrouwen kus!
  sus kunden sî dô vlehten
    ir munde, ir bruste, ir arme, ir blankiu bein.
      Swelch schiltaer entwurfe daz,
        geselleclîche als si lâgen, des waere ouch dem genouc.
        ir beider liebe doch vil sorgen trouc,
      si pflâgen minne ân allen haz. (ll. 21–30)

The final strophe of "Ez ist nu tac" likewise describes the effect that the thought of parting has on intimacy: "He took his leave so that it was fitting; now mark how:/ A game went along with the lament ("urlop er nam, daz dâ wol zam; nu merket wie:/ dâ ergíe ein schimpf bî klage" [ll. 29–30]). In "Sîne klâwen," too, day's imminence inspires a sexual leave-taking in the concluding lines:

  her little breast to his she pressed.
    The knight did not forget prowess
      though the watchman wanted to forestall this:
    leave-taking near and even nearer
      with kiss and other things gave them love's reward.

  ir brüstlîn an brust si dwanc.
    Der rîter ellens niht vergaz;
      des wold in wenden wahtaers dôn:
    urloup nâh und nâher baz
      mit kusse und anders gap in minne lôn. (ll. 46–50)

The thought of parting becomes the impetus for further intimacy in "Von der zinnen" and serves, as in all of Wolfram's lyrics, to conclude the poem:

> "Sadness never marred
>   so utterly one man's
>   new-found joy."
>   However, soon it dawned;
>   the dauntless knight
>   won from her those delights
>   that put their cares to flight.
>   close caress,
>   intimate embrace
>   their breasts press
>   and even more besides
>   gave farewell, of which the worth was high.

> "allen mannen
>   trûren nie sô gar zerstôrte
>   ir vröiden vunt."
>   Swie balde es tagete,
>   der unverzagete
>   an ir bejagete,
>   daz sorge in vlôch.
>   unvrömedez rucken,
>   gar heinlîch smucken,
>   ir brüstel drucken
>   und mê dannoch
>   urloup gap, des prîs was hôch. (ll. 34–45)

Lines 34 to 35, nicely translated by Richey—"However swift the dawn, the dauntless man took such award from her as put their cares to flight" (1969, 94)—again evoke the knight's martial valor.

For Wolfram, the lovers' "fears and griefs at parting are themselves the strongest possible erotic incentives; the farewells become high moments of sexual passion" (Dronke 1977, 179). Wolfram correlates the lovers' fears of discovery, their sorrows, with their reawakened desire, "a sensuality born out of the danger itself" (Dronke 1977, 179), and their courage. The approaching separation forces the lovers' recognition of the swift passage of time, compelling them to renew intimacy and joy: "It is the very fact of being imbedded in reality, time and danger that makes the pleasure so poignant and so intense" (Saville 1972, 210). This portrayal invites the audience's compassionate view of the lovers; we are drawn in by their desperate desire and inspired by their heroism.

Wolfram's tagelieder consistently take up two themes: the singularity—in the physical sense as well as its literary originality—of the lovers' closeness and the parting that sparks a renewal of their intimacy. His obsession with the lovers' courage is partially explained by his inclination for displaying the martial aspect of knighthood whether he is writing narrative or love lyric. In love poems, the knight's valor is manifest in his dauntless prolongation of love's farewell while the danger quickens: "Not since Kurenberg's lover called for his horse and armour, had the martial note in the Minnesang been thus decisively sounded. . . . Here knightly valour and knightly honour are objective realities; and this secret nocturnal love is an adventure of the chivalrous life involving both" (Richey 1969, 94). Wolfram's use of the word "ellens" ("battle prowess") in characterizing the knight's love making in "Sîne klâwen" evokes knightly prowess in a way that can be interpreted as either serious or parodic. In "Ez ist nu tac," on the other hand, the martial note sounded in the lover's plea to his lady that her virtue "shield" him is doubtlessly sincere: "May your womanly goodness behold me/ and be my shield coming and going/ today and always" ("dîn wîplîch güete neme mîn war/ und sî mî schílt híute hin und her noch zallen zîten" [ll. 35–36]). The lady's acting as a shield has a literal reference as well; wearing her colors—her handkerchief or sleeve—into battle serves as protection for her knight. This martial reference takes further shape in Wolfram's great narrative *Parzival*:

When the lover [of the tageliet] declares that the lady's goodness will be his shield to-day and at all times, we hear the forecast of Parzival's thought about Condwiramurs and of his advice to Gawan: "Friend, in thy hour of conflict, let a woman maintain the fight for thee, may she guide thy hand, one in whom thou hast found purity and womanly kindness."

> ['Friunt, an dînes kampfes zît
> dâ nem ein wîp für dich den strît:
> diu müeze ziehen dîne hant,
> an der dû kiusche hâst bekant
> unt wîplîche güete. . . .' *Parzival*, 332.9–13]
>
> (Richey 1969, 94)

With all this energy and exertion, Wolfram's tagelieder, unlike most Romance albas, are far from static: he complements the narratological and dialogic dimensions with visible action and flux. Even though the context is parting, the physical activity of the tagelieder creates togetherness rather than separation. Just as the thought of separation engenders the desire for closeness, so, too, does intimacy impel separation, dynamics that metaphorically reenact the sexual act. The resulting balance, an alternation between separation and union, prevents either from becoming permanent.

Consistent with his graphic evocation of sexuality, Wolfram's references to game and play are more obviously euphemisms for sexual activity than are such references in his Old Provençal models. In "Ez ist nu tac," the game that occurs during leave taking is explicitly sexual:

> A game went along with the lament.
>   They had both agreed so between them
>   that there was never such a close lying together
>   of which now yet Love has the renown.
>
> dâ ergíe ein schimpf bî klage.
>   Si hâten beide sich bewegen,
>   ez enwárt sô nâhen nie gelegen,
>   des noch diu minne hât den prîs. (ll. 28–31)

The more generalized joy, laughter, and play that abound in the Old Provençal and Old French versions are absent. Pleasure and its deprivation form the center of Wolfram's lovers' laments. But his poems, like all the others in the genre, do not take us beyond these intimacies to portray the actual leave taking.

With its bidirectional movements, the alba is symbolically concerned with transition. The passage from satisfaction to desire, from possibility to necessity exemplified in the alba also represents the passing from innocence to wisdom that, for Augustine, is vital to the process of human growth: "Thus, no mortal may become wise unless he passes from foolishness to wisdom. If the passage itself is foolishly made, it is not well done—but this sounds like senseless talk, for if the transition is wisely made, then the man was already wise before he passed from folly to wisdom. This is no less absurd. From this we can understand that there is an intermediate state which we cannot call by either name. Thus when the first man passed from the citadel of wisdom to folly, the passage itself was neither wise nor foolish. This is similar to sleeping and waking. Sleeping is not the same as going to sleep, and waking is not the same as being fully awake. There is a passage from one to the other" (*On the Free Choice of Will*, 145). One cannot attain wisdom without passing through the medial stage described as akin to waking but prior to complete awareness—a stage, in effect, of dawning.

Most albas conclude before the characters arrive at the maturity and wisdom implied by the idea of being fully awake, but the anguish they express does indeed lead to a sobering new knowledge. The lady of Walther's "Friuntlîchen lac" reveals her newly acquired wisdom: "This thing they call Love is nothing but pain and longing" ("daz si dâ heizent minne, deis niewan senede leit" [l. 8]). But for the most part, it is only where the narrative continues after the alba leaves off, as in Chaucer's *Troilus*, that we can view the lovers on their way to a new and broader, if more tragic, comprehension of the human condition. Kaske's astute observation highlights this comprehension: "In the courtly aube the curtain falls discreetly on the lovers' departure, preserving around it an air of ardor undiminished and heroism somberly undaunted in the face of the undescribed separation and hardships ahead. At the close of the alba in *Troilus and Criseyde* it is as though the curtain had momentarily stuck, affording a glimpse of a world in which flesh and spirit have, alas, their limitations" (1961, 175). Because it is embedded in narrative, the alba set piece in *Troilus* depicts life after dawn. Once the lovers part, we follow a grieving Troilus home:

> So harde hym wrong of sharp desire the peyne
> *f*orto ben eft there he was in plesaunce,
> That it may neuere out of his remembraunce.
>
> Retorned to his real paleys soone,
> He softe in-to his bed gan forto slynke,
> To slepe longe, as he was wont to doone;
> But al for nought—he may wel ligge and wynke,
> But slep ne may ther in his herte synke,
> Thynkyng how she, for whom desir hym brende
> A thousand fold was worth more than he wende.
> (III, 1531-37)

Although Chaucer here paints a joyful picture of flowering love, he portrays the lovers' journeys toward maturity and wisdom as long and painful.

The alba is a genre of potentiality on the threshold of change. Georges Poulet's summary of the medieval attitude toward the passage of time evokes the broad dualisms inherent in medieval life: "The Christian of the Middle Ages felt essentially then, that he was a man who endured. Nevertheless, within him and around him, he was unable to keep from seeing change. If he felt sure of his own permanence he was at the same time constrained to notice a profound lack of permanence. Paradoxically, he felt himself to be a permanent being and a transient being, a being who never changed and a being who always changed. . . . To change was to pass from potentiality to actuality" (1952, 4). This change from potentiality to actuality is implicit in the dawn symbolism of the alba.

Cruel Dawn

> And lovers were being tormented by that hour
> That by custom calls them to tears.
> Petrarch, "Già fiammeggiava l'amorosa stella"

> Hold back thy hours dark night, till we have done,
> The day will come too soon;
> Young Maids will curse thee if thou steal'st away,
> And leav'st their blushes open to the day.
> Beaumont and Fletcher, The Maid's Tragedy

Before the commitment the lovers must make to any contingency, they are free to contemplate a number of potential actions. The lovers of "Reis glorios, verais lums e clardatz" are out of view, seeming to ignore their plight altogether; it is the watchman's anxiety for them that we share. But the alba depicts that precise moment when action becomes imperative and potentiality lost to reality and then history. Once a decision is made, consequences will follow. Reality will swiftly replace desire.

Ovid's differing representations of Aurora conveniently illustrate dawn's dual aspects in the alba. In *Metamorphoses*, as I noted earlier in this chapter, she is the "keeper of the gates/ between the light and night," a static threshold marker separating night from day (238, l. 706). In *Amores* I.13, however, a poem predicated upon the lover's complaint that Aurora moves too swiftly, Dawn is a goddess of mobility, the flux of time itself: "Now over the ocean from her aged consort comes/ the golden one, who bears the day on her frosty axle./ Whither speed you, Aurora? Stay! ("Iam super oceanum venit, seniore marito,/ flava pruinoso quae vehit axe diem./ quo properas, Aurora? mane!" [1–3]). Like Ovid's Aurora, the alban dawn symbolizes both a threshold point—night and day, time, held in balance—but also light, the future, and separation. Realizing that day will gradually ascend, that decreasing dark cannot withstand encroaching light, prompts the lovers to use their time all the more fully. Cavalier poets such as Robert Herrick and Andrew Marvell later urged their coy mistresses to "make much of time." Marvell's persuasive poem concludes by focusing not on the prolonging of night but on a consuming of their days in pleasure: "Thus, though we cannot make our Sun/ Stand still, yet we will make him run" ("Coy Mistress," 45–46). Because it is futile to oppose cosmic movement, lovers should come together quickly. But the alba lover, like Aurora reluctant to part with her lover Cephalus, as envisioned by Ovid in *Amores* I.13, implores not the sun but the night to stand still: "slowly run, O steeds of night!" ("lente currite, Noctis equi!").

The brief time granted to alba lovers makes it all the more precious, a sentiment captured succinctly by Ovid's Leander in a letter to Hero: "the briefer the space given us for furtive love,/ the greater our care lest that space be idle" ("quo brevius spatium nobis ad furta dabatur,/ hoc magis est cautum, ne foret illud iners" [*Heroides,* 18:109–10]). The erotic aspect of the temporality of love is addressed most explicitly in Wolfram's tagelieder, as we have seen, but all albas incorporate this theme. The sentiment can be found outside the genre as well, most often in poems involving illicit love. Because the future is unpredictable and their next meeting may be far off, if it occurs at all, the lovers make the best of their meager allotment of time, determined to enjoy the fruits of love until the last possible moment. The lady of "En un vergier sotz fuella d'albespi" addresses a series of invitations to her lover in order of escalating intimacy. The carpe diem theme established, the lady beckons him to her "despite" her husband and "until the watchman plays his shawm": "Tot o fassam en despieg del gilos. . . . /Tro la gaita toque son caramel" (ll. 11, 15). The brevity of love, while it causes great anguish to the pair, further sparks their ardor.

The onslaught of day is a threat to the lovers' pleasure and fulfillment. Filtered through the light of day that spurs public life, their private world appears untenable. The gap between "the everyday world and the world of love" that, for Nichols, is a hallmark of the courtly lyric (1968, 350) is nowhere more explicit than in the alba; it clearly "dawns" on the audience as well as the lovers. The lovers must leave the secluded and joyous world of love to reenter the real, raptureless, public world. Ecstasy flees and, as in tales involving otherworldly nocturnal figures (vampires, ghosts, banshees), vanishes in day's light. When day breaks for the lovers of Heinrich von Morungen's "Owê, sol aber mir iemer mê," it is startling because it is somehow unexpected. Indeed, Heinrich's tageliet, like most dawn-songs, never takes us beyond the refrain "dô tagte ez" ("then it dawned"). Like the lovers, the audience is left reeling by the sudden dispersal of the marvelous, dreamlike encounter.

The motif of day scattering visions is made familiar in diverse forms, from Milton's devout and solemn sonnet, "I dreamed I saw my late espousèd saint" where the narrator laments, "I waked, she fled, and day brought back my night," to Bram Stoker's ever-popular horror story, *Dracula*. These creatures of the night are, in a sense, companions of alba lovers, who have few compatriots: "A common variation of the dawn-parting poem is to be found in the situation in which the dawn dispels merely the *dream* of enjoyment, not the reality. This is a minor literary genre in its own right, and depends upon two poems which came down from antiquity under the name of *Anacrean*. The poet dreams of being made happy by his beloved, but awakes (and tries to dream again)" (Hatto 1965, 527).

Walther von der Vogelweide cleverly plays on the alba situation and the typical dawn-scattering-joy motif in his lyric (not a tageliet), "Nemt, frowe, disen kranz," in which the narrator recalls his diurnal tryst with a beautiful girl. As the poem proceeds, it begins to dawn on us that he is recalling not an actual past event but a wonderful dream set during day. At the end of the lyric, in a phrase recalling Heinrich's refrain, "dô tagte ez," the narrator says, "day broke and I had to wake up" ("dô taget ez und muos ich wachen"), revealing that this idyllic wonder had really occurred at night in a dream.[4] For Walther, this beautiful, natural kind of love can occur only in a dream, as Goldin explains: "As things turn out, it was nowhere but in his sleep that Walther found this willing and perfect girl, and when he wakes he has to go round and round looking for her. He does not have much chance of finding her. His green girl is a wonderful dream: pure pleasure unadulterated by conscience; but she must remain a dream forever, the goal of an unfulfillable longing, like the brilliant lady of the minnesingers" (*German Lyrics* 99).

But alba lovers' disillusionment differs from those of dreamers. Although in retrospect their tryst may seem too wonderful to have been true, they have not dreamed or imagined their love affair: the idyllic love relationship is the more miraculous because it is real and shared. This "real" love is, of course, a poetic fabrication whose realism resides solely in the vividness and sensitivity of the portrayal, its truth to human feeling. Despite its brevity and danger, the nocturnal love experience is so wonderfully real that no dream could be its equal.

Instead of moving from "insubstantial dreams" to the greater reality of dawn, as Prudentius's dawn-hymn "Ales diei nuntius" exhorts us, alba lovers move from the substantial presence of the beloved to an empty, daytime solitude in which they are left with only vestiges: memories, promises, or other signs of the lover's actuality once he or she has gone. Without such tokens, alba love may come to seem an insubstantial dream in the light of day, especially to the listening audience whose envisioning of the scene is, after all, a function of sympathetic imagining.

Realistically, the dawn surprises no one in the sense that a spy or jealous spouse might. Yet alba lovers are incapable of viewing the cosmic cycle in which the coming dawn is merely a component of a gradual, daily, and predictable process. The particular dawn about which the alba revolves is perceived differently from all previous dawns—predictable, uneventful, and insignificant as those were. To the alba couple, as to Donne's awakened lover in "The Good-Morrow" (but to different effect), no prior dawn has ever been experienced in the same way. Within the context of alba love, this dawn is utterly new and dreadful; and its appearance is swift and sudden.

The lovers avoid recognizing dawn's imminence, trying to elude it by shutting themselves off from all signs of it. Hence, they belatedly bemoan its now fleet approach. The plaintive alba refrain expresses all lovers' dread: "Oh God, oh God, the dawn! How quickly it comes!" ("Oy Dieus, oy Dieus, de l'alba!/ Tan tost ve!" ["En un vergier sotz fuella d'albespi"]).

These emotions accord with what psychologists have learned about people in love: "In a state of love, real time gives way to psychological time which always converts bliss into less than an hour" (Bergmann 1987, 108). Thus, our lovers complain about how suddenly day comes: "It would well wound me to death/ If anyone has brought the time so soon" ("Bien m'avroit navreit a mort/ Ke si tost l'amoinroit ores" ["Est it jors?" ll. 3–4]). This lady also accuses the watchman: "you hasten [dawn] too much" ("vos lou hasteis trop" [l. 2]). In "Ab la gensor que sia," the sentiment is picked up in the lover's accusation to the watchman: "you hasten the day" ("cochas lo dia" [l. 21]). The lady of "Entre moi et mon amin" tells us: "How glad we should have been had that night lasted one hundred"; while the lady of "Ez ist nu tac" also expresses the anguish instilled by dawn's sudden imminence: "Should he separate from me now/ my lover, this sorrow is mine too early" ("Sol er von mir scheiden nuo,/ mîn vriunt, diu sorge ist mir ze vruo" [ll. 5–6]). Her lover similarly bewails: "I never yet knew so sad and sudden a separation./ Night hastens from us all too soon—/ Who measured it so short?" ("jôn erkande ich nie/ kein trûric scheiden alsô snel,/ und ist diu naht von hinnen alze balde./ wer hât sî sô kurz gemezzen? [ll. 18–21]). The narrator of "Von der zinnen" tells us "soon it dawned" ("swie balde ez tagete"), and the watchman of "Reis glorios, verais lums e clardatz" reiterates as regularly as the tolling of a bell "and soon it will be dawn" ("Et ades sera l'alba") in his refrain. Walther's lady makes an interesting variation on this theme in "Friuntlîchen lac," asking her lover, "whither do you go so soon?" ("war gâhest alsô balde?"), as if not only dawn and the watchman but even her lover conspire against her.

In the tageliet, dawn begins to assume the symbolic characteristics of the gilos—a character whose absence from the tageliet is striking. In his absence, the dawn itself comes to represent the lovers' fear of retribution. Sometimes it is perceived by the lovers as spying enviously, voyeuristically peering in at them, miming the role of the jealous husband in the eyes of the guilty couple. Thus, dawn in "Sîne klâwen" menacingly "glances . . . through the glass" ("blinken . . . tet durch diu glas") at the poem's conclusion. In the celebrated opening image from the same poem, dawn is seen not only as natural but animalistic, predatory, or even superhuman. Likened to the talons of a mighty falcon or eagle in the act of clawing through and piercing the cloud or veil of night, dawn swiftly, spectacularly ascends:

> His claws
> through the sky he draws,
> with great might aloft he soars;
> I see him growing gray,
> about to dawn:
> —the day!
>
> Sîne klâwen
> durch die wolken sint geslagen,
> er stîget ûf mit grôzer kraft;
> ich sich in grâwen

tagelîch, als er wil tagen:
den tac. (ll. 1–6)

This unparalleled personification of dawn as a bird of prey has generated critical admiration as well as explanation: in Dronke's view, the image dawns gradually, evoking the movement from numb apprehension to conscious fear in the lady's thoughts: "at first, for two lines, it is nothing but a cruel, monstrous animal of menacing strength—only in the third line does it grow 'day-like,' only in the fourth does it explicitly become day itself" (1977, 179). For Saville, this mysterious opening emphasizes dawn's great and violent natural power as it breaks through. He identifies the rising sun with the eagle rather than with a demon, as earlier critics had: "From the notion of the eagle mounting aloft to gaze on the sun with naked eye Wolfram has proceeded to a metaphorical identification of the eagle with the rising sun itself. The eagle's ferocity and his conventional associations with royalty are poetically transferred to the impression Wolfram wishes to give us of the dawn" (1972, 57–58).

Wolfram's portrayal, however, goes beyond the human side of the story, presenting not merely a powerful animal but one with superhuman features: day is "lordly, untarrying, relentless" in its approach, a "superhuman presence, irresistible and fateful, forerunner and champion of the hostile human forces which are not named" (Richey 1969, 91, 93). The opening lines are so rich, vivid, and allusive that they evoke a sense of disembodied vengeance; demon, eagle, superhuman day are all rolled into one avenging but unnamed force, the gilos. Rather than being scorned or mocked, this gilos is the embodiment of power. Like a dangerous weapon, dawn is sharp, cutting, penetrating; it is retribution "personified." Its violative force is reiterated when dawn rises aloft "mit grozer kraft," its sharp talons and darting glances severing the lovers' union.

Dawn blasts through the clouds in Wolfram's "Von der zinnen": "through the sky breaks/ the dawn's gleam ("durch wolken dringet/ tagender glast" [ll. 28–29]). It is equally mighty as it presses through the window in "Den morgenblic": "The day with power all through the window pressed./ Many locks they locked:/ That helped not: because of which they sorrowed" ("Der tac mit kraft al durch diu venster dranc./ vil slôze sî besluzzen./ daz half niht; des wart in sorge kunt" [ll. 11–13]). The dawn is cursed by Wolfram's lovers in "Ez ist nu tac": "cursed was the day" ("gevlouchet wart dem tage"). In Walther's "Friuntlîchen lac," the lady threatens dawn: "Woe betide you, dawn/ since you do not let me lie/

longer by my love" ("Wê geschehe dir tac,/ daz dû mich lâst bî liebe/ langer bliben nieht" [ll. 6–8]).

Of all alba characters, however, none personifies day more violently than Chaucer's Troilus. To him, day's light forcibly exposes the shrouded sacraments of love, invading not solely through windows (as in "Den morgenblic" or "Reis glorios") but through every cranny and crevice:

> O cruel day, accusour of the joie
> That nyght and love han stole and faste iwryen,
> Acorsed by thi comyng into Troye,
> For every bore hath oon of thi bryghte yen!
> Envyous day, what list the so to spien?
> What hastow lost, why sekestow this place,
> Ther god thi light so quenche for his grace?
>
> (III, 1450–56)

The dawn, personified as a marauding malevolence, measures the depth of the lovers' passion and their courage in cursing or fighting it. Such vivid depiction adds dramatic force to the lyric.

The more conscious the lover is of restricted time, the more quickly it seems to be passing. Dawn is a naturally gradual process of illumination, a literal enlightenment apparent in our metaphorical use of the word to describe our incipient glimmer of understanding when something dawns on us. But despite the lovers' attempts to escape time, they are, like all forms of life, completely subject to it. The necessity for definite departures and secrecy renders them all the more mastered by time. No matter how stridently they fulminate against it, they are caught in time's web. And just as dawn resolves itself ineluctably into day, alba lovers reluctantly yet necessarily resolve to separate.

The Dawn Descends: The Refrain

The refrain returns us again and again to the same starting or ending point, implying that on some level these are identical. The refrain establishes a cyclical pattern, a haunting echo that lingers long after everything else has faded from memory. Often found in female-voiced lyrics, the refrain, with its association with communal singing, harks back to an earlier society "in which the group had precedence over the individual self" (Earnshaw 1988, 135). In the alba, the refrain synthesizes the individual lover's expression with a more generalized or communal experience of lovers or sympathizers. Reintroducing communal sympathy, the refrain can reconnect the separating lovers to the world.

No matter how the lovers resist acknowledging day in the body of their songs, the refrain continually intrudes to measure time. If darkness abrogates the lovers' sense of time, the hours can still be sounded through the watchman's refrain-like cries. Like the regular tolling of a bell or the watchman's calling of the hour, the alba refrain functions—both in content and in form—as a reminder of time's passing.

Despite its cyclical and predictable nature, the refrain is also a fragmenting device, literally a rebreaking ("refrangere").[5] It fragments the alba lady's recollection of her rendezvous in "En un vergier sotz fuella d'albespi," reminding her of dawn's interruption of that meeting: "Oh God, oh God, the dawn! How quickly it comes!" ("Oy Dieus, oy Dieus, de l'alba!/ Tan tost ve!"). The watchman's refrain call in "Us cavaliers si jazia" interrupts not a recollection but the actual meeting:

> Ah!
> For I hear the watchman cry:
>   "Away!
> Rise! for I see day come
>   After dawn."
>
> Ai!
> Qu'ieu aug que li gaita cria:
>   "Via!
> Sus! qu'ieu vey lo jorn venir
>   Apres l'alba." (ll. 6–10)

Likewise, the refrain of "Reis glorios, verais lums e clardatz"—"and soon it will be dawn" ("et ades sera l'alba")—reminds the watchman-narrator as well as the audience of dawn's real imminence. The single-strophe lyric "Quan lo rossinhols escria" concludes with the refrain-like warning generalized to all lovers: "Lovers, rise!/ for I see the dawn and the clear day!" ("drutz, al levar!/ Qu'ieu vey l'alba e·l jorn clar!").

The lovers' obsession with the passage of time is manifest in the refrain. Through the insistent reiteration of the refrain, the structure of the poem conveys not only the fact that time moves swiftly but also that it gathers momentum as it hurtles forward. Consequently, the refrain generates the sensation of time's inexorable acceleration.

Paradoxically, the refrain, like dawn itself, signifies time's cyclical nature and its curtailment of present joys, implying both permanence and ending. What is established in the refrain is not the love relationship per se but its transience. Dawn's swift approach is continually signaled so that no matter how often the lovers manage to meet or shut out the light, during every one of those meetings, the natural cycle will regularly intrude: "the dawn, the dawn, yes the dawn!" ("l'alba,/ l'alba, oi l'alba!" ["Gaita be"]). No matter how fiercely the lovers attempt to ignore the destructive consequences of dawn, the refrain relentlessly intrudes: "then it dawned" ("dô tagte ez" ["Owê, sol aber mir iemer mê"]).

The refrain accrues significance with each repetition so that by the final strophe, the annunciation of dawn takes on additional, sometimes menacing, implications. One night of love has come to a close. There is a subtle warning, however, implicit in each recitation of the refrain—that love itself, for all its joys, must also have its ending. While the dawn initially signifies a literal dawning of day, by the conclusion of the alba, it foreshadows a more final parting. Alba love fuses a union between two separate bodies, but that union is not everlasting.

The song itself bridges the gap between union and separation. Like the refrain, the watchman's or bird's song calls the lovers back to reality. Such songs, true reveillés, rouse the couple in the poem from the realm of love. Yet the lyric, as the lovers participate in it, also serves to perpetuate the union. The secret, private love is given a public monument through the song, which becomes both its celebration and extension. The pleasure as well as the sorrow of the timebound tryst is transformed into lyric, made beautiful, and, through continual reenactment, immortal.

Conclusion

The Fractured Self
Songs of Mo(u)rning

> Should he part from me now
> my lover, this sorrow is mine too early.
> Wolfram von Eschenbach, *"Ez ist nu tac"*

At dawn, the still united lovers have to come to terms with their "undoing." The alba dramatizes the war between two competing consciousnesses: the lovers oscillate between a consciousness of time and a repression of that consciousness: performing a ritual in which all their protests, denunciations, and denials eventually resolve into acceptance of the necessity of parting. Their process of acknowledging the full impact of temporal change after having tried to suppress and deny all signs of it is the central drama of the alba. The lyric dramatizes the crucial decision-making dilemma: the lovers repress their awareness of time in order to enjoy love, but they must also allow reality to reassert itself in time for them to save themselves from harm. If they do not, their secret world of love would come into direct and shattering collision with the public world and be utterly desecrated or violently destroyed. To perpetuate their union and protect themselves, the lovers must put an end to their meeting.

Inevitably, naturally, day subjugates love. As one of Wolfram's lovers concedes, "day will not hold back" ("der tac wil niht erwinden" [*"Ez ist nu tac,"* l. 22]). Awareness of temporality impels the lovers' apprehension. Fluctuating between desire and necessity, they begin to acknowledge reality in advance of its crushing consequences.

Day's advent must be confronted no matter how desperately the lovers try to ignore it. After considering their alternatives, they must determine whether they will part voluntarily or throw all caution to the winds in an ecstatic, reckless denial of the consequences of discovery. By not bowing to the hegemony of law, they may face the consequences of having to bow to social justice and face ruin, perhaps even death, as a result. This latter alternative is never chosen in the alba because it is not a real choice—just as Troilus's proposal to Criseyde that they run away together is not a realistic alternative in their world. There are no options for alba lovers.

Alba lovers somehow always manage to part in the nick of time. They are never apprehended together, and the listener, caught up in the drama, has every reason to assume that the lovers escape unscathed. The husband's arrival is the "ever-present danger that constitutes the emotional frame of the poem, but in the alba the husband never arrives" (Saville 1972, 108). The urgency of the language creates tension and convinces us that the possibility of disaster is real; the audience's mere imagining that catastrophe could occur at any time keeps suspense, the drama, alive.

Just as dawn resolves itself ineluctably into day, alba lovers reluctantly yet necessarily resolve to separate. Alba poets' dramatization of the process of separation manifests their insight into psychological truths about the love experience. The lovers must extricate themselves from one another to become differentiated beings, each with his or her personal boundary visible in day's light. Alba lovers never express the fear (implicit in the Hermaphroditus legend) of losing themselves in union. Fusion has occurred so joyfully that the lovers put up no resistance to the psychological evisceration of their individual boundaries; the alba's symbiotic union is not presented as destructive. The difficulty and sorrow of separation rather than the threat of fusion become the pressing subjects that alba poets explore. The lovers' cries on parting reveal their agony at extricating themselves from their bond. Separation and the pain it entails invite inquiry into what precisely constitutes a self for such lovers (and their poets).

If alba lovers express the feeling that they have become one, if union refines, alters, or completes their sense of self, then separation must entail a kind of identity crisis. The identity constituted by their intimacy is threatened, for once they separate, they will no longer be able to define themselves as one. At dawn, the lovers must define themselves in terms that will somehow survive the physical rupture. A dissolution and deconstruction of the self occurs as the lover dismantles his or her body in an exchange of parts with the beloved. The exchange reenacts the sundering of self while also attempting to avert that sundering. Because their identities as lovers have been based upon physical union, the lovers now attempt to reconstitute identities that transcend the physical, redefining themselves along emotional and spiritual lines.

The imagery of dismemberment—of isolating and rearranging corporeal structures—in combination with a narrative scenario of passionate but short-lived love portray lovers who undergo dissolution and re-creation. The identity that alba lovers are left with at the completion of their song is diminished. The alba elegizes the lonely, fragmented futures they foresee.

On parting, the lovers must yield their newly assumed identity as a couple and equals. When they united, the social basis of their identities was dissolved, their social roles canceled. In psychological terms, the separation-individuation process involves a gradually emerging recognition of the separateness of the self from the other. In psychoanalytic terms, when an infant experiences an embryonic sense of self, it is accompanied by an awareness of an existent reality in the outside world: "The term 'separation' refers to the emergence of the child from being merged with the mother while the term 'individuation' refers to the child's awareness of his own particular characteristics. This feeling of self achieved in individuation constitutes the foundation on which a sense of identity is built" (Zweben-Howland 1993, 4). Alba lovers who merge together reenact this dynamic. Once they separate, a sense of the outside world is reestablished, and they will have to take up their positions in the world again. But when they do so, their social identity will be permanently altered, for they are now aware of its irrelevance to an important aspect of their lives or, indeed, of their true selves. Their experience of love engenders a confusion of identities. If social identity has become meaningless for illicit lovers, what constitutes true identity and how does love—and separation from the beloved—affect self-definition?

The frequency of references to particular body parts throughout the corpus of the alba manifests the poets' perception that the body is an object to be anatomized.[1] Obsessive love entails a dwelling on the beloved's various beauties and perfections. In the alba, hearts are shared, joined, torn asunder, taken, or pledged away; eyes, cheeks, mouths, breasts, ribs, arms, legs, and backs become the focus of isolated attention. The itemization of these *membra* serves to deconstruct the body, emphasizing the diversity and plethora of parts that constitute its collective form.[2]

The lovers' parting laments are pervaded with expressions that manifest their sense that the integrality of their bodies is being violated, as if separation from one another entails a correlative tearing apart of the individual self as well. The use of the reflexive in the lovers' plaints emphasizes not only how close the lovers are but also how difficult detachment is. In "En un vergier sotz fuella d'albespi," the lady prays that "my lover never part [himself] far from me" ("ni·l mieus amicx lonc de mi no·s partis" [l. 6]). In "S'anc fui belha ni prezada," the lady's phrasing emphasizes her attachment all the more: "for it would be/ ignorant vulgarity/ whoever should part ignobly/ her worthy lover/ from herself, before dawn" ("quar seria/ desconoissens vilania/ qui partia malamen/ son amic valen/ de si, tro en l'alba" [ll. 41–44]). The lover of "Friuntlîchen lac" explains: "I want to part [myself] from you: that is good for us both" ("ich wil mich von dir scheiden: daz ist uns beiden guot" [l. 11]). The German word order (literally, "I want me from you to part") further emphasizes the lovers' intertwinings and entanglings. Criseyde phrases her complaint in terms of severing when she says, "That day of vs moot make disseueraunce."

The pain of separation has been so deeply internalized that it is reenacted upon the self. Separation, like a kind of birth agony, entails an identity crisis in which the lovers feel disoriented, alienated, incomplete. Disunion in the alba recapitulates the human condition; it reenacts the first act of human disunion in which Eve was wrested from Adam's body. Separation involves individuation. That shattering moment of separation that is also the birth of self-awareness—when the self is first experienced as a separate entity—is the drama inherent in the alba. Metaphorical dismemberment becomes the correlative of physical separation.

In "Friuntlîchen lac," the lover is physically agonized: "his body was filled with longing" ("dô sente sich sîn lîp" [l. 50]). In his pledge, "thus my heart shall never leave you" ("sô enkumt mîn herze doch niemer von dir" [l. 28]), his heart is sundered from him and left in the lady's perpetual possession. The lady of Wolfram's "Sîne klâwen" complains to the watchman: "you have taken him from me often/ from my white arms, and not out of my heart" ("du hâst in dicke mir benomen/ von blanken armen, unde ûz herzen niht" [ll. 39–40]). The expression highlights the existence of two parallel but contrasting realms—one subject to time and loss (the lady's arms), the other eternal (her heart) (see Saville 1972, 208–9). Sayce observes that in "Den morgenblic" and "Sîne klâwen," "the bond between the lovers transcends physical absence. . . . These last two examples are variations on the familiar theme of the heart as dwelling-place" (1967, 257).

In the alba, the heart also functions metonymically for the act of memory. The lady of the tageliet "Slâfest du" laments that her joy vanishes along with the departing body of her beloved: "Alas, you take my joy together with you" ("owê, du vüerest mîne vröide sant dir!" [l. 12]). Joy belongs to the person of the beloved just as desire belongs to seeing the beloved in "Us cavaliers si jazia" ("if I did not see you/ soon believe that I would die/ for my great desire would kill me"). The lover incarnates joy and desire. Upon separating, the knight of the same lyric bequeaths his heart to his beloved:

> Gentle one, I take to the road,
> I am yours, wherever I may be.
> For God's sake, do not forget me one bit,
> for here remains my body's heart,
> and from you I will never part.
>
> Doussa res, ieu tenc ma via,
> vostres suy, on que ieu sia.
> Per Dieu, no m'oblidetz mia,
> que·l cor del cors reman sai,
> ni de vos mais no·m partrai. (ll. 28–32)

Although his body must move on, he separates out its essence; no matter where he roams, his best and most central part, his core, remains behind. The "cor/cors" ("body/heart") pun receives its full effect from the poet's play on the simultaneity of the body's leave taking and the heart's remaining. Yet the lover's assertion that he will never part from his lady denies the actuality. The vocabulary of union and presence is reforged along emotional, spiritual, and psychological lines. Physical separation is counteracted by emotional union. The lady of "Den morgenblic" addresses her lover in a similar way: "two hearts and one body have we:/ completely inseparable our trouthe/ with one another will be" ("zwei herze und ein lîp hân wir./ gar ungescheiden unser triuwe mit ein ander vert" [ll. 17–18]). The litotes characteristic of Wolfram is notable in his use of "gar ungescheiden" ("completely unbroken"), which stresses the strength and durability of the bond. Again a clear echo is found in Donne's poetry. The compass conceit of "A Valediction: Forbidding Mourning" demonstrates how the lovers' two souls, "which are one" (l. 21), are metaphysically united through their refined, transcendent love.

Chrétien de Troyes composes variations, both serious and comic, on this theme. He fastens on the idea of symbiotic attachment in *Lancelot*. When Lancelot, after a long pursuit of Guenevere, finally finds her, we are told, "Lancelot accompanies her with his eyes and heart as far as the door; but for his eyes it was a short journey as the room was very close by, and they would dearly have liked to go in after her, had it been possible. His heart, with its greater seniority and authority and being far more powerful, did pass through after her while his eyes, full of tears, remained outside with his body" (1987, 238). At the conclusion of the romance, when Lancelot returns to Arthur's court after his two-year imprisonment, Guenevere, overjoyed to see him, hangs back even while her heart is "kissing and making much" of her long-lost lover. Chrétien praises Guenevere's restraint in keeping her body from following her heart in welcoming Lancelot (276–77; cited in chapter 5).

Although Chrétien can write movingly of this disembodiment, he also parodies it. When Lancelot pulls away the iron bars that prevent his entry into Guenevere's chamber, he scrapes his fingers enough to create the telltale bloodstains on the bed linen that alert Meleagant to Guenevere's adultery: "His heart is ceaselessly drawn back to where the queen remains; and he has no power to take it away, for it finds in the queen such pleasure that it has no wish to leave her: the body goes, but the heart stays behind. He goes straight back to the window; but enough of himself remains behind for the sheets to be soiled and stained with the blood that dripped from his fingers" (1987, 247–48). Lancelot's physical wrenching of the iron bars has practical, material consequences, unlike the alba lovers' metaphorical use of language in which their body parts are voluntarily exchanged leaving no such physical traces.

But this kind of metaphorization does not go unremarked upon by Chrétien. Explaining how Cligés and Fenice exchange hearts, the poet muses on the language of anatomization:

> She fixed her eyes and heart on him, and in return he promised his own.—Promised? Rather gave outright.—Gave? No: to be sure I am lying, for nobody can give his heart away. I must put it differently.
>
> I shall not follow those who say there are two hearts united in one body, for it neither is true nor seems to be that there should be two hearts together in a single body; and even if they could come together, it would not appear true. But if you care to listen, I could explain to you how two hearts are united as one without actually coming together. They are joined as one only in that the desire of each passes from the one to the other so that they have one common wish; and because they share a single desire, there are those in

the habit of saying that each person possesses both hearts. But one heart is not in two places: the desire may well be one, yet each still has his own heart, just as many different men may sing a song or ditty in unison. By this analogy I prove to you that it is not by having two hearts that one person can know another's desire or that the other knows whatever the first loves and hates; no more can a body possess more than one heart than can those voices joining together so they seem like one belong to a single person. (130–31)

In analyzing this poetic conceit and concluding with a reference to harmonic music, Chrétien is tracing out the ramifications of a lyric tradition from which he clearly emerges. But whereas Chrétien critiques the "falsifications" of this poetic metaphor, alba poets are wedded to it. The physical world may be subject to time, decay, and separation, but the world of feeling is not. In the eternal realm of the heart, the alba beloved remains.

The affirmation of this power of love—the privileging of the reality of feeling over action—is reflected in a use of language that wills its own fiction into reality through the use of metaphor. In his verbal dismantling of the body, the speaker demonstrates the power of poetry to restructure the self. Language, operating on two planes, becomes simultaneously the vehicle of reality and fantasy. The poem is a metaphor for the union, a receipt of the transaction.

The focus on memory in the alba is related to the brevity of real time that the lovers actually spend together. Through memory, the past is retained and prolonged, brought into the present. The lover of "Ab la gensor que sia" plants the seeds of a lifelong love when he recounts:

> A sweet kiss she tendered me
> So pleasingly
> that I feel it still
> And all my life I will.
>
> Un dous bais mi tendia
> Tan plazenmen
> Qu'enquer lo·m sen
> E farai a ma via. (ll. 9–12)

The limits of love are here made explicit. It endures the length of life, "ma via." The emotions are admittedly secular: although they extend beyond physical presence, they do not extend, as in the writings of the mystics or the poetry of Donne, beyond the mortal life span.

The lovers' tryst is so brief that memory becomes an essential and almost concrete aspect of it. The relationship conducted primarily through conjunctions of opportunity and accessibility may not be able to perpetuate or renew itself except in the lovers' memories. In two dawn-songs, the Old French "Entre moi et mon amin" and Heinrich's "Owê, sol aber mir iemer mê," the tryst is entirely re-created, in retrospect, in the lovers' memories. This aspect of the alba has been much noted by critics (Saville 1972, 204n; Dronke 1977, 180–81). In "En un vergier sotz fuella d'albespi," the lady reminisces: "Through the sweet breeze that has come from there,/ From my lover, beautiful, courtly and gay,/ From his breath I have drunk a sweet ray" ("Per la doss'aura q'es venguda de lay,/ Del mieu amic belh e cortes e gay,/ Del sieu alen ai begut un dous ray" [ll. 17–19]). Noting the shift from the present to the past tense that occurs during this strophe, Dronke points out that "it is a memory of that orchard which has stirred [the lady] with such physical force that it seemed she was drinking in her lover's presence with the wind" (1977, 179). Dronke also observes that the poet passes "imperceptibly from the meeting of the lovers to the memories and longings of the woman alone, from event to daydream, outer to inner world" (1977, 175). It is the memory of the relationship that the lovers can possess and carry with them. Such possession makes the beloved a part of the lover.

Pledges of troth—verbal contracts—likewise prepare the lovers for separation, bestowing a promise of permanence that substitutes for physical presence. In the Christian dispensation, a word can miraculously be incarnated. Like their love, the promise is volitional, expressive, and sincere. The lovers' fidelity to their oaths, their faithfulness to love, forms the basis of their honor. The giving of one's word is an almost tangible token of oneself. After asking for his lady's pledge, the lover of "Us cavaliers si jazia" swears, "I am yours, wherever I may be" ("Vostres suy, on que ieu sia" [l. 32]), and pledges, "I shall soon return" ("ieu tost retornarai" [l. 44]). The lady of "Ab la gensor que sia" promises: "For I shall remain your lover" ("Qu'ieu remanh vostr'amia" [l. 26]). The pledge unites the separated lovers, anchoring and extending the relationship across time and space. Like Donne's "gold to ayery thinnesse beate" ("A Valediction: Forbidding Mourning" [l. 24]), their precious love endures spatial and temporal expansion.

The lover asserts the primacy of emotional attachment over physical separation. The lover's dichotomization of the physical and emotional redefines his or her love: love that has a spiritual component is less threatened by physical rapture. The disembodied heart represents the lover's transcendent love, a love that outlasts its physical consummation. The lover is also restructuring both the physical and psychological boundaries of the self. Physically, the lover's self-definition now incorporates the partner—only if they are one are exchanges of hearts possible without rupturing the self. Psychologically, the self is no longer purely physical; it has emotional boundaries that transcend physical delineation/ delimitation to include the beloved.

If Milton's Adam and Eve "took their solitary way" through Eden hand in hand—differentiated but together, as partners—the illicit alba lovers ending their perfect idyll must now take their solitary way individually, partnerless. "I take my way" ("ieu tenc ma via") laments the lover of "Us cavaliers si jazia." By bestowing vestiges of the self upon the beloved, the lover endeavors to retain some physical trace of attachment. The imagery of dismemberment that pervades the parting lovers' laments vividly attests to the ordeal brought on by separation. As the creation of Eve from Adam's rib is an act not only of disembodiment but also of individuation, so, too, the alba lovers' separation engenders a new sense of self. The lovers, torn asunder, undergo an act of parturition in which each lover is delivered anew and alone.

It is ironic that a poetry celebrating union also explores loneliness and desolation so deeply, but such isolation represents the tragic reality that underlies all human love. Separation from one another furnishes the lovers with reconstituted, distinct, if partial and shaken, identities. This agonizing ordeal is as painful as the birth act itself; the individual is left expressing a sense of incompletion, disorientation, and emptiness. Having experienced the absolute fulfillment of reciprocal love, the union of two into one, the lovers' anticipated separation is terrifying. The alba vividly portrays their dread of separation. Their morning/mourning song, however, is as much a song of mourning/morning for their newly born self as for their sundered love.

Notes

Introduction

1. Tennyson ("Tithonus"); Browning (in "Pippa Passes," "Meeting at Night," and "Parting at Morning"); Swinburne ("Before Dawn" and "At Parting"); Housman ("The Fairies break their dances"); Yeats ("The Dawn" and "Parting"); Sitwell ("Aubade" and "A Song at Morning"); Auden ("What's in your mind, my dove, my coney"); Ransom ("Parting at Dawn"); Williams ("Full Moon," "The Sun," and "Dawn"); Shapiro ("Aubade"); and Wilbur ("A Late Aubade").

2. Poe's "Three Modalities of the Old Provençal Dawn Song" and "New Light on the Alba: A Genre Redefined" give a comprehensive survey and discussion of the definitions of the alba. See also Woledge in Hatto 1965, 346 and n. 8.

3. The folk-song theory, formulated by the German Romantics, was forgotten for several generations and then revived in the twentieth century by Theodor Frings, Leo Spitzer, and others who amassed compelling examples to support their belief in the existence of a body of oral women's songs or Frauenlieder (Bragg 1989, 257–58). More recent work can be found in Malone's "Two English *Frauenlieder*"; Dronke's *Medieval Lyric* (86–108); Davidson's "Erotic 'Women's Songs' in Anglo-Saxon England"; Plummer's *Vox Feminae;* Bogin's *Women Troubadours;* Paden's *Voice of the Trobairitz;* and Earnshaw's *Female Voice in Medieval Romance Lyric.*

4. "Horum autem modorum cantionum modum excellentissimum esse pensamus; quare si excellentissima excellentissimis digna sunt, ut superius est probatum, illa que excellentissimo sunt digna vulgari, modo excellentissimo digna sunt, et per consequens in cantionibus pertractanda" (*De vulgari eloquentia* 376).

5. The pastourelle is, like the alba, a verse form composed by the early generation of troubadours. It tells of the chance encounter between a knight and a shepherdess and his attempt, successful or not, to seduce her (Paden 1987, iv). The genre was quite popular: Old Provençal has about 150 examples and Old French more than 100 (Earnshaw 1988, 90–94).

6. Paden (1975) has proposed that the gilos should not invariably be considered the lady's spouse. The alba's particular use of the term, however, has always been taken to refer to the lady's husband, and, as I shall argue in chapter 2, this assumption is correct.

7. For Bloch, the idealization of women in the ideology of courtliness should not be confused with love. The "invention of Western romantic love represented, above all, a usurping reappropriation of woman at the moment she became capable of appropriating what had traditionally constituted masculine modes of wealth.... Courtliness is, at bottom, a competing mode of coercion that will, alongside misogyny, continue to hide its disenfranchising effects behind the seduction of courtesy, and thus to dominate the discourse of lovers in the West" (1991, 196–97).

8. See Goldin, *Lyrics* (1973), 108–25; and 1975.

9. Such charges of misogyny are put forth in Bloch's comprehensive study *Medieval Misogyny and the Invention of Western Romantic Love* but can also be found in Gravdal, *Ravishing Maidens*, and "Rape," 363; Benton, "Clio and Venus," 35; Bruckner, "Fictions of the Female Voice," 869; Blumstein, *Misogyny and Idealization in the Courtly Romance*, 2; Cholakian, *The Troubadour Lyric*, 181; Burgwinkle, "Ethics and the Courtly Lady," 75; and Kay, *Subjectivity in Troubadour Poetry*, 85.

Chapter One. The Alba Lady: Literary Perspectives

1. Saville 1972; Fries 1981, 155–78. These works are all the more important in light of the paucity of critical attention to the alba.

2. Her pivotal role in the courtly utopia comes with conditions: she is designed to be one-dimensional, her silence and immobility make her susceptibility to authorial manipulation all the more conspicuous, and she exalts the singer who praises her. The problematic ways in which the domna is adored, silenced, manipulated, and nonparticipatory in the courtship ritual have been important subjects of recent lyric scholarship.

3. Overing's analysis of *Beowulf's* Modthryth is particularly enlightening on this subject; see *Language, Sign and Gender in Beowulf* (1990, 101–7). The rejection of female initiative and control is likewise conveyed in later, more romanticized works.

4. The unnamed second wife of Culwch's father in the Welsh tale puts a destiny on Culwch that leads to his joining Arthur's court and finding his future bride, Olwen.

5. The Old French fabliaux ("little fables") are funny stories in verse, perhaps derived from oral tradition but adapted by literary men who belonged to a cultured milieu. About 150 fabliaux survive, composed between 1200 and 1340 and preserved in manuscripts of the thirteenth and fourteenth centuries. Like courtly lyric, they were recited in both public and private places for audiences of both sexes. The humor of the fabliau is primarily sexual, involving various problems of sexual opportunity, privacy, potency, compatibility, rivalry, or obstacles to sexual satisfaction. Fabliau comedy is derived from obscene actions and language (see Muscatine 1957). Although both sexes are mocked in the fabliau, the fact that clerks are the

one group consistently admired has led to speculation that they composed and recited fabliaux along with jongleurs.

6. Alba poets make no reference or allusion to the *Heroides* and little to Ovid even though his works were widely disseminated and known in medieval Europe.

7. For an exploration of the origins of Chrétien's Enide that presents an entirely different view, see Bossy, 1986/1990.

8. Of Cadenet himself we know very little; twenty-five of his poems survive.

9. The music for this lyric, found in manuscript R (Paris, Bibl. nat., français 22543), has been published by J. Beck (*La musique des troubadours,* Paris, n.d., 99) and is the only one of Cadenet's melodies to survive. It is similar to the melody of Giraut de Bornelh's "Reis glorios."

10. Bloch sums up this view in his description of love in the courtly lyric, which, according to him, is virginal: "The connection between romantic love, virginity, and the ascetic impulse is even more apparent in the medieval lyric than in the short narrative form. . . . The perfection of the love object excludes or prevents her from desiring. To be loved, according to the logic of the courtly relation, the woman must be indifferent, unattainable, unsullied—in short, a virgin. . . . To the extent that the woman of the lyric seduces but is never seduced, she represents a virgin" (1991, 143, 147, 151). Bloch's interpretation excludes the alba, which is a courtly genre.

11. My understanding is that "schiltaer" (shield painter) was used to designate painter generally.

Chapter Two. The Alba Lady: Sex Roles and Social Roles

1. In the last twenty years, researchers have actively undertaken serious study of the female in the sciences and the humanities. More recent research into female biology, including physiology and behavioral traits, has shown that the female frequently plays an aggressive role in courtship and mating and that her role in animal societies is pivotal in ways that were previously overlooked (Shaw and Darling 1985, 3).

2. John Donne, whose verse uncannily echoes and plays brilliant variations upon troubadour motifs, including the alba's (see chapter 5), looks beyond gender in love relationships in "The Undertaking":

> If, as I have, you also doe
> > Vertue attir'd in woman see,
> And dare love that, and say so too,
> > And forget the Hee and Shee;
>
> And if this love, though placed so,
> > From prophane men you hide,

> Which will no faith on this bestow,
> Or, if they doe, deride:
>
> Then you have done a braver thing
> Then all the Worthies did;
> And a braver thence will spring,
> Which is, to keepe that hid. (ll. 17–28)

For Donne, as for alba poets, secreting this kind of love is a way of keeping it sacred.

3. A detailed analysis of how Chaucer reveals the differing personalities of Troilus and Criseyde through their dawn-songs is found in Sigal, "Benighted Love in Troy: Dawn and the Dual Negativity of Love in Chaucer's *Troilus*."

4. The text of Cercamon's "Ab lo pascor m'es bel q'eu chant" is from the Wolf and Rosenstein edition (1983, 54–59), as is the translation, with minor alterations of my own.

5. Texts of Marcabru's lyrics are taken from the Dejeanne edition. "Pois l'inverns d'ogan es anatz" (xxxix, 191–95), "Hueymais dey esser alegrans" (xxxiv, 165–68), "Al son desviat, chantaire" (v, 19–21), and "Bel més quan la rana chanta" (xi, 42–46); translations are from Gaunt (1990, 71nn. 34, 37) with slight alterations of my own.

6. Translation from Gaunt (1990, 71n.45) with alterations of my own.

7. Lazar believes that "the nature of *fin'amor* as poetically represented in the *cansos* remains adulterous beyond any doubt." Although Paden's theory has found acceptance among a small number of critics, many, including myself, agree with Lazar that Paden's attempt to "'unmarry' the married lady of the troubadours' songs and thus, *ipso facto*, to void the adulterous tenor of *fin'amor* . . . remains nevertheless a distortion of the evidence found both in the texts he dealt with and in those he did not consider" ("Carmina Erotica, Carmina Iocosa: The Body and the Bawdy in Medieval Love Songs," 250).

Chapter Three. Eros in the Socius

1. Duby characterizes the *compagno* of troubadour poetry as part of a new disinherited knightly class and literary courtly love as a great game in which young men were exhorted to demonstrate valor by seducing and abducting the lady of the house: "Undoubtedly the lord's wife was coveted, and the desire she inspired sublimated into a sophisticated form of love, was used as a means of disciplining young knights" (1987, 82; see also 1977, 118).

2. For an analysis of how the troubadours played with the literal and metaphorical levels of social hierarchy and sexual relations, see Sigal, "Courted in the Country."

3. Our lack of knowledge about the relationship between the fictive and historical context makes it problematic to speculate about real-life analogues. In his

History of Private Life, Duby justifies the use of literature to reveal certain historical dimensions, as does Boswell in *The Kindness of Strangers,* although he also warns against its misuse. If historians debate the applicability of literary texts, literary critics likewise debate the relevance of historical data. In speculating about historical underpinnings, we can add to our literary analysis information that may help confirm an interpretation. But when historical observation is drawn from literary sources, or vice versa, it must be used with care. I include these historians' theories to shed an interesting sidelight on the possible social contexts of the poetry.

4. As Régnier-Bohler comments in her chapter "Literary and Mystical Voices" in Duby 1987: "The theme of individual versus collectivity forms the heart of the [medieval] romantic adventure tale" (317); see also Hanning 1977.

5. Five of her songs, including a tenso, survive.

6. This is one of two possible interpretations of these lines (see Hatto 1965, 447).

7. Spousal abuse that leads to murder is statistically the greatest cause of death even among contemporary American women.

8. St. Augustine's view is more consoling to women whose chastity was taken from them violently: "violation of chastity, without the will's consent, cannot pollute the character" (*City of God,* I:16).

9. The history of the Church's attitude toward sexuality is continually being rewritten. The best introduction to the sexual mores of early Christianity is Peter Brown, *The Body and Society: Men, Women, and Sexual Renunciation in Early Christianity* (1988). On the subject of religious women and virginity, the work of Jane Tibbitts Schulenberg, especially "The Heroics of Virginity: Brides of Christ and Sacrificial Mutilation" (1986) and her forthcoming *Forgetful of Her Sex,* makes essential and fascinating reading. See also Ruether 1974; McNamara 1976; McNamara and Wemple 1987.

A secular analogue to the simultaneous negation and transcendence of womanhood is found in Gottfried von Strassburg's *Tristan,* who declares; "when a woman grows in virtue despite her inherited instincts and gladly keeps her honour, reputation, and person intact, she is only a woman in name, but in spirit she is a man!" (1967, 278).

10. In his *Commentary on Jonah,* St. Jerome states: "In persecutions it is not lawful to commit suicide except when one's chastity is jeopardized" (*Commentariorum in Jonam Prophetam Liber Unus,* P.L. 25:1129, quoted in Schulenburg 1986, 34); and in *Against Jovinianus,* he celebrates pagan virgins who killed themselves preserving their chastity. St. Ambrose, in *Concerning Virgins,* follows suit. In contrast, St. Augustine states that a violated woman has no reason to commit suicide and that guilt belongs only to the rapist, not to the woman who is raped (*City of God,* I:17–18, pp. 26–28). These early views were so prevalent that the fourteenth-century Chaucer provides both a classical and a more contemporary version of this attitude. In "The Physician's Tale" (a version of which is recounted in the thirteenth-century work *Le roman de la rose,* Chaucer's probable source), Virginia is decapitated by her father rather than suffered to lose her maidenhead along with the other indignities

involved in being given as a slave to the evil Apius. Virginius, her father, decides: "For love, and nat for hate, thou most be deed;/ My pitous hand moot smyten of thyn heed." Virgina accepts her father's sentence because he responds "No, certes" when she laments: "Is ther no grace, is ther no remedye?" She goes to her slaughter saying, "Blissed be God that I shal dye a mayde!/ Yif me my deeth, er that I have a shame" (248–49). In the more contemporary version presented in "The Franklin's Tale," Dorigen considers suicide, the only solution with which she is familiar, rather than carry out her oath to be Aurelius's lover until her husband commands her to keep her word despite its cost.

11. See Stuard, *Women in Medieval Society* (1976, 10) as well as "The Dominion of Gender: Women's Fortunes in the High Middle Ages"; Duby, *The Knight, the Lady and the Priest*; Gold, *The Lady and the Virgin*; Burns and Kreuger, intro., "Courtly Ideology and Women's Place in Medieval French Literature," 208; McNamara and Wemple, "The Power of Woman through the Family in Medieval Europe"; and Rose, *Women in the Middle Ages and the Renaissance*.

12. The transformation Kay refers to is the drastic change of view between earlier and more recent critics. Earlier critics held to Lewis's view that idealized love introduced a new feminine ideal by which women were empowered and revered (1976, 1–43). The new freedom enabled women's participation in the creative process by allowing them to circulate a new, more favorable literature of their own making (that is, the trobairitz and Marie de France) and by promoting the development of courtly love through patronage (for example, Eleanor of Aquitaine and Marie de Champagne). Women thus had a shaping influence over a new love ideal that included a justifying ideology for wifely adultery, which, as the double standard indicates, men in patriarchal society seldom required (Kelly-Gadol 1987, 146–48). The mutuality promoted by fin'amors was seen to have liberated aristocratic women to express their sexuality in passionate and loving forms. Such early views have come under increasing attack as scholars note that the uncritically positive reception of Lewis's idealized view of romantic love overlooks the many contradictions inherent in medieval conceptions of women.

Chapter Four. Eros and Dawning Identity

1. See Sarah Stanbury's essay, "The Lover's Gaze in *Troilus and Criseyde*," in which she elucidates the importance of the power of the female gaze in medieval poetry.

2. Troilus exclaims:

> O cruel day, accusour of the ioie
> That nyght and loue han stole and faste i-wryen [hidden],
> Acorsed be thi comyng in-to Troye,
> ƒor euery bore hath oon of thi bryghte yen.
> Enuyous day, what list the so to spien?

What hastow lost, why sekestow this place,
Ther god thi light so quenche for his grace? (III, 1450–56)

3. Giraut de Bornelh, the poet Dante praised as *poeta rectitudinis*, has the largest surviving corpus of any of the early troubadours; about fifty of his lyrics are extant. An earlier and shorter version of this discussion was published as "'Reis glorios': An Inverted *Alba?*" (1989–90).

4. One controversial strophe, accepted by several scholars as authentic (but considered by most as not having been composed by Giraut de Bornelh), dramatizes the male lover's response to his comrade's efforts, clearly demonstrating the futility of the watchman's service:

> Fair sweet friend, I am so richly resting
> That I wish neither dawn nor day would ever come,
> For the noblest ever born of mother
> I hold in my arms; wherefore I do not prize one bit
> Either the fool gilos nor the dawn!
>
> Bel dos companh, tan soy en ric soiorn
> Qu'ieu no volgra mays fos alba ni iorn,
> Car la gensor qu'anc nasques de mayre
> Tenc e abras, per qu'eu non prezi gayre
> Lo fol gilos ni l'alba! (Mss. T and R)
> (Bibl. nat. français 15211, Paris;
> Bibl. nat. français 22543, Paris)

In attempting to view the lyric as an artistic whole composed by Giraut de Bornelh, however, I follow the six-strophe arrangement (also followed by Kolsen, Goldin, and Woledge) that omits this questionable strophe. Kolsen's text is based on manuscript C, a fourteenth-century manuscript in the Bibliothèque Nationale (ms. C, français 856). Although I have used Sharman's edition because it is the most recent, Kolsen, Goldin, Woledge, and I prefer the omission of the additional seventh strophe (whose authenticity, as Sharman notes, is in doubt) because it breaks the anaphoric pattern with which strophes 2 through 6 begin as well as the pattern of *coblas doblas*. In this additional strophe, not only is the salutation altered but the speaker shifts from watchman to lover. In no other extant alba is the watchman addressed in such an endearing, intimate manner, one usually reserved for the beloved. The refrain "e ades sera l'alba!" consistent up to now, has also been altered in a way that disturbs the unity of the lyric: unlike the other strophes in which the refrain is a separate syntactic unit and a complete sentence (Spence notes that the refrain of strophes 1 through 6 "provides no logical conclusion to the strophe" [1981, 214]), the refrain in this questionable one is linked syntactically to the preceding line. The strophe, according to Wilhelm, "is not essential, and is even inimical to the poem's subtle tones" (1965, 200). Woledge's analysis of the manuscripts concludes: "The two mss. [with the additional strophe] are not . . . particularly good on the whole and Kolsen may well be nearer to Giraut's own text in giving us the highest common factor of the extant mss., which is at the same time a simple monologue formed of three pairs of stanzas" (in Hatto 1965, 383).

This strophe or any other additional strophe of "Reis glorios" found in medieval manuscripts is not to be dismissed as insignificant; these additional verses interest us insofar as their dialogue with the text illuminates aspects of poetic and thematic development. But in turning a dramatic monologue into a dialogue, strophe 7 is disjunctive and distracts from the dramatic force of the watchman's deliberations. It is, as Sharman notes, possible that "Giraut may have deliberately composed this single final stanza after the sequence of *coblas doblas* in order to contrast the lover's reply with the watchman's speech" (Giraut de Borneil 1989, 368n), but it is more likely to have been added by another poet.

The seven extant manuscripts of "Reis glorios" differ "not only in a number of details . . . but also in the number of stanzas they include and in the order in which they arrange them" (Hatto 1965, 381). In one manuscript (fourteenth century, cod. lat. 1759, Staatsbibliothek, Munich) the strophes are arranged in a different order. (What appears in Kolsen's text as the second strophe appears there as the penultimate strophe, followed by one additional strophe.)

5. Although he may have fallen prey to his culture's and his own antifeminist biases, Freud was the first to recognize and analyze infantile sexuality in relation to love. His careful and sensitive examination of the trauma of separation and the various neuroses of love and his interest in the sufferings of love have resonance for the alba.

6. Despite the fact that no manuscripts of Plato's works other than the *Timeus* were available, his ideas were well known: "It hardly matters that the [*Symposium*] manuscript was unknown in Europe until much later: Plato was studied elsewhere and his ideas were thoroughly disseminated throughout the Western world" (Singer 1984, 38). In fact, Singer conceives of the courtly tradition as a prolonged effort to resolve some of the problems raised by the *Symposium*.

7. Taylor argues that Dante purposefully reverses the gender roles of love lyric by transferring the speaking role to Francesca instead of giving it to Paolo; further, "Dante means her assumption of the lyric voice of love to be outrageous" (1992, 243). This view assumes that Dante was either unfamiliar with the female voice of Provençal lyric or discounted it.

8. Stuard's essay "The Domination of Gender" and the chapter on "Christianity, Sex and Women" in Bullough et al. 1988 are most enlightening on this subject.

9. Zweben-Howland's psychoanalytical approach to the idea of the emerging self in courtly lyric is especially insightful in its elucidation of Bernart de Ventadorn's "Can vei la lauzeta mover." I am indebted to her for sharing her unpublished essay,

"The Genesis of the Self in 'Can vei la lauzeta mover' by Bernart de Ventadorn," and for her lucid explanations of the psychological dimensions of the child-mother bond.

Chapter Five. First Light

1. Andreas Capellanus wrote the (in)famous treatise *De Arte Honeste Amandi* or *De Amore,* usually translated as *The Art of Courtly Love.* A mysterious figure about whom very little is known, he is considered by some a proponent and theoretician of courtly love and by others its greatest contemporary critic: "It is not yet been resolved and probably never will be finally settled whether *De Amore* is a serious account of love practices in courtly society in the late twelfth century, or an imaginative work, humorous and ironic, taking to the ultimate degree ideas about love already to be found in twelfth-century secular literature. . . . The once widely held view that [he] was Marie [de Champagne]'s chaplain (*capellanus*) is no longer a matter of certainty" (Lucas 1983, 176, 175).

2. This movement has been documented by many historians, beginning with Charles Homer Haskins in his pioneering *Renaissance of the Twelfth Century* (1927), a work that spawned numerous offspring. Walter Ullmann, in *The Individual and Society in the Middle Ages* (1966), explores twelfth-century political theory; Colin Morris's *The Discovery of the Individual* (1973) focuses on political, religious, and literary evidence of a rise in self-awareness among people at this time; John Benton concerns himself with the idea of self-discovery, self-examination, and individual potential in *Self and Society in Medieval France: The Memoirs of Abbot Guibert of Nogent.* For these scholars, the phrase "discovery of the individual" refers to a new interest in inner motivations, emotions, and psychological development. For Bynum, "the twelfth century 'discovers the self' in the sense that interest in the inner landscape of the human being increases after 1050 in comparison to the immediately preceding period; second, the twelfth century 'discovers the self' in the sense that knowing the inner core of human nature within one's own self is an explicit theme and pre-occupation in literature of the period" (1980, 4). In her view, the discovery of the self—"the inner mystery, the inner man, the inner landscape"—could not have happened without the concomitant "discovery of the group" (5, 15).

Essays collected by Benson and Constable (*Renaissance and Renewal in the Twelfth Century*) and Duby (*The History of Private Life,* vol. 2) as well as book-length works such as Hanning's *Individual in Twelfth Century Romance* demonstrate that a new impulse existed "on the part of literate men and women to understand themselves as single, unique persons—as what we call *individuals.* This impulse operated in three distinguishable but not totally distinct areas: the individual in relation to his own make up and character; the individual in relation to his society and institutional environment; the individual in relation to his God" (Hanning 1977, 1).

The Church's shift in focus from Christ as God triumphant to Christ as suffering man is, for Morris, another dimension of the new emphasis on the individual. By centering on Christ's humanity, the new approach bridged the vast distance separating human from God, a bridge manifest also in the dramatic reenactment in the emerging mystery plays. Monastic reformers "withdrew from society in order to cultivate the possibilities of their own inner selves," the inner self gradually becoming more and more an object of spiritual contemplation (Morris 1973, 36). Numerous studies following in the wake of broad-ranging works such as Morris's have made individuality in the Middle Ages a frequently debated topic.

3. Because literature of the period reflects this growing awareness of individuality, literary critics have been able to substantiate historians' theories. Southern first demonstrated these changes in a well-known chapter, "From Epic to Romance," in *The Making of the Middle Ages*. Morris's *Discovery of the Individual* adduces numerous factors, including the new kinds of aristocratic literary patrons, that influenced literature. Peter Dronke and Per Nykrog have substantiated this view (see "The Rise of Literary Fiction" in Benson and Constable 1982).

4. Walther von der Vogelweide, "Nemt, frowe, disen kranz"; English translation in Goldin 1973, 120–23.

5. Earnshaw notes that the refrain is "a regular pattern of interruption in dance songs, albas, and other songs of a popular and traditional character" (1988, 57).

Conclusion

1. Part of this discussion was published as "The Poetics of Dismemberment" (1990).

2. Interesting analogues are found in other genres. The lyric corpus contains a number of expressions of the idea that love controls the lover's body, separating it from his or her will. See Bernart de Ventadorn, "Non es meravelha s'eu chan" and "Tant ai mo cor ple de joya"; Jaufre Rudel, "Pro ai del chan essenhadors." The motif recurs in the romances of Chrétien de Troyes. Medieval theological debates about the use of saints' relics and attitudes toward body parts provide other interesting analogues (see Bynum 1991, 11–14).

Bibliography

Works Cited

Texts and Editions of Albas

All the albas discussed in this book are published with English translations in Arthur T. Hatto's *Eos: An Enquiry into the Theme of Lovers' Meetings and Partings at Dawn in Poetry* (see Works Consulted). Nevertheless, I have often taken the text of the poem from the standard edition rather than *Eos*. The following list details the albas and editions I have used as well as the pages on which they can be found in *Eos*. Many of the Old Provençal albas are included in the anthology *Provenzalische Chrestomathie*, edited by Carl Appel (see Other Primary Sources). Most citations of tagelieder are taken from *Des Minnesangs Frühling*, edited by Karl Lachmann, Moriz Haupt, Friedrich Vogt, and Carl von Kraus, revised by Hugo Moser and Helmut Tervooren (Stuttgart: S. Hirzel-Verlag, 1977; referred to henceforth as *MF*). I have also used Olive Sayce's *Poets of the Minnesang* (Oxford: Clarendon Press, 1967), which has notes and commentary in English and relies primarily on the texts in *MF*.

Anonymous. "Ab la gensor que sia." *Provenzalisches Lesebuch*. Edited by Karl Bartsch. Elberfeld, 1855, 102; Hatto, 363–64.
Anonymous. "En un vergier sotz fuella d'albespi." Appel, 90; Hatto, 358.
Anonymous. "Entre moi et mon amin." *Altfranzösische Romanzen und Pastourellen*. Edited by Karl Bartsch. Leipzig, 1870, 27; Hatto, 370.
Anonymous. "Eras diray co que·us dey dir." Edited by Martín de Riquer. *Revista de Filología Española* 34 (1950): 151–65; Hatto, 368–69.
Anonymous. "Est il jors?" *Receuil de motets français*. Edited by Gaston Raynaud and Henri Lavoix. 2 vols. Paris: F. Vieweg, 1881–83, 2:4–5; Hatto, 74.
Anonymous. "Gaite de la tor." Hatto, 372–74.
Anonymous. "Ich sich den morgenstern brehen!" Hatto, 446.
Anonymous. "L'abe c'apiert au jor." *Receuil de motets français*. Edited by Gaston Raynaud and Henri Lavoix. 2 vols. Paris: F. Vieweg, 1881–83, 2:4; Hatto, 375.
Anonymous. "Quan lo rossinhols escria." Appel, 90; Hatto, 364.

Appel, Carl. *Provenzalische Chrestomathie*. Leipzig: Reisland, 1907; Hatto, 364–65.
Bertran D'Alamanon or Gaucelm Faidit[?]. "Us cavaliers si jazia." *Les Poèmes de Gaucelm Faidit*. Edited by Jean Mouzat. Paris: A.G. Nizet, 1965, 555–56. Appel, 91; Hatto, 362–63.
Brulé, Gace. "Cant voi l'aube dou jor venir." *The Lyrics and Melodies of Gace Brulé*. Edited by Samuel N. Rosenberg and Samuel Danon. New York: Garland Publishing, 1985, 266–69; Hatto, 371–72.
Cadenet. "S'anc fui belha ni prezada." *Der Trobador Cadenet*. Edited by Carl Appel. Halle, 1920, 80–81; Hatto, 360–61.
Chaucer, Geoffrey. *Geoffrey Chaucer: Troilus & Criseyde. A New Edition of "The Book of Troilus."* Edited by Barry Windeatt. London: Longman, 1984.
Dietmar von Eist[?]. "Slâfest du, vriedel ziere?" *MF,* 66; Hatto, 446.
Giraut de Bornelh. "Reis glorios, verais lums e clardatz." *The Cansos and Sirventes of the Troubadour Giraut de Borneil: A Critical Edition*. Edited by Ruth Verity Sharman. Cambridge: Cambridge University Press, 1989, 365–68. Also in *Sämtliche Lieder des Trobadors: Giraut de Bornelh*. Edited by Adolf Kolsen. Halle, 1935, 1:342–47; Appel, 91–92; Hatto, 359.
Heinrich von Morungen. "Owê, sol aber mir iemer mê." *MF,* 276–77; Hatto, 447.
Margrave of Hohenburg. "Ich wache umbe eines ritters lîp." Hatto, 457–58.
Raimbaut de Vaqueiras. "Gaita be." *The Poems of the Troubadour Raimbaut de Vaqueiras*. Edited by Joseph Linskill. The Hague: Mouton, 1964, 25:261–63; Hatto, 365–66.
Raimon de las Salas. "Dieus, aydatz." *Provenzalisches Lesebuch*. Edited by Karl Bartsch. Elberfeld, 1855, 101; Hatto, 366–68.
Walther von der Vogelweide. "Friuntlîchen lac." *Die Gedichte Walthers von der Vogelweide*. Edited by Karl Lachmann and Carl von Kraus. Berlin, 1936, 88–89; Hatto, 455–56.
Wolfram von Eschenbach. "Den morgenblic." *MF,* 436–37; Hatto, 450.
———. "Der helden minne ir klage." *MF,* 441; Hatto, 454.
———. "Ez ist nu tac." *MF,* 445–47; Hatto, 448–49.
———. "Sîne klâwen." *MF,* 437–39; Hatto, 451–52.
———. "Von der zinnen." *MF,* 442–43; Hatto, 453.

Other Primary Sources

Anonymous. "At Parting." In *Seventeenth Century Lyrics from the Original Texts*. Edited by Norman Ault. London, 1928.
Aeschylus. *Eumenides*. Translated by Richard Lattimore. In *Aeschylus I: Oresteia*. Chicago: Chicago University Press, 1953.
Auden, W. H. "What's in Your Mind, My Dove?" In *The Collected Poetry of W. H. Auden*. New York: Random House, 1945.
Bernart de Ventadorn. *The Songs of Bernart de Ventadorn*. Edited by Stephen Nichols et al. Chapel Hill: University of North Carolina Press, 1962.

Béroul. *Le Roman de Tristan.* Edited by Ernest Muret. Paris: Firmin Didiot, 1903; reprint, Paris: Honoré Champion, 1962.
Boccaccio, Giovanni. *Il Filostrato.* Translated by Robert P. apRoberts and Anna Bruni Seldis. Edited by Vincenzo Pernicone. New York: Garland, 1986
———. *Il filostrato: Opere.* Edited by Vincenzo Pernicone. Bari: G. Laterza, 1938.
Broke, Arthur. *The Tragicall Historye of Romeus and Iuliet.* Edited by P. A. Daniel. London: New Shakspere Society, 1857.
Capellanus, Andreas. *The Art of Courtly Love.* Translated by John Jay Parry. New York: Columbia University Press, 1990.
Cercamon. *The Poetry of Cercamon and Jaufre Rudel.* Edited by George Wolf and Roy Rosenstein. New York: Garland, 1983.
Chaucer, Geoffrey. *The Riverside Chaucer.* Edited by Larry D. Benson. 3d ed. Boston: Houghton Mifflin, 1987.
Chrétien de Troyes. *Arthurian Romances.* Translated by D. D. R. Owen. London and Melbourne: Dent, 1987.
Dante Alighieri. *De vulgari eloquentia: Opere minore.* Milano: Rizzoli Editiore, 1960.
———. *The Divine Comedy.* Translated by Allen Mandelbaum. Berkeley: University of California Press, 1980–82.
Donne, John. "The Good-Morrow" 8; "The Undertaking" 10; "The Sunne Rising" 11; "Breake of Day" 19–20; "A Valediction: Forbidding Mourning" 38–39. In *The Complete and Selected Prose of John Donne.* Edited by Charles M. Coffin. New York: The Modern Library, 1952.
Folquet de Marseille. *Le troubadour Folquet de Marseille.* Edited by S. Stronski. Cracow, 1910.
Goldin, Frederick. *German and Italian Lyrics of the Middle Ages: An Anthology and a History.* New York: Doubleday, 1973.
———. *Lyrics of the Troubadours and Trouveres: An Anthology and a History.* New York: Doubleday, 1973.
———, trans. *The Song of Roland.* New York: Norton, 1978.
Guillaume de Lorris and Jean de Meun. *Le Roman de la Rose.* Edited by Félix Lecoy. Paris: Champion, 1965–70.
Homer. *The Odyssey of Homer.* Translated by Allen Mandelbaum. Berkeley: University of California Press, 1990.
Housman, A. E. "The Fairies Break Their Dances." In *The Collected Poems of A. E. Housman.* London: Cape, 1953.
Levy, Emil. *Petit dictionnaire provençal-français.* Heidelberg: Heidelberg University Press, 1973.
Marcabru. *Poésies complètes du troubadour Marcabru.* Edited by J. M. L. Dejeanne. Toulouse, 1909; New York: Johnson, 1971.
Marshall, J. H. *The Razos de Trobar of Raimon Vidal and Associated Texts.* London: Oxford University Press, 1972.
Marti, Bernart. *Il trovatore Bernart Marti.* Edited by F. Beggiato. Modena, 1984.

Marvell, Andrew. "To his Coy Mistress" 27–28. *The Poems and Letters of Andrew Marvell*. Edited by H. M. Margoliouth. Vol. I, *Poems*. Oxford: at the Clarendon Press, 1971.

Milton, John. *The Complete Poetical Works of John Milton*. Edited by Douglas Bush. Boston: Houghton Mifflin, 1965.

Molinier, Guillaume. *Las leys damors*. Edited by Adolphe Gatien-Arnoult. In *Monumens de la littérature romane*. Toulouse: J. B. Paya, 1841.

Ovid. *Amores*. Translated by Grant Showerman. In *Ovid in Six Volumes*. Cambridge: Harvard University Press; London: Heinemann, 1977.

———. *The Metamorphoses of Ovid: A New Verse Translation*. Translated by Allen Mandelbaum. New York: Harcourt Brace, 1993.

Paris, Matthew. *Chronica majora*. Edited by R. Luard. London, 1880.

Plato. *The Symposium*. Translated by W. Hamilton. Baltimore: Penguin, 1951.

Pound, Ezra. "Alba." "Alba inominata." "Langue d'oc." In *Selected Poems*. London: Faber and Faber, 1928.

Ransom, John Crowe. "Parting at Dawn." In *Selected Poems*. New York: Knopf, 1952.

Roques, Mario, ed. *Aucassin et Nicolette*. Paris, 1936.

Rudel, Jaufre. *The Poetry of Cercamon and Jaufre Rudel*. Edited by George Wolf and Roy Rosenstein. New York: Garland, 1983.

Scott, Sir Walter. *Castle Dangerous: Early Ballads and Lyrics and the Lay of the Last Minstrel*. Boston and New York: Houghton Mifflin, 1923.

Shapiro, Karl. "Aubades." In *Selected Poems*. New York: Random House, 1973.

Sitwell, Edith. "Aubade." "A Song at Morning." In *The Collected Poems of Edith Sitwell*. Edited by Karl Shapiro. New York: Vanguard, 1949.

St. Augustine. *The City of God*. Translated by Henry Bettenson. Edited by David Knowles. Harmondsworth: Penguin Books, 1972.

———. *On the Free Choice of Will*. Translated by A. S. Benjamin and L. H. Hackstaff. New York: Macmillan, 1964.

St. Jerome. "Against Jovinianus." Translated by W. H. Fremantle. Vol. 6. In *A Select Library of Nicene and Post-Nicene Fathers of the Christian Church*. 2d ser. 1892; rpt., Grand Rapids, Mich.: Eerdmans, 1978.

———. *The Letters of St. Jerome: Ancient Christian Writers*. Translated by Charles Christopher Mierow. Westminster, Md.: Newman, 1963.

Stampa, Gaspara. "Notte d'amore." In *Rime*. Edited by Abd-el-kader Salza. Bari, 1913.

Swinburne, Algernon Charles. "In the Orchard." In *The Complete Works of Algernon Charles Swinburne: Poetical Works*. Edited by Edmund Gosse and Thomas James Wise. New York: Russell and Russell, 1968.

Switten, Margaret. *The Medieval Lyric: Anthology I*. South Hadley, Mass.: Mount Holyoke College, 1988.

Tertullian, Quintus Septimius Florens. *Tertulliani opera*. Part 1. Edited by A. Kroymann. Turnhout: Brepols, 1954.

Virgil. *The Aeneid of Virgil*. Translated by Allen Mandelbaum. New York: Bantam, 1971.

von Strassburg, Gottfried. *Tristan.* Translated by Arthur T. Hatto. Baltimore: Penguin Books, 1967.
Waddell, Helen, trans. *Medieval Latin Lyrics.* New York: Norton, 1977.
Wilbur, Richard. "A Late Aubade." In *Walking to Sleep.* New York: Harcourt Brace Jovanovich, 1968.
Williams, William Carlos. "Full Moon." "The Sun." "Dawn." In *The Collected Poems of William Carlos Williams.* New York: New Directions, 1951.
Yeats, William Butler. "The Dawn." "Parting." In *The Collected Poems of W. B. Yeats.* New York: Macmillan, 1956.

Works Consulted

Anderson, Bonnie S., and Judith P. Zinsser. *A History of Their Own: Women in Europe from Prehistory to the Present.* New York: Harper and Row, 1988.
Arthur, Marilyn. "Early Greece: The Origins of the Western Attitude toward Women." In *Women in the Ancient World: The Arethusa Papers,* edited by John Peradotto and J. P. Sullivan, 7–58. Albany: State University of New York Press, 1984.
———. "From Medusa to Cleopatra: Women in the Ancient World." In Bridenthal, Koonz, and Stuard 1987, 79–105, q.v.
Aziza, Claude, et al. *Dictionnaire des symboles et des thèmes littéraires.* Paris: Nathan, 1978.
Baskerville, Charles Read. "English Songs on the Night Visit." *Publications of the Modern Language Association* 36 (1921): 565–615.
Bec, Pierre. "L'aube française 'Gaite de la tor': Pièce de ballet ou poème lyrique?" *Cahiers de Civilization Médiéval* 16 (1973): 17–33.
———. *La lyrique française au moyen age (XIIe–XIIIe siècles).* Poitiers: Picard, 1977–78.
———. *Petite anthologie de la lyrique occitane du moyen age.* 4th ed. Avignon: Aubanel, 1966.
Benson, Robert L., and Giles Constable, eds. *Renaissance and Renewal in the Twelfth Century.* Cambridge: Harvard University Press, 1982.
Benton, John F. "The Court of Champagne as a Literary Center." *Speculum* 36 (1961): 551–91.
———. *Self and Society in Medieval France: The Memoirs of Abbot Guibert of Nogent.* Toronto and London: University of Toronto Press, 1970. Reprint, 1984.
Bergmann, Martin. *The Anatomy of Loving.* New York: Columbia University Press, 1987.
———. "Psychoanalytic Observations on the Capacity to Love." In *Separation-Individuation.* Edited by John B. McDevitt and Calvin F. Settlage. New York: International Universities Press, 1971.
Bloch, R. Howard. *Etymologies and Genealogies: A Literary Anthropology of the French Middle Ages.* Chicago: University of Chicago Press, 1983.
———. *Medieval French Literature and Law.* Berkeley: University of California Press, 1977.

———. *Medieval Misogyny and the Invention of Western Romantic Love.* Chicago: University of Chicago Press, 1991.
Blumstein, Kahn Andrée. *Misogyny and Idealization in the Courtly Romance.* Bonn: Bouvier Verlag Herbert Grundmann, 1977.
Boase, Roger. *The Origin and Meaning of Courtly Love: A Critical Study of European Scholarship.* Manchester: Manchester University Press, 1977.
Bogin, Meg. *The Women Troubadours.* Scarborough: Paddington, 1976.
Bossy, Michel-André. "The Elaboration of the Female Narrative Functions in *Erec et Enide.*" In Busby and Kooper 1986/1990, 23–38, q.v.
Boswell, John. *The Kindness of Strangers: The Abandonment of Children in Western Europe from Late Antiquity to the Renaissance.* New York: Random House, 1988.
Bowlby, John. *Attachment.* 2d ed. New York: Basic Books, 1969.
———. *Attachment and Loss.* 2d ed. London: Penguin Books, 1991.
———. *The Making and Breaking of Affectional Bonds.* London: Tavistock, 1979.
Bragg, Lois. "'Wulf and Eadwacer,' 'The Wife's Lament,' and Women's Love Lyrics of the Middle Ages." *Germanisch-Romanische Monatschrift* (1989): 257–68.
Bridenthal, Renate, Claudia Koonz, and Susan Stuard, eds. *Becoming Visible: Women in European History.* 2d ed. Boston: Houghton Mifflin, 1987.
Briffault, Robert. *The Troubadours.* Edited by Lawrence F. Koons. Bloomington: Indiana University Press, 1965.
Brown, Emerson, Jr. "William Carlos Williams' 'Full Moon' and the Medieval Dawn Song." *Southern Humanities Review* 11 (1977): 175–83.
Brown, Peter. *The Body and Society: Men, Women, and Sexual Renunciation in Early Christianity.* New York: Columbia University Press, 1988.
Bruckner, Matilda Tomaryn. "Fictions of the Female Voice: The Women Troubadours." *Speculum* 67 (1992): 865–91.
Brundage, James A. *Law, Sex and Christian Society in Medieval Europe.* Chicago: University of Chicago Press, 1987.
Bullough, Vern L., Brenda Shelton, and Sarah Slavin. *The Subordinated Sex: A History of Attitudes Toward Women.* Athens: University of Georgia Press, 1988.
Burgwinkle, William E. "Ethics and the Courtly Lady." *Hawaii Review* 30 (1990): 72–129.
———. "Troubadour Song and the Art of Juggling." *Pacific Coast Philology* (1991): 13–24.
Burns, E. Jane. "The Man Behind the Lady in the Troubadour Lyric." *Romance Notes* 25 (1984): 254–70.
Burns, E. Jane, and Roberta Krueger, eds. "Courtly Ideology and Women's Place in Medieval French Literature." *Romance Notes* 25 (1985): 205–19.
Busby, Keith, and Erik Kooper, eds. *Courtly Literature: Culture and Context. Selected Papers from the 5th Triennial Congress of the International Courtly Literature Society.* Dalfsen, The Netherlands, 1986. Amsterdam/Philadelphia: Benjamins, 1990.

Bynum, Caroline Walker. "Did the Twelfth Century Discover the Individual?" *Journal of Ecclesiastical History* 31 (1980): 1–17.

———. *Fragmentation and Redemption: Essays on Gender and the Human Body in Medieval Religion.* New York: Zone, 1991.

Calabrese, Michael. "Ovid's Creation of the Female Voice." Paper, 1993 International Medieval Congress, Kalamazoo.

Cantarella, Eva. *Pandora's Daughters: The Role of Status of Women in Greek and Roman Antiquity.* Translated by Maureen B. Fant. Baltimore: Johns Hopkins University Press, 1987.

Cantor, Norman F. *The Meaning of the Middle Ages: A Sociological and Cultural History.* Boston: Allyn and Bacon, 1973.

Cardona, Martí Aurelli. "La détérioration du statut de la femme aristocratique en Provence (X^e–XIIIe siècles)." *Le Moyen Age* 91 (1977): 105–29.

Chaytor, H. J. *The Troubadours.* Cambridge: Cambridge University Press, 1912.

Cholakian, Rouben C. *The Troubadour Lyric: A Psychocritical Reading.* Manchester and New York: Manchester University Press, 1990.

Circlot, J. E. *A Dictionary of Symbols.* Translated by Jack Sage. New York: Philosophical Library, 1962.

Corti, Maria. *An Introduction to Literary Semiotics.* Translated by Margherita Bogat and Allen Mandelbaum. Bloomington: Indiana University Press, 1978.

Croce, Benedetto. *Esotetica.* 2d ed. Bari, 1902.

Daiches, David. *A Critical History of English Literature.* London: Secker and Warburg, 1961.

Davidson, Clifford. "Erotic 'Women's Songs' in Anglo-Saxon England." *Neophilologus* 59 (1975): 451–62.

Delcourt, Marie. *Hermaphrodite: Myths and Rites of the Bisexual Figure in Classical Antiquity.* London: Studio Books, 1961.

Denomy, A. J. "Courtly Love and Courtliness." *Speculum* 28 (1953): 44–63.

———. "An Inquiry into the Origins of Courtly Love." *Medieval Studies* 6 (1944): 68–80.

Deyermond, Alan. "Sexual Initiation in the Woman's-Voice Court Lyric." In Busby and Kooper 1986/1990, 125–58, q.v.

Dronke, Peter. *Medieval Latin and the Rise of the European Love Lyric.* 2d ed. Oxford: Clarendon, 1968.

———. *The Medieval Lyric.* 2d ed. London: Cambridge University Press, 1977.

———. *Women Writers of the Middle Ages.* Cambridge: Cambridge University Press, 1984.

DuBois, Page. "Sappho and Helen." In *Women in the Ancient World: The Arethusa Papers,* edited by John Peradotto and J. P. Sullivan. Albany: State University of New York Press, 1984.

Duby, Georges. *The Chivalrous Society.* Translated by Cynthia Postam. Berkeley: University of California Press, 1977.

———. *The Knight, the Lady and the Priest: The Making of Modern Marriage in Medieval France.* Translated by Barbara Bray. New York: Pantheon, 1983.

———. "Le modèle courtois." Edited by Christiane Klapisch-Zuber. *Le Moyen Age* (1991): 261–76.

———, ed. *The History of Private Life.* Vol. 2. Cambridge: Belknap Press of Harvard University Press, 1987.

Earnshaw, Doris. *The Female Voice in Medieval Romance Lyric.* New York: Lang, 1988.

Ebin, Lois, ed. *Vernacular Poetics in the Middle Ages.* Kalamazoo: Medieval Institute Publications, 1984.

Engels, Friedrich. *The Origin of the Family, Private Property and the State.* Translated by Ernest Untermann. Chicago: Kerr, 1902.

Erickson, Carolly. "The Vision of Women." In *The Medieval Vision,* edited by Carolly Erickson. New York: Oxford University Press, 1976.

Erikson, Erik. *Identity, Youth and Crisis.* New York: Norton, 1968.

Erler, Mary, and Maryanne Kowaleski. *Women and Power in the Middle Ages.* Athens: University of Georgia Press, 1988.

Feinstein, Sandy. "Whatever Happened to the Women in Folktales?" *Women's Studies International Forum* 9 (1986): 251–56.

Ferrante, Joan. "The Conflict of Lyric Conventions and Romance Form." In Ferrante and Economu 1975, 135–78, q.v.

———. "Male Fantasy and Female Reality in Courtly Literature." *Women's Studies* 11 (1984): 67–97.

———. "Public Postures and Private Maneuvers: Roles Medieval Women Play," In Erler and Kowaleski 1988, 213–29, q.v.

Ferrante, Joan, and George Economu, eds. *In Pursuit of Perfection: Courtly Love in Medieval Literature.* Port Washington, N.Y.: Kennikat, 1975.

Fisher, Elizabeth. *Woman's Creation: Sexual Evolution and the Shaping of Society.* Garden City, N.Y.: Anchor, 1979.

Flandrin, Jean-Louis. "Sex in Married Life in the Early Middle Ages." In *Western Sexuality: Practice and Precept in Past and Present Times,* translated by Anthony Forster, edited by Philippe Ariès and André Béjin. New York: Blackwell, 1985.

Forster, Leonard. "Conventional Safety Valves: Alba, Pastourelle, and Epithalamium." In *Lebende Antike: Symposion für Rudolf Sühnel,* edited by Horst Meller and Hans Joachim. Berlin: Erich Schmidt Verlag, 1967.

Frappier, Jean. *La poésie lyrique en France aux XIIe et XIIIe siècles.* Paris: Sorbonne, 1952.

Freud, Sigmund. *Civilization and Its Discontents.* Translated by James Strachey. New York: Norton, 1961.

———. "'Civilized' Sexual Morality and Modern Nervous Illness." In James Strachey, ed. and trans., *Sigmund Freud,* 9:181–204. London: The Hogarth Press, 1959.

———. *Group Psychology and the Analysis of the Ego.* Translated by James Strachey. New York: Bantam, 1960.

Fries, Maureen. "The 'Other' Voice: Woman's Song, Its Satire and Its Transcendence in Late Medieval British Literature." In Plummer 1981, 155–78, q.v.

Frings, Theodor. *Minnesinger und Troubadours*. Berlin: Berlin Deutsche Akademie der Wissenschaften, 1949.

Gaunt, Simon B. "Marginal Men, Marcabru and Orthodoxy: The Early Troubadours and Adultery." *Medium Aevum* 1990 (49): 55–72.

———. *Troubadours and Irony*. Cambridge: Cambridge University Press, 1989.

Georgiana, Linda. *The Solitary Self: Individuality in the "Ancrene Wisse."* Cambridge: Harvard University Press, 1981.

Goldin, Frederick. "The Array of Perspectives in the Early Courtly Love Lyric." In Ferrante and Economu 1975, q.v.

———. *German and Italian Lyrics of the Middle Ages: An Anthology and a History*. New York: Doubleday, 1973.

———. *Lyrics of the Troubadours and Trouveres: An Anthology and a History*. New York: Doubleday, 1973.

———. *The Mirror of Narcissus in the Courtly Love Lyric*. Ithaca: Cornell University Press, 1967.

Grandsen, K. W. "Lente currite, noctis equi: Chaucer, *Troilus and Criseyde* 3.1422–70, Donne, 'The Sunne Rising,' and Ovid, *Amores* I.13." In *Creative Imagination and Latin Literature*, edited by David West and Tony Woodman. Cambridge: Cambridge University Press, 1979.

Gravdal, Kathryn. "Camouflaging Rape: The Rhetoric of Sexual Violence in the Medieval Pastourelle." *Romanic Review* (1985): 361–73.

———. "Chrétien de Troyes, Gratian, and the Medieval Romance of Sexual Violence." *Signs* 17 (1992): 558–85.

———. *Ravishing Maidens: Writing Rape in Medieval French Literature and Law*. Philadelphia: University of Pennsylvania Press, 1991.

Hanning, Robert W. *The Individual in Twelfth Century Romance*. New Haven: Yale University Press, 1977.

———. "Poetic Emblems in Medieval Narrative Texts." In Ebin 1984, q.v.

Harvey, Ruth E. *The Troubadour Marcabru and Love*. London: Westfield College, 1989.

Haskins, Charles Homer. *The Renaissance of the Twelfth Century*. Cambridge: Cambridge University Press, 1927.

Hatto, Arthur T. "An Early 'Tagelied.'" *Modern Language Review* 46 (1951): 66–68.

———. *Eos: An Enquiry into the Theme of Lovers' Meetings and Partings at Dawn in Poetry*. The Hague: Mouton, 1965.

———. "On the Beauty of Numbers in Wolfram's Dawn Song." *Modern Language Review* 45 (1950): 58–72.

Hatzichronoglou, Lena. "Euripides' Medea: Woman or Fiend?" In *Woman's Power, Man's Game: Essays in Honor of Joy K. King*, 1–31. Wauconda, Ill.: Bolchazy-Carducci, 1993.

Hazen, Cindy, and Phillip Shaver. "Romantic Love Conceptualized as an Attachment Process." *Journal of Personality and Social Psychology* 52 (1987): 511–24.

Heilbrun, Carolyn. *Toward a Recognition of Androgyny*. New York: Knopf, 1973.

Herlihy, David. *Medieval Households*. Cambridge: Harvard University Press, 1985.

———. *Women in Medieval Society*. Houston: University of Saint Thomas, 1971.

Hill, Thomas D. "Half-waking, Half-sleeping: A Tropological Motif in a Middle English Lyric and Its European Context." *Review of English Studies* 29 (1978): 50–56.

Huchet, Jean-Charles. "La Dame et le troubadour: 'Fin'amors' et mystique chez Bernart de Ventadorn." *Littérature* 49 (1982): 13.

———. "Obscénité et 'fin'amor': le comte de Poitier, premier troubadour." *Revue des Lanques Romanes* 88 (1984): 243–66.

Hueffer, Francis. *The Troubadours: A History of Provençal Life and Literature in the Middle Ages.* London: Chatto and Windus, 1878.

Huizinga, J. *Homo Ludens: A Study of the Play Element in Culture.* Boston: Beacon, 1955.

Jackson, W. T. H. *The Challenge of the Medieval Text.* Edited by Joan Ferrante and Robert Hanning. New York: Columbia University Press, 1985.

———, ed. *The Interpretation of Medieval Lyric Poetry.* New York: Columbia University Press, 1980.

Jackson, William E. "The Woman's Song in Medieval German Poetry." In Plummer 1981, 47–94, q.v.

Jauss, Hans Robert. *Toward an Aesthetic of Reception.* Translated by Timothy Bahti. Minneapolis: University of Minnesota Press, 1982.

Jeanroy, Alfred. *La poésie lyrique des troubadours.* 2 vols. Toulouse: Privat, 1934.

———. *Les origines de la poésie lyrique en France au moyen age.* 3d ed. Paris: Champion, 1925.

Jochens, Jenny M. "The Medieval Icelandic Heroine: Fact or Fiction?" *Viator* 17 (1986): 35–50.

Kaske, Robert E. "The Aube in Chaucer's *Troilus.*" In *Chaucer Criticism II,* edited by Richard J. Schoeck and Jerome Taylor, 167–79. Notre Dame: University of Notre Dame Press, 1961.

———. "An Aube in the *Reeve's Tale.*" *English Literary History* 26 (1959): 295–310.

———. "January's 'Aube.'" *Modern Language Notes* 75 (1960): 1–4.

Kay, Sarah. *Subjectivity in Troubadour Poetry.* Cambridge: Cambridge University Press, 1990.

Kelly-Gadol, Joan. "Did Women Have a Renaissance?" In Bridenthal, Koonz, and Stuard, eds. 1987, 175–202, q.v.

Kendrick, Laura. *The Game of Love: Troubadour Wordplay.* Berkeley: University of California Press, 1988.

Kochs, Theodor. *Das deutsche geistliche Tagelied.* Munster: Aschendorft, 1928.

Köhler, Erich. "Observations historiques et sociologiques sur la poésie des troubadours." *Cahiers de Civilisation Médiévale* 7 (1964): 25–51.

———. "Marcabru und die beiden 'Schulen.'" *Cultura Neolatina* 30 (1970): 300–311.

Lazar, Moshé. *Amour courtois et "fin'amors" dans la littérature du XIIe siècle.* Paris: Librairie C. Klincksieck, 1964.

———. "Carmina Erotica, Carmino Iocosa: The Body and the Bawdy in Medieval Love Songs." In Lazar and Lacy 1989, 249–76, q.v.

Lazar, Moshé, and Norris J. Lacy, eds. *Poetics of Love in the Middle Ages: Texts and Contexts*. Fairfax, Va.: George Mason University Press, 1989.

Lewis, C.S. *The Allegory of Love: A Study in Medieval Tradition*. 1936. Reprint, London: Oxford University Press, 1976.

Lucas, Angela M. *Women in the Middle Ages: Religion, Marriage and Letters*. New York: St. Martin's, 1983.

Lucka, Emil. *The Evolution of Love*. Translated by Ellie Schleussner. London: Allen and Unwin, 1922.

Mahler, Margaret, Fred Pen, and Anni Bergman. *The Psychological Birth of the Human Infant*. New York: Basic Books, 1975.

Malone, Kemp. "Two English *Frauenlieder.*" *Comparative Literature* 14 (1962): 106–17.

Marx, Karl, and Frederick Engels. *Literature and Art*. New York: International Publishers, 1947.

McCash, June Hall. "Mutual Love as a Medieval Ideal." In Busby and Kooper 1990, 429–548, q.v.

McLeod, Glenda. *Virtue and Venom: Catalogs of Women from Antiquity to the Renaissance*. Ann Arbor: University of Michigan Press, 1991.

McNamara, JoAnn. "Sexual Equality and the Cult of Virginity in Early Christian Thought." *Feminist Studies* 3, no. 3/4 (1976): 145–58.

McNamara, JoAnn, and Suzanne F. Wemple. "The Power of Woman through the Family in Medieval Europe: 500–1000." *Feminist Studies* 1 (1973): 126–41.

Moller, Herbert. "The Meaning of Courtly Love." *Journal of American Folklore* 73 (1964): 39–52.

Monter, William E. "The Pedestal and the Stake: Courtly Love and Witchcraft." In Bridenthal, Koonz, and Stuard 1987, 121–36, q.v.

Moore, John C. *Love in Twelfth-Century France*. Philadelphia: University of Pennsylvania Press, 1972.

Morris, Colin. *The Discovery of the Individual, 1050–1200*. New York: Harper, 1973.

Muscatine, Charles. *Chaucer and the French Tradition: A Study in Style and Meaning*. Berkeley: University of California Press, 1957.

Newman, F. X., ed. *The Meaning of Courtly Love*. Albany: State University of New York Press, 1973.

Nichols, Stephen G., Jr. "Medieval Women and Writers: *Aisthesis* and the Powers of Marginality." *Yale French Studies* 75 (1988): 77–94.

———. "Toward an Aesthetic of the Provençal *Canso*." In *The Disciplines of Criticism: Essays in Literary Theory, Interpretation, and History*, edited by Peter Demetz, Thomas Greene, and Lowry Nelson, Jr., 349–74. New Haven: Yale University Press, 1968.

———. "Working Late: Marie de France and the Value of Poetry." In *Women in French Literature*, edited by Michel Guggenheim, 7–16. Palo Alto: Anima Libri, 1988.

Overing, Gillian R. *Language, Sign, and Gender in Beowulf*. Carbondale: Southern Illinois University Press, 1990.

Paden, William D. "The Troubadour's Lady: Her Marital Status and Social Rank." *Studies in Philology* 72 (1975): 28–50.

———, ed. *The Medieval Pastourelle*. New York: Garland, 1987.

Paris, Gaston. "Etudes sur les romans de la table ronde: Lancelot du Lac." *Romania* 12 (1883): 459–534.

Payne, Robert O. *The Key of Remembrance: A Study of Chaucer's Poetics*. New Haven: Yale University Press, 1963.

Petroff, Elizabeth Alvilda. *Body and Soul: Essays on Medieval Women and Mysticism*. New York: Oxford University Press, 1994.

———. *Medieval Women's Visionary Literature*. New York: Oxford University Press, 1986.

Piquet, Edgar. *L'évolution de la pastourelle du XIIe siècle à nos jours*. Bern, 1926.

Pillet, Alfred, and Henry Carstens. *Bibliographie der troubadours*. Halle, 1933. Reprint, New York: Franklin, 1968.

Plummer, John F., ed. *Vox Feminae: Studies in Medieval Woman's Song*. Kalamazoo: Medieval Institute, 1981.

Poe, Elizabeth Wilson. "New Light on the Alba: A Genre Redefined." *Viator* 15 (1984): 139–50.

———. "The Three Modalities of the Old Provençal Dawn Song." *Romance Philology* 37 (1983): 259–72.

Poggioli, Renato. "Tragedy or Romance? A Reading of the Paolo and Francesca Episode in Dante's *Inferno*." *Publications of the Modern Language Association* 72 (1957): 313–54.

Pomeroy, Sarah B. *Goddesses, Whores, Wives, and Slaves: Women in Classical Antiquity*. New York: Schocken Books, 1975.

Poulet, Georges. *Etudes sur le temps humain*. Paris: Sorbonne, 1952.

Power, Eileen. *Medieval Women*. Cambridge: Cambridge University Press, 1975.

Purcell, Sally, trans. *Literature in the Vernacular (De Vulgari Eloquentia)*. Manchester: Carcanet New Press, 1981.

Restori, A. "La gaite de la tor." In *Festschrift Petraglioso Serrano*. Messina, 1904.

Richey, Margaret Fitzgerald. *Essays on Medieval German Poetry*. New York: Barnes & Noble, 1969.

———. *Medieval German Lyrics*. Translated by Margaret Fitzgerald Richey. London: Oliver and Boyd, 1958.

Rieger, Dietmar. *Gattungen und Gatttungsbezeichnungen der Trobadorlyric*. Tubingen: Max Niemeyer Verlag, 1976.

Riquer, Martín de. "Alba trovadoresca de autor catalan." *Revista de Filología Española* 34 (1950): 151–65.

———. *Les albas provenzales*. Barcelona: Entregas de Poesia, 1944.

Roncaglia, Aurelio. "Trobar clus: Discussione aperta." *Cultura Neolatina* 29 (1969): 5–51.

Rose, Mary Beth. *Women in the Middle Ages and the Renaissance: Literary and Historical Perspectives*. Syracuse: Syracuse University Press, 1986.

Rosen, Tova. "On Tongues Being Bound and Let Loose: Women in Medieval Hebrew Literature." *Journal of Jewish History* 8 (1988): 67–87.

Ruether, R. R., ed. *Religion and Sexism: Images of Women in the Jewish and Christian Traditions*. New York: Simon and Schuster, 1974.

Saintsbury, George. *The Flourishing of Romance and the Rise of Allegory*. Edinburgh: Blackwood, 1897.

Saïz, Próspero. *Personae and Poiesis: The Poet and the Poem in Medieval Love Lyric*. The Hague: Mouton, 1976.

Sargent-Baur, Barbara Nelson. "Truth, Half-Truth, Untruth: Béroul's Telling of the Tristan Story." In *The Craft of Fiction: Essays in Medieval Poetics*. Rochester, Mich.: Solaris Press, Inc., 1984.

Saville, Jonathan. *The Medieval Erotic Alba: Structure as Meaning*. New York: Columbia University Press, 1972.

Sayce, Olive. *Poets of the Minnesang*. London: Oxford University Press, 1967.

Scaglione, Aldo D. *Knights at Court: Courtliness, Chivalry, and Courtesy from Ottonian Germany to the Italian Renaissance*. Berkeley: University of California Press, 1991.

———. *Nature and Love in the Late Middle Ages*. Berkeley: University of California Press, 1963.

Schotter, Anne Howland. "Woman's Song in Medieval Latin." In Plummer 1981, 19–34, q.v.

Schulenburg, Jane Tibbetts. "The Heroics of Virginity: Brides of Christ and Sacrificial Mutilation." In Rose 1986, q.v.

Scudieri-Ruggieri, Jole M. "Per la origini dell'alba." *Cultura Neolatina* 3 (1943): 191–202.

Sedgwick, Eve Kosofsky. *Between Men: English Literature and Male Homosocial Desire*. New York: Columbia University Press, 1985.

Shahar, Shulamith. *The Fourth Estate: A History of Women in the Middle Ages*. Translated by Chaya Galai. London: Methuen, 1983.

Shapiro, Marianne. "The Figure of the Watchman in the Provençal Erotic Alba." *Modern Language Notes* 91 (1976): 607–35.

Shaw, Evelyn, and Joan Darling. *Female Strategies*. New York: Walker, 1985.

Sigal, Gale. "Benighted Love in Troy: Dawn and the Dual Negativity of Love in Chaucer's *Troilus*." In *Voices in Translation: The Authority of "Olde Bookes" in Medieval Literature*, edited by Deborah Sinnreich and Gale Sigal, 191–206. New York: AMS, 1992.

———. "Courted in the Country: Women's Precarious Place in the Lyric Landscape." In *Text and Territory*, edited by Sylvia Tomasch and Sealy Gilles. Forthcoming.

———. "Dignity and Desire: The *Alba* Poet's Liberation of the Courtly Lady." In *Papers on Romance Literary Relations: The Creation of Female Voices by Male Writers in Romance Literatures*, 9–22. Brockport: SUNY, 1987.

———. "The Pit or the Pedestal?: The Dichotomization of the Lady in Troubadour Lyric." *The Romanic Review* 84 (March 1993): 109–42.

———. "The Poetics of Dismemberment: *Eros* and Identity in the Medieval Dawn-Song." *Tenso* 5 (1990): 133–52.

———. "'Reis glorios': An Inverted *Alba?*" *Medieval Perspectives* 4–5 (1989–90): 185–95.

Simonelli, Maria Picchio. *Lirica moralistica nell'Occitania del XII secolo: Bernart de Venzac.* Modena, 1974.

Singer, Irving. *The Nature of Love.* Chicago: University of Chicago Press, 1984.

Slater, Philip. *The Glory of Hera.* Boston: Beacon Press, 1968.

Smith, Nathaniel B., and Joseph T. Snow. *The Expansion and Transformation of Courtly Literature.* Athens: University of Georgia Press, 1980.

Southern, Richard W. *The Making of the Middle Ages.* New Haven: Yale University Press, 1953.

Spence, Sarah. "'Au Criator!': The Subversive Role of the Watchman in *Gaite de la Tor.*" *Philological Quarterly* 63 (1984): 116–25.

———. "*Et ades sera l'alba:* Revelations as Intertext for the Provençal *Alba.*" *Romance Philology* 35 (1981): 212–17.

Spitzer, Leo. "The Mozarabic Lyric and Theodore Frings' Theories." *Comparative Literature* 4 (1952): 1–22.

Stanbury, Sarah. "The Lover's Gaze in *Troilus and Criseyde.*" In *Chaucer's Troilus and Criseyde "Subgit to alle Poesye,"* edited by R. A. Shoaf. Binghamton, N.Y.: Medieval and Renaissance Texts and Studies, 1992.

Stuard, Susan. "The Dominion of Gender: Women's Fortunes in the High Middle Ages." In Bridenthal, Koonz, and Stuard 1987, 153–74, q.v.

———, ed. *Women in Medieval Society.* Philadelphia: University of Pennsylvania Press, 1976.

Sutherland, D. R. "L'élément théatral dans la canso chez les troubadours de l'époque classique." *Revue de Lanque et de Littérature d'Oc* 12–13 (1962–63): 95–100.

Taylor, Karla. "*Inferno 5* and *Troilus and Criseyde* Revisited." In *Chaucer's Troilus and Criseyde: "Subgit to alle Poesye,"* edited by R. A. Shoaf, 239–56. Binghamton, N.Y.: Medieval and Renaissance Texts and Studies, 1992.

Topsfield, L. T. *Troubadours and Love.* Cambridge: Cambridge University Press, 1975.

Ullmann, Walter. *The Individual and Society in the Middle Ages.* Baltimore: Johns Hopkins University Press, 1966.

Valency, Maurice. *In Praise of Love: An Introduction to Love-Poetry of the Renaissance.* New York: Macmillan, 1961.

Van Vleck, Amelia E. *Memory and Re-creation in Troubadour Lyric.* Berkeley: University of California Press, 1991.

Wemple, Suzanne F. "Sanctity and Power: The Dual Pursuit of Medieval Women." In Bridenthal, Koonz, and Stuard 1987, 90–118, q.v.

Wilhelm, James J. *The Cruelest Month.* New Haven: Yale University Press, 1965.

———. *Seven Troubadours: The Creators of Modern Verse.* University Park: Penn State University Press, 1970.

Woods, W. S. "The 'Aube' in *Aucassin et Nicolette.*" In *Medieval Studies in Honor of Urban Tigner Holmes, Jr.,* edited by John Mahoney and John E. Keller, 209–15. Chapel Hill: University of North Carolina Press, 1965.

Zumthor, Paul. *Essai de poétique médiéval.* Paris: Klincksieck, 1972.

———. *Toward a Medieval Poetics.* Translated by Phillip Bennett. Minneapolis: University Press of Minnesota, 1992.

Zweben-Howland, Lynda. "The Genesis of the Self in 'Can vei la lauzeta mover' by Bernart de Ventadorn." Paper, 1993 Southeastern Medieval Association Conference.

Index

"Ab la gensor que sia" (anon.): dawn in, 189; equality in, 99; husband in, 89; love in, 201; playfulness in, 156; pledges in, 202; prayers in, 121; rank in, 101; sex roles in, 55–57; sexual activity in, 41–42

"Ab lo pascor m'es bel q'eu chant." *See* Cercamon

Achilles, 25

Adam, 164–65, 198, 203

adultery: and alienation, 171; attitudes toward, 78–79; in cansos, 208n.7; encoding of, 86–88; and illegitimacy, 79–81, 86, 119; justification for, 32, 39; punishment for, 112–13; role of, 76–77, 90–91, 120, 123; ubiquitousness of, 80–81, 85–86

adynata, 48

Aeneas, 25

Aeschylus, *Eumenides*, 98

Agamemnon, 25

albas: characteristics of, 18, 54, 58–59, 87–88, 105, 110; classification of, 4–9; context of, 72–76; imagery in, 170, 197–203; influences on, 10, 16–17; music for, 2, 207n.9; origins of, 8–9, 27; plot in, 61–62, 87–88, 94, 169–70, 195; potentiality of, 180, 186; refrain in, 192–94; structure in, 147, 179–81, 184, 192–94, 202; studies of, 11–12; as subversive, 19, 75–76, 107–8, 125; terms in, 152; themes of, 1–4, 36. *See also* knight; lady; setting; sex roles; voice

"Alba," translation of (Ezra Pound), 3

Alcmene, 136

Alice of Bath (Chaucer), 109

alienation, 120, 129–30, 170–71

Alix (countess of Blois), 116

Ambrose, Saint, 9, 209–10n.10

Anacrean, 188

Anchises (character in Virgil's *Aeneid*), 25

androgyny, 162–63, 166

"Angel of the Morning" (song), 2

Aphrodite, 161

Aristophanes, 160–62, 164–65

Arnaut Daniel, 96–97

Arthur (king), 26, 104, 171, 200

artistic endeavors, analogies to, 45–48

Arveragus (character in Chaucer's "The Franklin's Tale"), 106–7

Ascanius (character in Virgil's *Aeneid*), 25

Athena, 98

aube/aubade, 5, 7–8, 52–54. *See also* albas

Aude (character in *Song of Roland*), 26

Auden, W. H., 2

Augustine, Saint, 124, 184–85, 209n.8, 209–10n.10

Aurora (goddess), 72, 136, 179–80, 186–87

Baskerville, Charles Read, 8–9
Bec, Pierre, 7, 180
Benson, Robert L., 213n.2
Benton, John F., 127–28, 213n.2
Beowulf, 25
Bernart de Ventadorn, 96–97, 212–13n.9
Bernart Marti, 81–82
Béroul, 173
biology: and creation myth, 164–65; and gender, 51–52
Bloch, R. H.: on adultery, 86; on courtly love, 207n.10; on idealization of lady, 14–18
Blumstein, Kahn Andrée, 128
Boccaccio, Giovanni, 6
body: anatomization of, 197–98, 200–201; of the lady, 134–35, 140–41, 144–45
Boswell, John, 85–86, 209n.3
Bowlby, John, 167
Brangane (character in *Tristan* legend), 103–4
Briseis (character in the *Iliad*), 25
Broke, Arthur, 179
Brown, Peter, 209n.9
Browning, Robert, 2
Brundage, James A., 127
Burgwinkle, William E., 86, 128
Burns, E. Jane, 96–97
Bynum, Caroline Walker, 13, 213n.2

Cadenet, "S'anc fui belha ni prezada": emotions in, 37; husband in, 87–88, 90, 109; marriage in, 111; playfulness in, 156; separation in, 198; sex roles in, 58; and time's passage, 178–79; watchman in, 33–35, 137–39; women in, 30–33, 78, 117–18

Camilla (character in Virgil's *Aeneid*), 25
cansos: adultery in, 208n.7; definition of, 10–11, 17, 19, 28–29, 105–6; humanization of, 29–30; the lady in, 13–15, 24, 27–29, 96–99, 104, 128–29; love in, 120; rank and status in, 96–99, 107; role of, 15–16; sex roles in, 53
"Cant voi l'aube dou jor venir." *See* Gace Brulé
Capellanus, Andreas, 127, 171
celibacy, 123–24
Cercamon, "Ab lo pascor m'es bel q'eu chant," 78–79
chanson de geste, the lady in, 25–26
chanson de toile, sentiments in, 85
characters. *See* gayta; gilos; knight; lady
Charlemagne, 26
Chaucer, Geoffrey: on courtliness, 109; on dawn, 133, 136, 192; "The Franklin's Tale," 106–7; on love, 66–68, 90, 105–7; on separation, 185–86; on sex roles, 52–54, 62–66; on virginity, 209–10n.10; "Wife of Bath," 109. *See also* Criseyde; Troilus
chivalry: adoption of, 4; components in, 76; and individualism, 174; and women's status, 127–28. *See also* courtly love
Cholakian, Rouben C., 128
Chrétien de Troyes: influences on, 77–78; on love, 125–26, 201–2; on lovers' dilemma, 118, 171–73; on mutuality, 104–5; on separation, 199–200; on test for lover, 26. *See also* Cligés; Enide; Fenice; Guenevere; Lancelot
Christianity: changes in, 213–14n.2; and cult of the Virgin, 122, 128; defiance of, 119, 125–26, 130; and

gender relations, 112, 164–65; history of, 209n.9; influence by, 104–5, 111, 176; and marriage laws, 113, 116–19, 124–25, 130, 165; and salvation, 154; and sexuality, 123–24. *See also* God
clerics, lyrics by, 26–27
Cligés, 200–201
Constable, Giles, 213n.2
courage, 39–40
courtly love (fin'amors). *See* fin'amors
Creusa (character in Virgil's *Aeneid*), 25
Criseyde: motive for her alba, 90; night addressed by, 65–67, 133, 136–37, 146; passion of, 68, 105; role of, 52–54, 62–64; and separation, 198
Croce, Benedetto, 5
cult of the Virgin, 122, 128

Dante Alighieri: on adultery, 77; on canso, 10–11; *Divine Comedy*, 10–11, 77, 163–64; on love, 163–64; on poets, 211n.3
Darling, Joan, 51–52
dawn: bifurcation of, 65–67; dual aspects of, 186–87; as enemy, 38, 114–15, 158–59; invocation of, 168; merging in, 163; as reality, 188–90; refrain of, 192–94; as symbol, 1, 63–65, 72, 175–80, 191–92; as transition, 184–85
dawn-hymns, 9–10, 139, 189
dawn-songs. *See* albas; dawn
day: alienation from, 170; personification of, 65–66; role of, 144–46, 187–88; versus night, 71–72; watchman's desire for, 151
"Den morgenblic" (Wolfram von Eschenbach): dawn in, 191; emotions in, 36, 60; and identity, 170; intimacy in, 177, 180–81; love in, 168; separation in, 198–99; sexuality in, 45–48
"Der helden minne ir klage" (Wolfram von Eschenbach), 36, 91–93
Dia, Contessa de, 111
Dido, 23, 25, 123
Dietmar von Eist [?], "Slâfest du, vreidel ziere," 142, 157–58, 198–99
"Dieus, aydatz." *See* Raimon de las Salas
difference, representation of, 13
discretion, 45–46, 170–73
dismemberment, 170, 197–203
domna. *See* cansos, the lady in
Donne, John: alba used by, 2, 143–46; on love, 109, 143–45, 207–8n.2; on separation, 199; works: "Breake of Day," 2, 145–46; "The Good-Morrow," 2, 145, 189; "The Sunne Rising," 2, 143–45; "A Valediction," 199
Dorigen (character in "The Franklin's Tale"), 106–7
Dronke, Peter: on adultery, 88; on albas, 9, 12, 39, 68; on dawn, 191; on individualism, 214n.3; on the lady, 158; on memory, 202; on setting, 134–35
Duby, Georges: on courtly love, 127, 178; on emergence of self, 213n.2; on rank and status, 98, 102; on social roles, 72–73; on use of literature, 209n.3

eagle, as sun, 191
Earnshaw, Doris, 13, 156, 214n.5
Eleanor of Aquitaine, 116
emotions: expression of, 35–40, 44–45, 48; and fusion, 163, 175–78, 196; and gender roles, 58–61; of love and separation, 167–68, 201–3; and sense of self, 129–30. *See also* fin'amors; love

"En cest sonet coind'e leri." *See* Arnaut Daniel
Engels, Friedrich, 4, 76
English literature, alba's role in, 1–2, 143
Enide (character in Chrétien de Troyes, *Erec et Enide*), 207n.7
"Entre moi et mon amin" (anon.): dawn in, 189–90; night in, 134–35; playfulness in, 156; reality in, 48–49; sex roles in, 57–58; sexual activity in, 43–44; structure of, 202
"En un vergier sotz fuella d'albespi" (anon.): emotions in, 37; equality in, 100; fusion in, 178; husband in, 88, 90; the lady in, 39, 49, 171; playfulness in, 156; prayers in, 121, 136–37; separation in, 198; setting in, 120, 193; sexual activity in, 42–43, 140; structure in, 202; time's passage in, 48, 187; translation of, 2–3
Eos (goddess), 72
epics, women in, 24–26
equality, 94–96. *See also* lovers, equality between; rank and status
"Eras diray ço que·us dey dir" (anon.), 116, 121–22
Erikson, Erik, 169–70
"Est il jors?" (anon.): emotions in, 133; lausengiers in, 115–16; symbiotic love in, 168
Etienne de Meaux, "Trop est mes maris jaloux," 82–85
Eve, 164–65, 198, 203
Everly Brothers, 2
eyes, and power, 141, 144–45
"Ez ist nu tac" (Wolfram von Eschenbach): dawn in, 191; emotions in, 36, 60; intimacy in, 176, 181; knight in, 102–3, 108, 183–84; "now" in, 142; prayers in, 121; sexuality in, 48, 141; and time's passage, 190; watchman in, 38

fabliau/fabliaux, 19, 26, 206–7n.5
Fenice (character in Chrétien de Troyes, *Cligés*), 200–201
Ferrante, Joan, 26, 173
fin'amors (courtly love): attitudes toward, 33; components of, 95–96, 102, 108–10, 163; definitions in, 15–16, 76, 78, 116, 120; definition of, 116, 122, 125; effects of, 127–29; emergence of, 18–19, 76; goal of, 123; idealization of women in, 4, 14, 39, 105–6, 206n.7; and individualism, 174–75; psychodynamics of, 175–76; rejection of, 92–93; representation of, 13–16, 18–19; role of, 86, 102; as social climbing, 97–99; as threat, 126; versus society, 118–20. *See also* adultery; emotions; knight; lady; love
folk-song theory, and alba's origins, 8
Folquet de Marseilles, "Vers Dieus, el vostre nom et de sancta Maria," 10
Forster, Leonard, 40–41, 45, 94, 101
Francesca da Rimini (character in Dante's *Divine Comedy*), 77, 163–64
Franklin, 105–7
French literature: albas in, 6–8; pastourelle in, 205n.5; poetry's role in, 3–4
Freud, Sigmund: on alienation, 129–30; on civilization, 119–20; on love, 155, 172–73, 177–78; on narcissism, 167
friendship, 152–54
Fries, Maureen: on the lady, 13, 23, 56–57, 73; on sex roles, 51, 54, 59, 61–62, 71–72
Frings, Theodor, 8
"Friuntlîchen lac" (Walther von der

Vogelweide): dawn in, 190–92, 198; equality in, 100; honor in, 114; the lady in, 36, 38, 49, 185; and love's definition, 49; prayers in, 121; separation in, 166–67, 198; sex roles in, 58; sexual activity in, 42, 140

Fromm, Erich, 167

Gace Brulé, "Cant voi l'aube dou jor venir": dawn in, 159; emotions in, 35–37; equality in, 100; husband in, 87; intimacy in, 178; lausengiers in, 115; "now" in, 143; prayers in, 121; sex roles in, 61; sexual activity in, 43; society in, 110–11

"Gaita be" (Raimbaut de Vaqueiras): dawn in, 114–15, 159; emotions in, 60; husband in, 89–90, 101; love in, 109; playfulness in, 156; society in, 112

"Gaite de la tor" (anon.): dawn in, 159; equality in, 99–100; night in, 138; "now" in, 142; prayers in, 121, 138; sexual activity in, 42; society in, 114; theft in, 103

gayta, watchman: abuse of, 37–38, 40; loyalty of, 151–53; and night's passage, 138–39, 178–79; and "now," 142; prayers of, 121–22, 150–54; role of, 33–35, 71, 89–92, 147, 149–52; and sex roles, 56–57; theme of, 6

gender: biblical texts on, 164–65; construction of, 52–53, 62–63; definitions of, 160; fluidity of, 54–61; and rank and status, 94–103; theories on, 51–55. *See also* men; sex roles; women

genres: evolution of, 5, 7–8; and marginalization, 15–16

German literature: alba's role in, 1–2, 4, 6; themes in, 36

gilos (husband): defiance of, 37, 88, 90; definition of, 76–77, 87–88, 205n.6; derision of, 26; fear of, 88–90; as God, 154; power of, 90–91, 101–4, 111–12, 115–16, 191; representation of, 14, 78–79, 82–85, 109; role of, 74–75, 87–88, 102; as silenced, 57; symbols for, 190; as unfaithful, 80–81

Giraut de Bornelh, "Reis glorios, verais lums e clardatz": husband in, 88–89; as inverted alba, 153; and lovers' allegiances, 154–55; and lovers' choices, 186; music for, 207n.9; "now" in, 142; piety in, 10; plot in, 147–50; prayers in, 121–22, 139; and time's passage, 190, 193; watchman in, 147–54

God: changes in relationship with, 122; creation by, 164–65; gilos as, 154; invocation of, 61. *See also* Christianity; prayers

Goldin, Frederick, 11, 188, 211–12n.4

Gottfried von Strassburg: on lovers' dilemma, 118–19; on passion, 166–68; on rank and status, 103–4; on secrecy, 172–73; setting created by, 140; <u>Tristan,</u> 103–4, 140, 166–68, 173, 209n.9; on women's sexuality, 209n.9

Grandsen, K. W., 136

Gratian, 124

Gravdal, Kathryn, 128

Guenevere: adultery of, 77; dilemma of, 171–72; Lancelot's love for, 104, 164, 199–200; and Lancelot's mysticism, 125–26

Gui d'Ussel, 95

Guillaume IX, "Mout jauzens me prenc en amar," 98–99

Hanning, Robert W., 157, 174, 213n.2
Haskins, Charles Homer, 213n.2

Hatto, Arthur T.: on albas, 5, 7; on lovers, 11–12, 46–47; on Wolfram, 92–93
Hazen, Cindy, 167–68
heart, as memory, 198–99, 201–2
Heilbrun, Carolyn, 25, 162, 166
Heinrich von Morungen. *See* "Owê, sol aber mir iemer mê"
Helen of Troy, 25
Henry II (king of England), 116
Hercules, 136
hermaphroditism, 160–62, 164
Hermaphroditus, 161–62, 164
Hermes, 161
Herrick, Robert, 187
holy spirit, invocation of, 139
Homer, *Iliad*, 25
Housman, Alfred Edward, 2
"How Culwch Won Olwen," 26
Hueffer, Francis, 4
humanization, 29–30
husband (gilos). *See* gilos

"Ich sich den morgensterne brehen" (anon.), 112, 142–43
"Ich wache umb eines ritters lîp." *See* Margrave von Hohenburg
identity: crisis of, 196–97; formation of, 169–70, 174; and social roles, 171–73; transformation of, 175. *See also* individualism; self
illegitimacy, 79–81, 86, 119
individualism: emergence of, 173–74; and intimacy, 175–77, 180–83; and separation, 198
infantile sexuality, 155
intimacy, 175–78, 180–84
Isolde (character in Tristan legend), 103–4, 140, 166–68, 173
Ivo of Chartres, 113

Jackson, W. T. H., 5, 175–76
James, Saint, 138

Jauss, Hans Robert, 7
Jeanroy, Alfred, 5–6, 11
Jerome, Saint, 123–25, 209–10n.10
Jesus, on marital union, 165
Jove, 135

Kaske, Robert E.: on lovers' prayers, 61; on separation, 185; on sex-role theories, 51–54, 62
Kay, Sarah, 95, 97, 210n.12
kharja, theme of, 6
Kilydd (character in "How Culwch Won Olwen), 26
knight: characteristics of, 101–2, 108, 183; emotions of, 59–60; gilos feared by, 115; power of, 160; role of, 51–58, 72–74, 169–70; terms for, 74, 101
Köhler, Erich, 95, 97–98, 102
Kolsen, Adolf, 211–12n.4

"L'abe c'apiert au jor" (anon.): emotions in, 38; night in, 135–36; prayers in, 121, 138
lady: body of, 134–35, 140–41, 144–45; characteristics of, 12–15, 18–19, 38, 76, 101, 169; desire of, 140–42; emotions of, 35–40; honor of, 113–14; as literary construct, 8; love defined by, 49; multidimensionality of, 29–30; power of, 129; rationales for, 30–33; role of, 51–59, 72–76, 169–70; stereotype of, 23–24; as superlative, 39. *See also* knight; lovers
Lancelot: deception by, 173; and love, 77, 104, 164, 199–200; mysticism of, 125–26; return of, 171–72; and seduction, 26
"Langue D'Oc," translation of (Ezra Pound), 3
Latin language, use of, 27
Latin lyrics, women in, 26–27

lausengiers (liars, slanderers), as threat, 115–16
"L'autrier jost'una sebissa." *See* Marcabru
Lavinia (character in Virgil's *Aeneid*), 25
laws, on marriage, 113, 116–19, 124–25, 130, 165
Lazar, Moshé, 122, 208n.7
Lewis, C. S., 210n.12
love: affirmation of, 201–3; code of, 33; definitions of, 49, 76–78, 104–5, 139, 160–61, 203; effects of, 27, 157, 163–66; expansion of, 145; exploration of, 28–29, 77; loyalty to, 39; mutuality of, 15, 28, 58, 71–72, 100, 105; negativity of, 65–68; and reality, 189; subjugation of, 195; symbiotic nature of, 71, 161, 166–68. *See also* intimacy; passion; sexual activity
lovers: allegiances of, 154–55; characteristics of, 55–59, 65–67, 75–76; choices of, 186–88, 195; dilemma of, 57, 118–20, 129–30, 142, 169–73, 195–96; equality between, 94–96, 99–101, 104–6, 129–30; false versus true, 33–35; identity of, 169–70; isolation of, 142–44; merging of, 160–68, 175–78, 196; playfulness of, 155–58; prayers of, 120–23, 136–39; rage of, 158–59; and reality, 54, 188–89; reciprocity of, 62–63, 67–71; separation of, 166–68, 179–87, 194–99, 202–3; terms for, 58, 74, 101–2; and time, 142–47. *See also* knight; lady; sex roles; sexual activity

Mahler, Margaret, 167
Maimonides, 164
Marcabru: on marriage, 78–81; works: "L'autrier jost'una sebissa," 80; "Pois l'inverns d'ogan es anatz," 79
Margaret de Rivers, 119
Margrave von Hohenburg, "Ich wache umb eines ritters lîp," watchman in, 38
Maria de Ventadorn, 95
Marie de Champagne, 116–17, 127
Marie de France, 26, 78
Mark (king) (character in Tristan), 103–4
Marlowe, Christopher, 143
marriage: attitudes toward, 78–80, 95–96, 124; changes in, 127; conception of, 80, 95–96, 124; effects of, 50, 85, 107, 116–18; freedom from, 127; influences on, 111; laws on, 113, 116–19, 124–25, 130, 165; love in, 106–7, 116–17; and monogamy, 113, 125; opposition to, 118–20, 129; representation of, 14, 18–19, 30–31, 91–92, 111. *See also* adultery; gilos; wife
Marvell, Andrew, 187
Medusa, and power of sight, 141–42
Meleager, 136
memory, heart as, 198–99, 201–2
men: emotions of, 59–60; role of, 51–58; women feared by, 164–65. *See also* gilos; knight
Menelaos, 25
Middle Ages: characteristics of, 18; developments in, 173–74; dualisms in, 186; and human potential, 143. *See also* Christianity; social order
Milton, John, 188
Moller, Herbert, 86
monogamy, 113, 125
monologues, interlaced, 68–71
Moore, George, 2–3
Morris, Colin, 213–14nn.2–3
mother/child relationship, 167–68, 197

"Mout jauzens me prenc en amar." *See* Guillaume IX
music, and albas, 2, 207n.9

narcissism, 167, 175, 178–79
Nichols, Stephen G., Jr., 11, 187
night: creatures of, 187–88; personification of, 65–66; as setting, 134–35; as symbol, 133–34; and time's passage, 135–38; versus day, 71–72
"No m'agrad'iverns ni pascors." *See* Raimbaut de Vaqueiras
Norse literature, women in, 25
Nykrog, Per, 214n.3

oaths, 202
Odysseus, 25
Ogrin (character in Béroul's Tristan), 173
Overing, Gillian R., 206n.3
Ovid: on dawn, 179–80, 186–87; on merging of sexes, 161–62, 164–65; on women, 17–18, 27, 49. *See also* Aurora
"Owê, sol aber mir iemer mê" (Heinrich von Morungen): dawn in, 188; lovers in, 68–71, 168; "now" in, 142; setting in, 134–35; sexual activity in, 141; structure in, 201

Paden, William D.: on gilos, 76–77, 87, 205n.6; on love, 76; on lovers' relationship, 61; on marriage, 76–77, 208n.7; on rank and status, 98
Paolo Malatesta, 77, 163–64
Paris, Gaston, 14, 116
Paris, Matthew, 119
Parzival (Wolfram von Eschenbach), 92, 183–84
passion: and equality, 166–68; focus of, 104–7; as threat, 125

pastourelle: misogyny in, 19; rank and status in, 107; sex roles in, 53; shepherdess in, 13–14, 27–28
Paul, Saint, 112, 123
Peire Vidal, 97
Peter Lombard, 165
Plato, 160–65
playfulness, 155–58
pledges, 202
Poe, Elizabeth Wilson, 6–8, 9
poets: description of, 16–19; identity of, 35; interests of, 166; redefinitions by, 157; role of, 3–4, 75–76. *See also* voice
point of view, and sexuality in albas, 46–47
"Pois l'inverns d'ogan es anatz." *See* Marcabru
Poulet, Georges, 186
Pound, Ezra, 2–3
prayers: of lovers, 120–23, 136–39; of watchman, 121–22, 150–54
Prudentius, 9, 189. *See also* dawn-hymns

"Quan lo rossinhols escria" (anon.), 3, 193

Raimbaut de Vaqueiras: and dawn, 114–15, 159; on emotions, 60; on husband, 89–90, 101; on love, 109; "No m'agrad'iverns ni pascors," 109; on playfulness, 156; on society, 112. *See also* "Gaita be"
Raimon de las Salas, "Dieus, aydatz": equality in, 100; the lady in, 37; playfulness in, 156; prayers in, 121; sexual activity in, 42, 140–41
rank and status, 94–103, 107. *See also* women, rank and status of
Ransom, John Crowe, 2
rape, attitudes toward, 123

reality: acknowledgment of, 48–49; resistance to, 57, 75, 186–88. *See also* time
refrain, of dawn-song, 192–94
Régnier-Bohler, Danielle, 209n.4
Reik, Theodor, 167
"Reis glorios, verais lums e clardatz." *See* Giraut de Bornelh
Renaissance, 143–44
Richey, Margaret Fitzgerald, 47, 182
Rieger, Dietmar, 9
Roland, 26
romances, heroes/heroines in, 29, 174
romantic love. *See* fin'amors

Saintsbury, George, 4
Saïz, Próspero, 48–49, 153
Salmacis (character from Ovid's *Metamorphoses*), 161–62
salvation, 154. *See also* dawn-hymns
"S'anc fui belha ni prezada." *See* Cadenet
Sargent-Baur, Barbara Nelson, 173
Saville, Jonathan: on adultery, 86–87, 90; on albas, 6, 9, 11–12; on dawn, 175–76, 191; on the lady, 13, 23, 72–73; on love relationship, 28–29; on prayers, 120–21; on rank and status, 94, 101; on sacred in alba, 153–54; on sex-role theories, 51, 53–54; on watchman, 150
Sayce, Olive, 47, 147, 198
Scaglione, Aldo D., 98, 102, 109–10
Schotter, Anne Howland, 27
Schulenberg, Jane Tibbitts, 209n.9
Scott, Sir Walter, 139
secrecy, 45–46, 170–73
Sedgwick, Eve, 153
self: development of, 167; discovery of, 173–74; as fractured, 171–73, 195–200; and growth of wisdom, 184–85; restructuring of, 201–3;

and symbiotic love, 167, 177–78. *See also* identity; individualism
semiotic codes, adaptation of, 5
setting: insignificance of, 139–40, 142, 146–47; meaning of, 120; night as, 133–35; and watchman's role, 147. *See also* dawn; time
sex roles: absence of, 62, 74–75; fluidity of, 59–61; and "role reversal," 51–65. *See also* androgyny; hermaphroditism
sexual activity: denunciation of, 123–24; description of, 40–48; as ideal, 126–27; playfulness of, 155–58; regulation of, 124–25; as subject, 26
Shakespeare, William, *Romeo and Juliet*, 90, 179
Shapiro, Karl, 2
Shapiro, Marianne, 35
Sharman, Ruth Verity, 211–12n.4
Shaver, Phillip, 167–68
Shaw, Evelyn, 51–52
shield, as metaphor, 103, 183
Sibyl, 25
"Sîne klâwen" (Wolfram von Eschenbach): emotions in, 37; intimacy in, 181–83; the lady in, 40; "now" in, 142; separation in, 198; social order in, 113–14; and threat to lovers, 91; and time's passage, 190–91; watchman in, 38, 152
Singer, Irving, 105, 127, 161, 212n.6
sirventes (genre), 4
Sitwell, Edith, 2
"Slâfest du, vreidel ziere." *See* Dietmar von Eist
Smith, Nathaniel B., 86
Snow, Joseph T., 86
social order: acceptance of, 92–93, 151; critique of, 75–76; and

240   Index

illegitimacy, 79–81, 86, 119; and love, 171–73; maintenance of, 111; mobility in, 109–10; roles in, 72–75, 169–70; subversion of, 107–8, 130

society: importance of, 71–72; representation of, 110–11; versus romantic love, 112, 118–20, 154–55

Southern, Richard W., 214n.3

Spanish literature, and alba's role, 6

Spanish Peninsula, albas sung in, 6

Spence, Sarah, 150, 180

status and rank, 94–103, 107. *See also* women, rank and status of

Stoker, Bram, 188

Swinburne, Algernon Charles, 2

symbiosis, and love, 71, 161, 166–68

tageliet/tagelieder: absence of gilos from, 90–91; adultery in, 90–91; emotions in, 36–37, 60–61; equality in, 100; intimacy in, 176, 178; knight in, 108; the lady in, 40; marriage in, 91–92; playfulness in, 157–58; society in, 112; studies of, 12; symbols in, 190; terms used in, 58; types of, 68; watchman in, 38. *See also* albas; Dietmar von Eist; Heinrich von Morungen; Margrave von Hohenburg; Walther von der Vogelweide; Wolfram von Eschenbach

Taylor, Karla, 212n.7

Tennyson, Alfred, 2, 28

Tertullian, 123

time: and dawn, 178–80; escape from, 147; immunity to, 144; limitations of, 153–54; passage of, 186–88, 192–94; perception of, 135, 195; significance of, 140, 146–47. *See also* dawn; day; night

Topsfield, L. T., 11

Tristan (Béroul), 173

Tristan (Gottfried von Strassburg), 140, 166–68, 173. *See also* Brangane; Isolde; Mark

trobairitz, 111

Troilus: day addressed by, 65–67, 144, 146; passion of, 68, 105; as personification of day, 192; role of, 52–53, 62–64; and separation, 185–86

Trojan War, 25, 66

"Trop est mes maris jaloux." *See* Etienne de Meaux

troubadour lyrics: adultery in, 76–78; development of, 5, 8; genres of, 2, 15–16; hidden meanings in, 86–87; the lady in, 24; misogyny in, 15–18; prototypes for, 72–76; rank and status in, 94–103; sacred and secular in, 9–10; and self-expression, 174–75; and self-legitimation, 102. *See also* albas; cansos; pastourelle; poets; voice

Ullmann, Walter, 213n.2

"Us cavaliers si jazia" (anon.): night in, 137–38; prayers in, 121; separation in, 199, 203; sex roles in, 58–61; symbiotic love in, 168; time in, 193

Van der Waals, H.G., 178

"Vers Dieus, el vostre nom et de sancta Maria." *See* Folquet de Marseilles

victimization, portrayal of, 32

Virgil, <u>Aeneid,</u> 25

virginity, 123–24

voice: authenticity of, 50; construction of, 18–20, 28, 32–33; criticism on, 14–15; as empowerment, 57; and female idealization, 4; Ovid as father of, 27; range of, 7; and sex roles, 53; shifts in, 31–32

"Von der zinnen" (Wolfram von Eschenbach), 60, 101, 182, 190–91

Wagner, Richard, 2
"Wake Up, Little Susie" (Everly Brothers), 2
Walther von der Vogelweide: on dawn, 188, 190–92; on equality, 100; on honor, 114; on the lady, 36, 38, 49, 185; on love's definition, 49; "Nemt, frowe, disen kranz," 188; on prayers, 121; on separation, 166–67, 198; on sex roles, 58; on sexual activity, 42, 140. See also "Friuntlîchen lac"
watchman. See gayta
wechsel, 68. See also "Owê, sol aber mir iemer mê"
Welsh literature, the lady in, 26. See also "Owê, sol aber mir iemer mê"
Western literature, women in, 24–26
Widsith, 25
wife, status of, 111–12, 116–17. See also lady; women
Wilbur, Richard, 2
Wilhelm, James J., 150, 153–54
Williams, William Carlos, 2
Woledge, B., 6, 211–12n.4
Wolfram von Eschenbach: artistic representation by, 47–48; on dawn, 191; on emotions, 36–37, 60–61; and identity, 170; on intimacy, 176–77, 180–84; on knight, 101, 102–3, 108, 183–84; on the lady, 40; on love, 91–92, 168; on marriage, 78; on "now," 142; on prayers, 121; on separation, 198–99; on sexuality, 45–48, 141, 184; on social order, 113–14; terms used by, 58; on threat to lovers, 91; on time's passage, 190–91, 195; on watchman, 37–38, 152. See also "Den morgenblic"; "Der helden minne ir klage"; "Ez ist nu tac"; Parzival; "Sîne klâwen"; "Von der zinnen"
women: attitudes toward, 24, 123; beatings of, 117; idealization of, 4, 14, 39, 105–6, 206n.7; oral songs by, 205n.3; rank and status of, 94–103, 107, 111–12, 116–17, 127–28, 210n.12; representation of, 12–18, 24–28; rights of, 118, 128, 141–42; role of, 30–33, 51–58; and sexual desire, 127; as trobairitz, 111; and virginity, 123–24. See also lady

Yeats, William Butler, 2

Zeus, 160
Zumthor, Paul, 11
Zweben-Howland, Lynda, 212–13n.9